AF757519

To David, Kate, and Laura
who make it all worthwhile

Contents

List of Tables

Preface and Acknowledgements

This study addresses several puzzles surrounding the Council for Mutual Economic Assistance (CMEA). Why did the Soviet Union create a trading system based on economic autarky and bilateral, state-controlled trade? Although it satisfied short-term Soviet interests, there were long-term negative consequences. Second, when the negative consequences of the initial choice became apparent, why did it prove to be so difficult for the Soviet Union to reform CMEA to better reflect its interests? Finally, why was CMEA disbanded in 1991 when the criticisms of its performance were not new, and there was still a need for regional economic cooperation?

In designing this study, I was driven by the belief that CMEA is not a unique phenomenon and that these puzzles could be explained by theories used to explain economic cooperation among other states. Therefore, this study draws upon the debate in political science about the factors that lead to the creation of a particular type of trading system and to change in that system. In particular, I argue that the creation of and change in CMEA can be explained by the intereaction of two sets of variables: structural (the power and interests of the actors) and cognitive (norms and principles, usage and custom, and knowledge). I also argue that once CMEA was created, the choices made affected the subsequent evolution of regional economic cooperation. This is known as path dependence. However, I do acknowledge that CMEA was "nested" in a broader context and that it is impossible to completely isolate it from the broader context of Soviet and East European relations because the power asymmetry was so great. The Soviet Union had developed intruments of control which allowed it to participate in the decision-making of the East European states as more than an external constraint. These instruments existed in each of the four contexts which comprised the relationship: the multilateral, national, institutional, and personal. Changes in this broader context then affected CMEA itself.

The study uses a standard comparative case study methodology developed by Alexander George which is known as structured-focused comparison. The cases selected represent the attempt of each major Soviet leader to reform CMEA to conform with his own vision of Soviet and East European relations. The information is drawn from the voluminous writings on CMEA in the Soviet and East European presses and academic journals.

As is usual, many people have contributed to this study in many ways. Jan Triska, Steve Krasner, Condoleezza Rice, and Nina Halpern challenged me to master not only the study of this region but also the theoretical literature. Mark Peceny, Alison Brysk, Scott Johnson, Cheryl Boyer, Jeff Knopf, Patrick James, and Dale Smith read numerous drafts and encouraged me to clarify my thinking. Needless to say, I alone remain responsible for the shortcomings that remain. I would also like to acknowledge the generous financial support of the Center for International Security and Arms Control at Stanford and the Berkeley Stanford Program on Soviet Studies.

Chapter One

Introduction

The formation of the Council for Mutual Economic Assistance (CMEA) was announced in a communique published in *Pravda* on January 25, 1949. CMEA was charged with

> the implementation of broader economic cooperation between the countries of people's democracy and the U.S.S.R. . . . -- on the basis of equal representation, for the purpose of exchanging economic experience, rendering technical assistance to one another, rendering mutual aid in raw materials, food, machines, equipment and so forth." [1]

Like the United States, the Soviet Union was relatively free to organize trade within its sphere of influence on whatever basis it chose due to the disruption of the world economy by World War II and its own power capabilities. Yet the two great powers chose to organize trade in very different ways. The U.S. created a trading system based on "specialization, multilateral free trade, and an international division of labor" which was codified in the General Agreement on Trade and Tariffs (GATT) and which formed the basis for the European cooperation fostered by the Marshall Plan. The Soviet Union, on the other hand, created a trading system based on economic autarky and bilateral, state-controlled trade within the framework of CMEA.[2]

Initially, the trading system that the Soviet Union created satisfied its interests. However, despite arguable advantages such as economic planning and political hegemony, the pattern of trade that emerged gradually became costly for the Soviet Union. As a net exporter of raw materials and a net importer of over priced, low quality, and often technologically obsolete manufactured products, many economists argued that the Soviet Union was granting Eastern Europe significant trade subsidies. Estimates of these subsidies 1972-1984 are as high as $114 billion.[3] In an effort to improve its terms of trade by improving the quality and technical level of East European manufactured products, the Soviet Union attempted to reform CMEA. Khrushchev recommended that it be granted supranational authority over planning and investment, Brezhnev attempted to reinterpret the decision rule, and Gorbachev pursued mutual convertibility of the members' currencies. Despite some success in reinterpreting the decision rule, the Soviet Union was unable to fundamentally alter this pattern of trade to better reflect its interests. The East European revolutions in the fall of 1989 led to domestic economic reforms and increased demands for reform of CMEA. In June 1991 while the European Union (EU) was embarking on a transition to a more intensive form of regional integration, the members of CMEA met without fanfare to disband the organization.

As this brief history illustrates, an examination of CMEA produces several puzzles. Why did the Soviet Union create this particular type of trading system? Although it satisfied short-term Soviet interests, there were long-term negative consequences associated with it. Second, when the negative consequences of the initial choice became apparent, why did it prove to be so difficult for the Soviet Union to reform CMEA to better reflect its interests? Finally, why was CMEA disbanded in 1991?

Why Study CMEA?

CMEA deserves closer examination because the puzzles it presents are not unique to that organization. In fact, they illustrate several of the central anomalies in the study of Soviet-East European relations. Historically, many scholars "viewed Soviet dealings with the East Europeans as international relations of *no* type--as sufficiently Soviet-controlled that the very phrase 'international relations' was misleading."[4] However, over time it became apparent that despite the power disparity, the Soviet Union "found itself far from able to translate this military and economic advantage into corresponding political influence and control," not only in CMEA but in the Warsaw Pact as well.[5] Also, the complete abandonment of regional cooperation in the wake of the East European revolutions in the fall of 1989 merits explanation because it was contrary to the emerging global trend of increased regional cooperation exemplified by the EU, and the economic impact was enormous. As one Hungarian economist phrased it, "the immediate market loss expressed in terms of total exports or GDP was equivalent to France losing her German and Italian markets overnight."[6]

CMEA is uniquely suited to analyze these anomalies for several reasons. First, much more information is available on CMEA than on other multilateral organizations in the bloc, such as the Warsaw Pact. Second, CMEA was "the first formal assembly of the Soviet Union and its associates as states,"[7] and it is the only organization which spans the history of the socialist bloc from Stalin to Gorbachev. As the literature on the "new institutionalism" suggests, understanding the initial choices made about the socialist trading system is important because "the initial identification of interests and decision-making procedures will have a major influence on subsequent policy choices, alternatives deemed possible, and actual state behavior."[8] Thus, the choices made when CMEA was created affected the subsequent evolution of regional economic cooperation as well as the structure of other international organizations in the bloc. This is known as path dependence.[9] Finally, foreign trade played a significant role in the economies of the small East European states, and their economies were adapted and developed to meet the demands of their CMEA trade partners so the socialist trading system is an important component of the economic problems that played a significant role in the collapse of Communism in 1989.

Despite these advantages, CMEA has been understudied by political scientists. The literature has been dominated by economists who have concentrated on the economic rather than the political aspects of the organization. Most political science analyses of CMEA are political histories.[10] The major theoretical attempt to study it was the application of regional integration theory in the early 1970s. In a review of this literature, Roger Kanet concludes that "there is little in the collection of analytic studies that either informs us about integration processes in Eastern Europe or adds to the general theory of political integration."[11]

More recently William Reisinger and Randall Stone have applied bargaining theory to CMEA.[12] Although both studies contribute greatly to our understanding of CMEA, they do not address the causes of the Soviet choice to create a particular type of trading system or the consequences of that initial choice.

How To Study CMEA

Political scientists have written extensively about the liberal trading system created by the U.S. In contrast, they have written little about the radically different trading system created by the Soviet Union, even though this led to what Robert Gilpin terms "the greatest breach ever in the interdependent world economy."[13] Framing a study of the creation of CMEA in terms of the theoretical debate in political science about the factors that lead to the creation of a particular type of trading system and to change in that trading system can increase our understanding of the puzzles surrounding CMEA. It can also shed light on this theoretical debate by expanding the universe of cases to include a radically different trading system.

In *Power and Interdependence*, Robert Keohane and Joseph Nye proposed that the term international regimes be used to refer to the procedures, rules, or institutions that governments create or accept to "regulate and control transnational and interstate relations."[14] A special issue of *International Organization* further refined the term.[15] Two schools of thought on regime creation and change have emerged: structural and cognitive.[16]

The structural approach (neorealism) draws upon the realist tradition which posits "an international system of functionally symmetrical, power-maximizing states acting in an anarchic environment."[17] It explains the creation and change of regimes as the result of the power and interests of states. Power is defined in terms of capabilities, generally size of population and territory, resource endowment, economic capability, military strength, political stability and competence.[18] The term interests refers to "autonomously calculated self-interest."[19] The primary interest of states is assumed to be ensuring their survival because "survival is a prerequisite to achieving any goal that states may have."[20] However, states may pursue other interests when their survival is not at stake.

The most general formulation of neorealism asserts that the trading system which emerged after World War II was a reflection of the interests of the most powerful state, the U.S. A more specific formulation known as hegemonic stability theory has two major theoretical propositions. The first relates "particular distributions of potential economic power, defined by the size and level of development of individual states, to the structure of the international trading system, defined in terms of openness."[21] Specifically, it posits that a hegemonic distribution of potential economic power will lead to an open international trading system. The second proposition relates the distribution of power to the strength of international regimes. It posits that "hegemonic structures of power, dominated by a single country, are most conducive to the development of strong international regimes whose rules are relatively precise and well obeyed."[22]

However, structural approaches lack such clear propositions about regime change. In general, it is posited that regime change is caused by changes in the distribution of capabilities across states or by changes in the interests of the regime's members, especially the most powerful. However, there is some disagreement as to how quickly change will occur and as to whether regimes can have an independent impact on outcomes. For example, some analysts observed that in the 1970s international regimes were not collapsing as rapidly as the theory would predict given the perceived decline of the hegemon, the U.S. There were four responses to this apparent anomaly. The first was that U.S. power capabilities had not declined so there was nothing to explain.[23] The second attributed the anomaly to lags; "once policies have been adopted, they are pursued until a new crisis demonstrates that they are no longer feasible."[24] The third proposed a differentiated, issue-specific version of the theory where "declines in resources available to the United States for use in a given issue area should be closely related to the weakening of the international regime (*circa* 1967) in that area."[25] The fourth acknowledged that "under certain restrictive conditions involving the failure of individual action to secure Pareto-optimal outcomes, international regimes may have a significant impact even in an anarchic world."[26]

The cognitive approach, which draws upon the liberal tradition in political science, is more difficult to specify completely because it includes a disparate group of approaches. However, they are generally grouped together because they use some combination of norms and principles, custom and usage, and knowledge as the explanatory variables. Norms are "standards of behavior defined in terms of rights and obligations", and principles are defined as "specific prescriptions or proscriptions for action."[27] "Usage refers to regular patterns of behavior based on actual practice; custom to long-standing practice."[28] Knowledge is "the sum of technical information and of theories about that information which commands sufficient consensus at a given time among interested actors to serve as a guide to public policy designed to achieve some social goal."[29]

The cognitive approaches are rooted in the conceptualization of regimes as social institutions which arise from "the conjunction of convergent expectations and patterns of behavior or practice."[30] They see regimes as a pervasive characteristic of the international system that can have an independent impact on outcomes. In particular, they focus on the role of regimes in defining or redefining the interests of the states.

Regimes can alter states' calculations of how to maximize their interests as well as the interests themselves. For example, the very existence of a regime can change the states' calculations of their interests because of the sunk costs involved and the informational advantages provided by the regime. A hegemon may decide that its interests are better maximized in the current regime even though it no longer perfectly reflects its power and interests because of prior investments which are probably irretrievable. Also, the information provided by the regime may be valuable enough to the states to ensure its continued existence.

A regime can change the interests themselves by "increasing transactions flows, facilitating knowledge and understanding, and creating property rights."[31] Regimes regulate transactions flows and, by providing a degree of certainty, often increase them. Therefore, the existence of a regime can alter interests by increasing the opportunity costs of change. Regimes can also create new interests when they "gather and disseminate different and usually more complex information, highlighting cause and effect relationships that had not been previously understood."[32] Much research has focused on the role of epistemic communities, networks of "professionals with recognized expertise and competence in a particular domain and an authoritative claim to policy-relevant knowledge within that domain or issue area," in this process.[33] Finally, regimes can change interests by creating new property rights. For example, joint investment projects such as the Yamburg pipeline may be created or it may be recognized that states have certain rights.

Cognitive theorists emphasize that regimes are resistant to change because

> new arrangements require actors to assimilate alternative procedures or patterns of behavior and to accept (initially) unknown outcomes. Additionally, planned changes in regimes require not only the destruction of existing institutions but also the coordination of expectations around new focal points.[34]

Thus, cognitive theories posit that regime change is likely to lag behind changes in the distribution of power or the interests of states. However, they recognize that there comes a time when the costs of changing the regime become lower than the costs of continuing the old pattern of cooperation. At that point, the regime must either change or collapse.

Increasingly, scholars are asserting that there may be a complex interaction between the system-level factors identified by the neorealists and the unit-level factors identified by the cognitive approaches. For example, Vinod Aggarwal argues that the structural and cognitive approaches "should not be seen as being mutually exclusive, competing models to explain the transformation of international regimes: cognitive theories more successfully explain the development of principles and norms (meta-regime), while structural theories more successfully explain the development of rules and procedures."[35] In the *International Organization* special issue devoted to epistemic communities, the authors

> acknowledge that systemic conditions and domestic pressures impose constraints on state behavior, but we argue that there is still a wide degree of latitude. How states identify their interests and recognize the latitude of actions deemed appropriate in specific issue-areas of policymaking are functions of the manner in which the problems are understood by the policymakers or are represented by those to whom they turn for advice under conditions of uncertainty.[36]

In this study, I argue that the third approach has the greatest explanatory capacity, but I also stress the importance of path dependence.

The creation and initial structure of CMEA can best be understood as the result of the interaction between structural and cognitive factors. While the power and interests of the states explain the impetus for the creation of CMEA and the Soviet Union's capability to determine the form of the trading system, they are not a sufficient explanation for the trading system which emerged. A variety of institutional arrangements were compatible with those interests. Instead I argue that the Soviet Union drew upon its ideology and experience for a design for economic reconstruction which was associated with its own economic development and rise to power.[37]

By the mid-1950s, it was apparent that the pattern of trade which had emerged within the socialist bloc was not in the Soviet Union's economic interest. Nonetheless, attempts to reform CMEA met with limited success. Structural factors explain the pressure for reform (a change in Soviet interests), but they cannot explain the limited success of those attempts because Soviet power capabilities had not declined. I argue that two choices the Soviet Union made in creating CMEA affected the evolution of economic cooperation by narrowing the future choice set in particular ways.

First, the Soviet Union chose to base regional economic

cooperation on the principle of the autarkic development of each state. Cooperation based on this model of development proved to be less efficient than cooperation based on economic integration and specialization as in the EU, but once selected inefficient institutions can persist. The path to greater efficiency is not necessarily clear when "decision makers operate on the basis of incomplete information and their subjective and ideologically conditioned views of how the world ought to be,"[38] as was the case in the socialist bloc. Technical information on costs of production which could have served as a basis for decisions on specialization was lacking in Soviet-style centrally planned economies, and ideology inhibited economic reforms which could have generated that information. Also, over time industrial capacities had been developed in the states, and particular transactions flows had emerged so there were states and organizations within the states "with a stake in the existing constraints" which resisted change.[39] The Soviet Union was unable to impose reforms over the objections of other members because of the second choice that it made when creating CMEA.

Economic cooperation in the socialist bloc was not based on "'the abnegation of sovereignty in a limited but decisive field'" as in the EU but on national sovereignty which was reflected in the institutional structure of CMEA.[40] Each state had equal representation, voting was based on a unanimity decision rule, and CMEA was not granted any supranational authority so its decisions were not binding on the members. Thus, the decision making procedures empowered the small states by giving them voting power which was not congruent with their power capabilities. This made it possible for them to resist Soviet attempts to reform CMEA.

The emphasis on national sovereignty in CMEA also impeded learning at the international level. Ernst Haas asserts that "international organizations are exposed to knowledge through the medium of epistemic communities."[41] However, in the case of CMEA, the specialists in the Secretariat were chosen on the basis of nationality quotas, and although the charter stated that "the Secretariat personnel act as international officials when carrying out service responsibilities," the members retained "the right to recall their citizens from the Secretariat whenever they wish[ed], without explanation."[42] One Czech official phrased it thus: "Going to negotiate at the CMEA was like the reverse of Dante. He wrote that the gate to Hell bears the inscription, 'Entering here, forget when you came.' Instead going to the CMEA, you had better not forget that you have to go home!"[43] Since the states were the sole employer, the professionals were subject to "institutional pressures on their careers, which may result in deviations from stipulated norms of behavior in the production of knowledge." This inhibited the formation of a consensus on reform of CMEA.[44]

It was only after the 1989 revolutions in Eastern Europe that a consensus was reached on the need for fundamental changes in the socialist trading system. Due to the economic reforms, a disjuncture had arisen between the new domestic economic structures and the old pattern of transactions flows. However, the differing pace and goals of reform made reaching a new consensus on the norms and principles of cooperation impossible, and the members disbanded CMEA without creating a successor organization. Knowledge of the history of CMEA is important, though, for understanding the future evolution of economic cooperation in this region because "earlier experiences with regimes and with one's prospective partners affect an actor's willingness to create new regimes."[45]

Was CMEA a Regime?

The next question to be asked is whether the application of regime theory to CMEA is concept stretching. After all, CMEA is generally considered to have been imposed on Eastern Europe rather than emerging "when rational self-interested calculation leads actors to abandon independent decision making in favor of joint decision making."[46] The form of economic cooperation which was embodied in CMEA was not the result of bargaining or negotiation and was in that sense imposed. However, I argue in the next chapter that the degree of imposition is generally overstated in the literature. There was strong interest among the East European states in regional economic cooperation as a response to their own domestic problems. Also, CMEA is not the only case where a "dominant actor openly and explicitly articulates institutional arrangements and compels subordinate actors to conform to them." Oran Young cites the example of the role of the United States in the regime for the continental shelves that emerged after World War II.[47]

It is important, though, to specify more clearly the broader environment in which CMEA was situated. During the Stalin period, the East European states are generally regarded as being less than fully sovereign because the Soviet Union had developed instruments which allowed it to participate in their decision-making as more than an external constraint. These instruments existed in each of the four contexts which comprised the Soviet-East European relationship: the multilateral, national, institutional, and personal contexts. The instruments in the multilateral context were the various multilateral organizations in the Soviet bloc, and the instruments in the national context were the interactions between the states of Eastern Europe and the Soviet Union "as sovereigns in the international environment." The instruments in the institutional context consisted of the "transgovernmental channels of communications," and the instruments in the personal context consisted of the "personal networks that function both formally and informally."[48] However, there were significant changes in the degree of Soviet penetration from the Stalin period to the post-Stalin period so I treat this as a variable.

Methodology

This study follows a comparative case study methodology rather than a standard statistical approach in order to examine the cases in more detail. However, this does not mean that the creation of and changes in CMEA can only be described in a historical fashion. The method of structured, focused comparison developed by Alexander George provides a means of designing and implementing comparative case studies to enhance their relevance and utility for theory development.[49] The analysis is "'focused' in that a historical case must be converted for analytic purposes: certain aspects of the case which are interesting from a theoretical perspective provide the focus. This contrasts with the use of a historical period simply for the purposes of describing as many aspects of the period as possible."[50] Furthermore, the analysis is "structured" in that the data requirements of the case studies are defined and standardized through the design of the study. This is achieved by "formulating theoretically relevant general questions to ask of each case."[51] Rather than pursuing an inductive analysis and using questions to discover a potential causal pattern, I use the theoretical framework presented earlier to investigate regime creation and regime change in a socialist setting.

Organization of the Study

Chapter Two examines the creation and the initial structure of CMEA. The power capabilities which made it possible for the Soviet Union to create CMEA and the interests which led it to do so are examined. However, I argue that structural factors are not a sufficient explanation for two key decisions made by the Soviet Union: the decisions to base regional trade on the autarkic development of each state and to select a weak institutional structure. Cognitive factors (Soviet ideology and experience) are necessary to explain why these alternatives were chosen when others could have satisfied Soviet interests at least as well. This case also establishes a baseline from which changes in CMEA can be assessed.

Chapters Three through Five contain case studies of decisions on proposals to reform CMEA. The first case study examines the CMEA decision not to adopt a 1962 Soviet proposal to endow CMEA with supranational authority. Through this proposal the Soviet Union was attempting to change the organizing principle of intra-bloc trade from autarky to a socialist division of labor. Although the Soviet Union was interested in reform, and its power capabilities had not declined, it was unable to secure adoption of its reform proposal. The success of the Romanian opposition to the Soviet reform proposal demonstrates how the changes in the instruments by which the Soviet Union exerted influence, coupled with the weakness of CMEA's institutional arrangements, impeded reform. It also demonstrates the difficulties of reaching agreement on a change in the underlying principles of economic cooperation.

The second case study examines the reinterpretation of Article IV (3) of the CMEA charter which permitted "interested parties" to pursue cooperation without the participation of all members. This reinterpretation was codified in the 1971 "Comprehensive Program for the Intensification and Improvement of Cooperation and the Development of Socialist Economic Integration of Comecon Member Countries." This case demonstrates one set of conditions under which reform could be achieved. Interest in reform of CMEA had grown because the underlying economic problems which had led to the first attempt to reform CMEA had not been resolved. The Soviet Union was able to secure Romanian approval for the adoption of the interested-party principle because it was able to argue that this was supported by the language of the CMEA Charter and that it did not violate the national sovereignty of the members.

The third case study examines the collapse of CMEA in 1991. Although the criticisms of CMEA's performance were not new, several changes distinguish this reform effort from previous ones. A new economic infrastructure needed to be created because of the changes in domestic economic structure which resulted from the revolutions of 1989. Faced with this challenge, the Soviet Union did not provide the leadership necessary to create a new infrastructure. Finally, in the absence of hegemonic leadership, it was necessary to achieve unanimous agreement on the principles on which future economic cooperation would be based. This proved to be impossible.

The sixth chapter examines the prospects for new forms of regional economic cooperation. Regional trade has collapsed, and it has become apparent that, despite the hopes of the East Europeans, negotiations on membership in the EU will be a long, difficult process. Although progress has been made in creating new forms of economic cooperation, there are obstacles to further development, and purely regional solutions to the trade problems are unlikely to emerge. As a result of their past experiences, the states are wary of the impact of regional cooperation on their economies, and there is not a leader in the region with the willingness and capability to induce others to cooperate. Also, the states vary greatly in size, level of development, and speed of reform so convergent expectations and patterns of behavior are unlikely to emerge.

Notes

1. Establishment of the Council for Mutual Economic Aid," p. 11.

As a result of its increasing estrangement from the Soviet Union, Albania ceased to participate in 1961, while Mongolia joined in 1962, Cuba in 1972, and Vietnam in 1978. The non-European Communist states were granted membership to make it easier to coordinate economic assistance to them, and their positions in the debates on reform are rarely mentioned, even in the literature of the member states. Therefore, this study concentrates on the Soviet Union and the East European members of CMEA which continued to comprise the core of the organization. Two other common abbreviations for CMEA are Comecon and CEMA.

2. Gilpin, "Economic Interdependence," p. 31.

3. Marrese and Vanous, *Soviet Subsidization of Trade*. Alternative estimates of Soviet subsidies are discussed in the chapters that follow.

4. Reisinger, *Energy and the Soviet Bloc*, p. ix.

Vlad Sobell, for example, uses an imperial model in his study of CMEA. *The CMEA in Crisis*, Chapter 2. Reisinger rejects this approach because it "denies ab initio what analysts are most interested in understanding: the *politics* of Soviet-East European relations" (p. 14).

5. Moreton, "Foreign Policy Goals," p. 145. For example, there is evidence that the East Europeans refused to extend the defensive commitments of the Warsaw Pact to the Sino-Soviet border, despite pressure from the Soviet Union to do so (p. 152).

6. Inotai, "Transforming the East," p. 26.

7. Kaser, *Comecon*, p. 11. The Cominform was created in 1947, but it was composed of the European communist parties, not states.

8. P. Haas, "Introduction," p. 33. Examples of the "new institutionalism" are: March and Olsen, "The New Institutionalism," and *Rediscovering Institutions*.

9. For more on path dependence, see North, *Institutions*.

10. Two examples are: Korbonski, "Comecon" and Schaefer, *Comecon and the Politics of Integration*.

11. Kanet, "Integration Theory," p. 388.

12. Reisinger, *Energy and the Soviet Bloc* and Stone, *Satellites and Commissars*.

13. Gilpin, "Economic Interdependence," p. 48.

14. Keohane and Nye, *Power and Interdependence*, p. 5.

15. Reprinted as Krasner, ed., *International Regimes*.

16. There is no real agreement in the literature as to what the second school should be called. In his volume on regimes, Krasner refers to this school as the Grotians, and Keohane refers to it as the reflective approach. However, Haggard and Simmons use the label cognitive in their review of the literature as do others. Therefore, the term cognitive is used despite certain drawbacks. Krasner, ed., *International Regimes*. Keohane, "International Institutions". Haggard and Simmons, "Theories of International Regimes."

Good general overviews of these approaches can be found in P. Haas, "Introduction," pp. 20-34 and Hansenclever, Mayer, and Rittberger, "Interests, Power, Knowledge."

17. Krasner, "Structural Causes," p. 2.

18. See, for example, Waltz, *Theory of International Relations*, p. 131. Waltz argues that this conceptualization of power is better than that of power as control over outcomes. "The intention of an act and its result will seldom be identical because the result will be affected by the person or object acted on and conditioned by the environment within which it occurs" (p. 192).

19. Stein, "Coordination and Collaboration," p. 132.

20. Waltz, *Theory of International Relations*, p. 91.

21. Krasner, "State Power," p. 343.

22. Keohane, "The Theory of Hegemonic Stability," p. 132.

23. See, for example, Strange, "The Myth of Lost Hegemony" and Russett, "The Mysterious Case of Vanishing Hegemony."

24. Krasner, "State Power," p. 343.

25. Keohane, "The Theory of Hegemonic Stability," p. 144.

26. Krasner, "Structural Causes," p. 2. This last response becomes neoliberal institutionalism or interest-based theories of regimes. See Hansenclever, Mayer, and Rittberger, "Interests, Power, Knowledge."

27. Krasner, "Structural Causes," p. 2.

28. Krasner, "Structural Causes," p. 18.

29. E. Haas, "Why Collaborate?" pp. 367-68.

30. Young, "Regime Dynamics," p. 94.

31. Krasner, "Regimes and the Limits of Realism," p. 363.

32. Krasner, "Regimes and the Limits of Realism," p. 363.

33. P. Haas, "Introduction," p. 3. This issue of *International Organization* contains a series of case studies on the impact of epistemic communities on international cooperation.

34. Young, "Regime Dynamics," p. 96.

35. Aggarwal, *Liberal Protectionism*, p. 19.

36. P. Haas, "Introduction," p. 2.

37. For a similar argument about the U.S., see Goldstein, "Ideas, Institutions, and American Trade Policy."

38. North, *Institutions*, p. 97.

39. North, *Institutions*, p. 99.

40. Quoted in Nugent, *The Government and Politics of the European Community*, p. 32.

I will discuss the Soviet concept of national sovereignty, which differed significantly from the Western concept, in detail in later chapters.

41. E. Haas, *When Knowledge is Power*, p. 40.

42. Nicolae, "CMEA in Theory and Practice," pp. 42, 84.

43. Interview with Vladislav Cihar in Stone, *Satellites and Commissars*, pp. 216-17.

44. Thus, CMEA was characterized by an organizational structure which Haas associates with turbulent non-growth. In contrast, the EU has an organizational structure which more closely approximates managed interdependence which Haas associates with learning. It has some supranational authority. The decision rule varies from a simple majority to unanimity although consensus is generally used, and there is an international civil service with some concessions to nationality quotas. E. Haas, *When Knowledge is Power*, p. 41.

45. Hansenclever, Mayer, and Rittberger, "Interests, Power, Knowledge," pp. 186-87.

46. Stein, "Coordination and Collaboration," p. 132.

47. Young, "Regime Dynamics," p. 100.

48. Rice, *The Soviet Union and the Czechoslovak Army*, p. 18.

49. George, "Case Studies and Theory Development," p. 25. See also Lijphart, "The Comparable-Case Strategy" and Eckstein, "Case Study and Theory."

50. Aggarwal, *Liberal Protectionism*, p. 39.

51. George, "Case Studies and Theory Development," p. 25.

Chapter Two

The Creation of CMEA

The formation of the Council for Mutual Economic Assistance was announced in a communique published in *Pravda* on January 25, 1949, but its origins and early activities are still largely shrouded in secrecy. There is no consensus on seemingly trivial questions such as the founding date.[1] Soviet sources generally confine themselves to vague statements like: "the [first] session gave practical form to the CMEA as an international organization of socialist states, approved a plan for the functioning of the Council for 1949, and also examined a number of organizational questions having to do with the activity of the CMEA."[2] Even the quasi-official history of CMEA by Nikolai Faddeev, who was head of the Secretariat 1958-83, has little information on the early activities of CMEA.[3] A few sources are more detailed, and there is evidence that discussions of significant economic integration such as plan coordination and multilateral clearing occurred.[4] However as a result of Soviet intervention, these proposals were abandoned in favor of barter trade based on long-term bilateral agreements, and CMEA lapsed into inactivity.

In creating CMEA, the Soviet Union made two key decisions that are puzzling: the decision to base regional trade on the autarkic development of each state and the decision to select a weak institutional structure. While autarky may have served short-term Soviet economic interests, in the long-term it led to parallel development and the unnecessary duplication of capacities in the region. The decision to create an economic organization with a weak institutional structure and to rely upon informal procedures to ensure that its decisions corresponded with Soviet interests is also puzzling because over time this made it more difficult for the Soviet Union to control decision-making within CMEA.

I argue that the creation and initial structure of CMEA can best be understood as the result of the interaction between structural and cognitive factors. While the power and interests of the actors explain the impetus for the creation of CMEA and the Soviet Union's capability to determine the form of the trading system, they are not a sufficient explanation for the trading system which emerged. A variety of institutional arrangements were compatible with those interests. Instead I argue that the Soviet Union drew upon its ideology and experience for a design for economic reconstruction which was associated with its own economic development and rise to power. These cognitive factors then helped determine the precise form of the trading system which the Soviet Union created.

Structural Factors: Power and Interest

East European Interests

The literature on the creation of CMEA has paid little attention to East European interest in economic cooperation, and the creation of CMEA is generally regarded as something of a *fait accompli* by the Soviet Union.[5] However, there is considerable evidence that the East Europeans demonstrated an early interest in subregional political and economic cooperation as a solution to their economic and security problems. As small to medium-sized states sandwiched between two great powers -- Germany and Russia -- the East Europeans believed that cooperation was necessary if they were to maintain their independence. Also, in a region of widespread irredentism, subregional cooperation provided a possible solution to the nationality problem. Finally, the East European states were war-ravaged and still largely underdeveloped. Most lacked significant natural resources and faced the problem of a large, unskilled agricultural population. They also feared the reemergence of "the beggar-thy-neighbor protectionist policies" activated in the 1930s with such devastating effect.[6] Thus, economic cooperation was viewed as a means to recover from the devastation of the war and to overcome the region's underdevelopment.

At first the East Europeans tried to organize political and economic cooperation among themselves. Proposals for the federation or confederation of states in the region were made both during and immediately after World War II. Two of the most far-reaching were the plans for the confederation of Poland and Czechoslovakia and for a Balkan federation by Yugoslavia and Bulgaria. Both plans envisioned significant economic cooperation through the creation of customs unions. Although the negotiations would have been difficult due to historical animosities and territorial disputes, both proposals were ultimately abandoned because of Soviet opposition.

In November 1940, the Polish and Czechoslovak governments in London published a joint declaration expressing their desire for a confederation of the two countries "based on a customs union with a common currency, a joint general staff, coordinated foreign policy and a common ministerial council."[7] The Czechoslovak President Eduard Benes and the Polish Premier and Commander in Chief General Wladslaw Sikorski hoped to prevent Soviet attempts to impose communism on both states through the creation of a confederation. However, Benes insisted that any confederation not be anti-Soviet and kept the Soviets informed of the progress of the negotiations. On January 23, 1942 the text of an agreement was published which allowed for the accession of other East European states in addition to the provisions mentioned above. The next month "Soviet radio stations began to broadcast unfavorable comments on the confederation plans, calling them meaningless because not a confederation but only Soviet Russia could save Poland and Czechoslovakia from Germany."[8] In July the Soviet Ambassador Bogomolov informed the Czechoslovaks that the Soviet Union opposed their negotiations with Poland. Anxious to secure Soviet good will, the Americans and the British did not provide support in the face of Soviet opposition so Benes felt compelled to abandon the idea of a confederation, and he proposed an alliance instead. However, the Soviets opposed this also, and in May 1943 Czechoslovakia suspended negotiations with Poland.

After the war, Poland and Czechoslovakia made another attempt at economic cooperation. They signed an Economic Collaboration Convention in July 1947 which "provided for a permanent economic council, with eight specialized commissions, to guide industrial development collaboration in the Silesian basin, jointly develop energy resources, and eventually establish a waterways system linking the Oder and the Danube."[9] Through this, Poland and Czechoslovakia sought "to specialize in those industries in which they had a comparative cost advantage, so that they could supply each other's markets with goods produced at lower costs."[10] They also hoped for future Hungarian participation. However, they were forced to abandon their plans once again due to Soviet opposition.

Meanwhile, after the liberation of Bulgaria in September 1944 by the Red Army, the temporary government and Central Committee of Yugoslavia began to correspond with the government and Central Committee of Bulgaria on the question of unification.[11] Bulgarian Premier Georgi Dimitrov and Yugoslav leader Josip Tito were not anti-Soviet; rather, they were striving "to combine the long-lived tendencies toward Balkan unity with Leninist precepts of federalism as a solution of nationality problems" and as a means to promote the economic development of the region.[12] The Soviet Union was kept informed and initially endorsed the plan. However, when Yugoslavia and Bulgaria prepared to sign a joint declaration of unity in January 1947, the Soviets demanded that it be postponed because of American and British concerns. (Bulgaria was an enemy state, and no peace treaty had been signed.) After the Bulgarian Peace Treaty was signed in February 1947, plans for the Balkan federation moved forward once again. At a conference in Bled later that year, both governments agreed to "develop economic cooperation by 'laying the groundwork for a customs union and by coordinating their economic plans'; to create a regime for the frontier properties and to simplify travel and citizenship regulations; to expand cultural cooperation; to concert their policies on the Greek question and on 'all other major international problems which affect their interests, ...'"[13] The Soviets supported this proposal until Dimitrov began to talk of extending participation to Romania, Czechoslovakia, Poland, and Greece. A *Pravda* editorial published in January 1948 stated that "'these countries do not need . . . an artificial and problematic federation, confederation or union, but a strengthening and a defense of their independence and sovereignty through a mobilization and organization of their internal popular-democratic forces . . .'"[14] The Yugoslav and Bulgarian delegations were called to Moscow in February where Stalin condemned a larger Balkan federation and ordered them to speed up the conclusion of the federation of Yugoslavia and Bulgaria. This made the Yugoslavs suspicious that Moscow wanted to use the federation as "a snare -- to crack the unity of the Yugoslav Communists."[15] Relations between the Soviet Union and Yugoslavia continued to deteriorate, and all plans for a Balkan federation ceased with the expulsion of Yugoslavia from the Cominform in June 1948.

During 1947 it also became clear that the Soviet Union would not allow the East Europeans to cooperate economically with the West. In a speech at Harvard University on June 5, 1947, Secretary of State George Marshall announced that the U.S. would provide "friendly aid in the drafting of a [joint] European program [for economic recovery] and . . . later support of such a program so far as it may be practical for us to do so."[16] Although the Soviet Union refused to participate in the Marshall Plan, the seven East European states were invited "to meet in Paris on July 12 to set up a 'committee of cooperation' which would draw up a report on Europe's resources, prospects and needs, for transmission to the United States."[17] Most of the East Europeans declined the invitation echoing the language of the Soviet refusal. However, on July 8 Czechoslovakia, which was still under coalition rule, accepted the invitation apparently acting on the basis of the Soviet Union's initial advice to participate and the belief that Poland would also participate. However, that same day the Soviet Union changed its position on East European participation, and the next day Poland declined the invitation stating that "the Paris conference was 'more or less set' beforehand, that there were 'political strings' attached to proposed American aid and that it would be the aim of the Western powers under the Marshall plan to revive a 'strong Germany.'"[18]

The Czech Foreign and Prime Ministers immediately flew to Moscow for "already scheduled trade talks", and on July 10, Czechoslovakia also declined the invitation to the Paris conference. As the chairman of the Czech Social Democratic Party wrote,

> 'When we learned, however, that our participation in Paris might be construed as an act that infringed our ties of alliance with the Soviet Union and when our participation in the conference in Paris had also become an issue involving our alliance with the U.S.S.R., we could not take the republic's economic interests as our sole guide but had first of all to think about ensuring its political existence. There is, of course, no need to stress how important the alliance with our great neighbor is for us. Everyone recognizes that without this alliance with a state able to render us prompt and effective aid, we should be defenseless in the face of the German threat, ...'[19]

Thus, it became clear that if the East Europeans wanted to pursue economic cooperation, they would have to approach the Soviet Union because it would not allow them to cooperate either among themselves or with the West.

Indeed the East Europeans' interest in economic cooperation was so strong that they began to propose plans for organizing regional economic cooperation which included the Soviet Union. Based on his examination of the Archives of the Czechoslovak Ministry of National Planning, the Czech historian Karel Kaplan attributes the following summary of the events which led to the creation of CMEA to the Soviet Foreign Minister Vyacheslav Mikhailovich Molotov:

> "Last autumn," he recalled, "our Rumanian friends raised the question of closer ties among the People's Democracies and the Soviet Union." It involved a coordination of their activities and included the proposal "that there be a coordination of their respective plans. At first we had our doubts about the usefulness of this suggestion, whether it wasn't premature. Enemies might take advantage of it. But when others came with the same idea, Comrade Stalin expressed the opinion that the time was ripe. Gottwald had spoken of it and the Romanian comrades, but also comrades from other People's Democratic countries .... (then) the question was discussed by the Politburo of the Central Committee of the Czechoslovak Communist Party and in response, we agreed in principle." The Rumanians worked out detailed draft proposals "which we then considered and found to be correct. As

> a result, a document emerges on close cooperation between the Soviet Union and the countries of the new democracies."[20]

From the available evidence, it appears that many of the East European states favored "economic cooperation through plan coordination and regional planning in which trade and specialization indicators would play a role."[21] Czechoslovakia was a particularly outspoken proponent of economic cooperation based on a division of labor. It proposed that the CMEA members "'coordinate their economic plans, establish joint investment programs, [and] begin joint production programs . . . from the point of view of setting up a division of productive forces according to the requirements of each country and its natural and historical conditions.'"[22] In a January 1949 conversation with U.S. embassy officers in Warsaw, the Director General of the Economic Department of the Polish Foreign Office stated that CMEA was formed for the "'predominate purpose [of] achieving rationalization in industrialization' of participating orbit countries and centralizing economic planning for [the] area."[23] Working documents were formulated on this basis. However according to Sandor Ausch, a Hungarian economist who was a member of the CMEA Bureau at that time, Stalin "intervened and, . . ., and put an end to the activities of the CMEA apparatus in this field."[24] Economic integration was replaced by another program of development: autarky.

Soviet and East European Power Capabilities

The East Europeans were not powerful enough to pursue their vision of economic cooperation in the face of Soviet opposition. By any one of five measures of capability, the Soviet Union was clearly the regional hegemon in 1949 although it was still recovering from the devastation of World War II. It had extended its Western borders at the expense of Poland, Czechoslovakia and Romania. These border adjustments left the Soviet Union with an area of 22,403 thousand square kilometers and the East European states with a combined area of 991 thousand square kilometers. The Soviet population was more than twice as large as that of the East European states (193,200,000 versus

88,501,000) as was its gross domestic product (69.4 billion 1950 U.S. dollars versus 32.4).[25]

The Soviet army was one of the victors of the war while the East Europeans were still in the process of rebuilding their militaries. East Germany, Romania, Hungary, and Bulgaria were all former enemy states, and the sizes of their militaries were restricted by the provisions of the peace treaties. According to an agreement approved by the Allied Control Council at Berlin on September 20, 1945, all German land, naval, and air forces as well as military organizations were abolished. Military training, propaganda, and activities were also prohibited.[26] However, in December 1949 there was a para-military police force in the Soviet zone which consisted of about 35 units of 12,000 men each. "These units are not employed in ordinary police duties; they are staffed by former German generals, and recruiting is chiefly done among former members of the *Wehrmacht* and the Communist Free German Youth organization."[27] Bulgaria was limited to total armed force personnel of 65,500, Hungary to 70,000, and Romania to 138,000 by the peace treaties signed in Paris on February 10, 1947. These included combat, service, and overhead personnel. It was also forbidden for any persons not in the army, navy, or air force to receive military training. These provisions were to remain in force until modified with the approval of the Allied and Associated Powers or the United Nations Security Council.[28] Poland and Czechoslovakia were under no restrictions, but their militaries had been virtually destroyed in the war. According to the best available estimates, Soviet military personnel numbered 2,874,000 while those of Eastern Europe numbered 1,262,000.[29]

The Soviet Union was also blessed with abundant natural resources. It was a significant exporter of manganese ore, iron ore, chromite, aluminum, precious metals, and crude petroleum.[30] In contrast, the East European states were relatively resource poor, and many of their ore deposits were of low quality. Lead, zinc, and low-rank coal were Bulgaria's principal mineral products. Czechoslovakia's principal mineral resources were magnesite, coal, limestone and kaolin. East Germany's were potash, coal, salt, and silver. Hungary's principal mineral resource was bauxite;[31] Poland produced high-rank coal and zinc; and Romania had significant petroleum deposits.

Soviet Interests

The Soviet Union's economic and security interests led to its desire to create CMEA. Although it was in military control of Eastern Europe, the Soviet Union could not compete economically with the U.S. for influence in the region. For this reason, the Marshall Plan represented a major threat to Soviet security interests which could only be parried by isolating the East European economies from the world economy.

The Soviets were invited to participate in the Marshall Plan themselves, but they objected to two key provisions which they viewed as violations of their sovereignty. They refused to accept "the exchange of information and definite commitments in respect of production and exports, perhaps even continental planning or a European customs union" with capitalist nations which were an essential part of the American plan.[32] The Soviets instead proposed "first, to ascertain the reality, terms, and amount of the proposed credits; second, to ask European countries what credits they require; and third, to draw up a program combining requirements which should be met as far as possible out of US credits."[33] They also did not want ex-enemy states, especially Germany, to be equal participants because they feared that this would lead to the rebirth of Germany's military potential as well as the permanent end of reparations. Both sides refused to compromise, and the conference broke up with the Soviets announcing that they would not participate in the Marshall Plan.

Despite the Soviet refusal, Britain and France invited the seven East European states to the July 1947 meetings in Paris. As the Soviets recognized, this represented an attempt to undermine the unity of the socialist camp and to extend Western influence in a region which the Soviets viewed as vital to their security. They then pressured the East Europeans not to participate. Once it became apparent that the Marshall Plan would be a success, however, the Soviets decided that the bloc must strive for maximum economic independence from the capitalist world to prevent renewed Western attempts at economic incursion. The creation of a bloc trade organization to rival the Organization for European Economic Cooperation (OEEC) would promote economic independence from the West and perhaps prevent future East European participation in West European economic cooperation unless approved by the bloc organization.

A bloc trade organization could also be used to coordinate a trade embargo with Yugoslavia. The socialist countries had signed extensive trade agreements with Yugoslavia before its expulsion from the Cominform in 1948. For example in May 1947, Hungary and Yugoslavia had signed an agreement by which Hungary would construct aluminum plants in Yugoslavia in exchange for deliveries of caustic soda and guaranteed purchases of alumina. Later that year an agreement on plan coordination between the two countries was also signed.[34] The Soviets hoped that severing economic relations would break Yugoslavia's resolve as well as limit the other East Europeans' contact with the heretics.

In terms of its economic interests, the Soviet Union needed a massive influx of capital goods and resources to rebuild its war-ravaged economy. The Soviets had looked to German reparations as a principal source. At Yalta Roosevelt had agreed "to consider 'as a basis for discussion' the Soviet proposal for $20 billion in reparation (one-half of which would go to Russia)."[35] At the end of the war, the Soviets began shipping German industrial equipment and even entire factories to the Soviet Union as reparations. However, the Americans halted all deliveries from their zone in 1946 because the Soviets and the French would not abide by the decision to treat Germany as a single economic unit. The U.S. was also concerned about the cost of occupation and saw the rebuilding of the German economy as a solution. As the Soviets recognized, "to proclaim a new expanded plan for industrial production means to cut sharply, if not to halt completely, shipments of German industrial equipment as reparations."[36] The failure of the March 1947 Conference of Foreign Ministers in Moscow to reach a decision on any important aspect of the German question made it quite clear that the resumption of reparations deliveries from the Western zones was highly unlikely.

On June 24, 1948, the Soviet Union began a blockade of the Western zones in an attempt to block the West's planned creation of its own German state. In March 1948, the U.S. had instituted "an export licensing system for American exports to the entire [Soviet] Bloc in order to prevent their receiving 'armaments and strategic goods.'"[37] The latter phrase was interpreted liberally, and the U.S. responded to the Berlin Blockade by persuading the Europeans to cooperate with the embargo. As a result, Soviet imports of machinery valued at $155 million in 1947 dropped to about $50 million by 1950.[38] This made it difficult for the Soviets to satisfy their demands for capital goods through trade with the West. The role that the Western embargo played in the creation of CMEA was acknowledged in the 1949 communique announcing its formation.

> The conference further observed that the Governments of the United States of America, England, and certain other countries of Western Europe are in effect boycotting trade relations with the countries of people's democracy and the U.S.S.R., because these countries do not consider it possible to subordinate themselves to the dictate of the Marshall Plan, since this plan violates the sovereignty of the countries and the interests of their national economies.
>
> Taking this fact into consideration, the conference discussed the question of the possibility of organizing broader economic cooperation between the countries of the people's democracy and the U.S.S.R.[39]

It was by default that by 1949 the East European states were the most likely source of the capital goods and resources necessary to rebuild the Soviet economy.

However, major changes in the pattern of trade and production in the region were necessary before the Soviet Union's economic and security interests could be met. Before World War II, the East European states had primarily traded with Germany. Although the war had disrupted regional trade and increased the role of the Soviet Union, East European trade with the West soon began to revive. By 1947-48, the

Soviet share of Czechoslovak, Hungarian, and Polish trade had fallen to just over 30 percent, and it was continuing to fall.[40] Moreover, the Western embargo on strategic exports led to greater East European demands for imports of the very items that the Soviet Union wanted to import from them: raw materials and capital goods (See Table 2.1).

Table 2.1: The Share of the USSR in Total Imports of Major Commodities of European People's Democracies, 1950 (in %)

Machinery and equipment	28.6
Iron ore	65.0
Pig iron	68.1
Rolled steel and pipes	48.9
Non-ferrous metals	26.5
Oil	47.3
Oil products	62.6
Timber materials	12.7
Cotton	79.3
Grains	77.9

Source: N. Orlov, "The Foreign Trade of the Soviet Union Under Present Conditions," *Voprosy ekonomiki*, May 1959 in *Problems of Economics* 2 (September 1959), p. 30.

Satisfaction of their own and Soviet demands for these goods required major changes in the pattern of production because even the most industrially advanced East European state, Czechoslovakia, had primarily produced textiles, footwear, glassware, and other light industry products while the others had produced food, raw materials, and semi-finished goods.

The Soviet Union was interested in the creation of a regional trading system for the reasons listed above, and it clearly had the power to determine the substantive nature of that system. However, Soviet power and interests do not constitute a sufficient explanation for the decisions to create a trading system based on economic autarky and to select a weak institutional structure for CMEA. Soviet security interests clearly required that the trading system be isolated from the world economy, yet they did not require that each state within the trading system pursue economic autarky. Other forms of economic cooperation within the region could have satisfied Soviet economic and security interests at least as well as, if not better than, autarky. For example, CMEA could have been created as a supranational planning organization with the goals of promoting specialization and a division of labor. This would have allowed the Soviet Union to determine the pattern of economic development while avoiding the potential problems associated with autarky. An additional advantage of this choice was that it was closer to the East European vision of economic cooperation. In fact as the next chapter demonstrates, Khrushchev attempted to reform CMEA along these lines in the early 1960s when the economic costs to the Soviet Union of a trading system based on the autarkic development of each state became clear.

Since the major Soviet criticism of the Marshall Plan was that it violated the sovereignty of the participants,[41] it is not surprising that the Soviets selected a more egalitarian institutional structure for CMEA. However, there are many permutations of decision rules that could have satisfied Soviet interests at least as well as, if not better than, unanimity. Traditional international law provided support for unanimity, but international economic organizations had been moving toward majority decision rules because of the limitations unanimity places on effective action: a single member can block a decision, and it tends to lead to least common denominator decisions. For example, the IMF has a weighted voting system which gives the U.S. a virtual veto, and even the GATT rules provide for majority decision-making, with certain exceptions.[42] The Soviet Union could have opted for a decision rule which required an extraordinary majority or at a minimum, it could have made CMEA decisions binding on the members. To understand why these particular choices were made, it is necessary to look at cognitive factors such as ideology and experience.

Cognitive Factors: Ideology and Experience

Autarky

As the first socialist state and one of the victors of World War II, the Soviet Union was able to offer the East Europeans both theoretical and practical guidance for economic development. Soviet ideology was based on Karl Marx's dialectical materialism, a method of interpreting the past and predicting the direction of future developments based on the primacy of economics. However, the first successful communist revolution did not occur in a developed capitalist country as Marx had predicted, but in the least developed European power, Russia.[43] Therefore, the Russian communists paid inordinate attention to building the material basis of socialism through rapid industrialization. Marxist theory had little to say about how to achieve this except a belief that "created factors of production will play an ever-growing role in sustaining steady growth."[44]

Under the pressure of circumstances, a model of economic development, generally referred to as the Stalinist model, emerged. It consisted of three major elements. First, state authority as expressed in highly centralized plans replaced the market in the management of the economy. In the Soviet Union, these plans were based on quantity-term calculations and ignored the relative scales and costs of production. Second, the goal of the state in managing the economy was to achieve rapid industrialization. Third, in order to achieve this rapid industrialization, Stalin "laid the emphasis on the development of heavy industry. Within this, he stressed as the decisive link of the chain the development of the complete spectrum of metallurgy and engineering, with a priority given to the manufacturing of equipment serving the output of the means of production."[45]

Circumstances also led the Soviet Union to strive for self-sufficiency. The introduction of central planning in 1928 had changed the economic calculations in favor of autarky. The government maintained a monopoly of foreign trade, and the foreign trade corporations operated within a foreign trade plan. Since Soviet plans were taut, any disruption in supply could reverberate through the whole economy. This led to a preference for domestic sources of supply rather than uncertain foreign ones. And "in the absence of any serious interest in the relative scales and costs of production, in the late thirties trade came to be regarded as something in the nature of a burden on the economy, a physical drain of commodities out of the country."[46] Thus, foreign trade was conducted to obtain essential goods which were unavailable, either temporarily or permanently.[47] In the uncertain atmosphere of the 1930s, the Soviet Union also wanted to secure and maintain its military and economic independence from a hostile capitalist world. According to Stalin,

> 'the country of the dictatorship of the proletariat, in conditions of capitalist encirclement, cannot remain economically independent if it does not produce at home the instruments and means of production. . . . Without this, no one can speak of the assurance of the economic independence of our country.'[48]

This model of economic development was remarkably successful initially. The Soviet Union's resource endowment made it possible to develop the complete spectrum of metallurgy and engineering without massive imports of raw materials, and the size of the domestic market made it possible to benefit from economies of scale in production. However, by 1949 the Soviet economy faced new tasks. Rather than industrializing, it needed to rebuild infrastructure which had been destroyed in World War II. The emergence of Communist governments in Eastern Europe also meant that it was no longer necessary to build socialism in one country. Finally, there were valid reasons to suppose that the Stalinist model of economic development might not be as successful in Eastern Europe as it had been in the Soviet Union. For example, the East European states' internal markets were too small to support the production of the complete spectrum of engineering at economies of scale, and they lacked the extensive mineral resources to support metallurgical production. For these reasons, discussions on an appropriate model of economic development for the post-war period began.

Nikolai Voznesenskii, the Chairman of the State Planning

Commission (Gosplan), argued that the socialist state sets the goals for the national economy which are then expressed through the plans and that the proportions of the different sectors of the Soviet economy which had been appropriate before the war would not necessarily be appropriate in the post-war period.[49] Finally, he asserted that "the state plan makes use of the law of value for the correct distribution of social labor between the different branches of the economy in the interests of socialism."[50] Thus, Voznesenskii believed that planning priorities could change as state policy changed and that it was necessary to consider the profitability of various sectors when allocating resources through the plan.

On the other hand, Stalin argued that "the laws of political economy reflect law-governed processes operating irrespective of the will of men" so the planning priorities of the socialist state were a reflection of those laws rather than state policy.[51] While he acknowledged that the law of value was relevant to the production of commodities such as consumer goods, he argued that the means of production were not subject to the law of value because they were not bought and sold.[52] Therefore, he concluded that "the law of value cannot be a 'regulator of the proportions' in the distribution of labor between the different branches of production."[53] Stalin believed that planning priorities were unchangeable unless there was a change in the underlying structure of the economy and that considerations of value should not drive changes in the allocation of resources between the sectors of the economy.

The outcome of this discussion was significant for the development of the socialist trading system because, as Michael Kaser observes, without value planning there were no "criteria for the rational specializations undertaken in the context of co-ordinated long-term planning."[54] Although there is evidence that discussions of plan coordination and multilateral clearing occurred in the early meetings of the CMEA Council Session, the March 1949 dismissal and denunciation of Voznesenskii signaled the Soviet rejection of this course.[55] The proposals for plan coordination and multilateral clearing were abandoned in favor of economic autarky and bilateral barter trade. Stalin did not respond creatively to the new situation in the post-war period. Instead he responded as cognitive psychology would lead us to expect. He "identif[ied] and interpret[ed] problems within existing frameworks and according to past protocols and then tr[ied] to manage the problems according to operating procedures that [he had] applied in analogous cases."[56]

Institutional Structure of CMEA

The formal arrangements of CMEA were egalitarian. It was provided with a limited organizational structure, and the brief founding communique apparently served in lieu of a formal charter. The highest organ was the Council Session which consisted of "representatives of the countries participating in the conference, on the basis of equal representation." It was to "gather in periodic meetings by turns in the capitals of the participating countries, under the chairmanship of the representative of the country in whose capital the meeting is being held."[57] A permanent Bureau composed of one delegate from each member and the general secretary of CMEA, A. Loshchakov a Soviet citizen, was added at the first Council Session "'to further mutual economic work.'"[58] The Bureau was headquartered in Moscow and supported by a technical secretariat composed of Soviet experts. According to Loshchakov, a third body, a commission on the coordination of foreign trade which was composed of the deputy ministers of foreign trade, was also formed.[59] Each member was given one vote, and decisions had to be unanimous. Moreover, CMEA decisions were not binding on the members; they were adopted "only with the consent of the interested country."[60] The Soviet Union found these institutional arrangements attractive because they reflected Soviet ideology and experience.[61]

The principle of national sovereignty was well-established in Soviet thought and practice so it is not surprising that it was embodied in CMEA. Self-determination for the nationalities of the Russian empire "was an important element in Bolshevik propaganda before November

1917, and was reaffirmed after the seizure of power."[62] In theory, the Soviet constitution guaranteed the right of the national republics to secede from the union; "this principle of sovereignty finds its embodiment in the creation of the socialist multinational state on elements of free will and equality of nations. The multinational state protects the sovereign rights of the Soviet national union republics."[63] The emphasis on sovereignty was also not unusual in Soviet-East European relations. As Brzezinski notes, the treaties of friendship, collaboration, and mutual aid which the Soviets had already signed with the East Europeans "went quite far in stressing the latter's sovereignty, equality, and independence."[64]

However, it is important to realize that the Soviet concept of national sovereignty was very different from the Western bourgeois concept in that it had a class content. Marxist-Leninist theory relates different historical types of states, which are distinguished by the nature of the means of production to different types of sovereignty. The program of the Eighth Party Congress adopted in March 1919 states that "the question of who in any particular case must be regarded as the bearer of the will of a nation on the issue of separatism must be decided 'according to the historical stage of development of that nation.'"[65] Thus, the Soviets emphasized "the secondary importance of national elements with respect to the class struggle and the class interests of the proletariat." Also, the October Revolution signified the birth of a new historical type of state, and "under conditions of the present historical epoch, the principle of sovereignty signifies first of all the complete independence of states within the socialist system (. . .) from the states within the imperialist system in all their domestic and foreign affairs."[66] Given that the Soviets ascribed to a two camp view of the world in which states were either allied with the Soviet Union or with imperialism, this implied that "utterances against the Soviet Union must inevitably serve the interests of imperialism and betray national interests."[67] Thus in Soviet theory, national sovereignty was limited by the interests of the proletariat defined as socialism and by the interests of international socialism defined as the interests of the Soviet Union.

The Soviets also drew upon their domestic experience for the unanimity decision rule. As Stephen Zamora observes, "the borrowing of international voting rules from domestic experience is characteristic, and probably logical, since the experience of most world leaders is first formed in their respective national arenas."[68] In the Soviet Union, fear of factionalism had led to a situation where decisions were typically unanimous. Uncontested slates of candidates received 99 percent of the vote with 99 percent of the electorate voting. There had not been a negative vote cast in the major legislative body, the Supreme Soviet, since the early 1930s, and Stalin had even gone to the extreme of insisting that all decisions of the Politburo "be recorded as unanimous and forbidding the opposition leaders to air their differences publicly."[69]

Finally, the Soviet Union drew upon its domestic experience for the informal procedures which characterized CMEA's operation. The formal organization was divested of its policy-making power. The highest organ of CMEA, the Council Session, met three times (Moscow, April 26-28, 1949; Sofia, August 25-27, 1949; and Moscow, November 24, 1950) and then ceased meeting until after the death of Stalin. The work of the Council Session was assumed by its administrative organ, the Bureau, and policy was made in Moscow. Karel Kaplan claims that

> When the Bureau was considering more important questions, Mikoyan attended too as a member of the Soviet Politburo. His political authority guaranteed in advance that the proposals he made, would be accepted. Everybody realized that his speeches and views were directives from Moscow and they all behaved accordingly, including the governments they were representing.[70]

Soviet institutions in the Stalin Era are generally referred to as transmission belts, that is they "were progressively divested of executive policy-making power and converted into administrative arms of the executive, here defined narrowly as the Politburo, or more precisely still, as Stalin."[71] This is demonstrated by how seldom the policy-making institutions met. Although the CPSU party statutes stated that Party Congresses were to meet every three years at which time they would select the Central Committee which would in turn select the Secretariat, the Politburo, etc., there was a gap of almost fourteen years between the

18th Party Congress (March 1939) and the 19th (October 1952). In his Secret Speech at the 20th Party Congress, Khrushchev stated that in the last years of Stalin's life "the Central Committee plenary sessions [which should have been held twice a year] were not convened and that the sessions of the Political Bureau occurred only occasionally."[72] Thus, the principle of national sovereignty, the decision rule, and the informal procedures of CMEA were clearly drawn from Soviet ideology and domestic experience.

Soviet Instruments

Rather than relying upon a strong institutional structure to ensure that CMEA decisions were in its interest, the Soviet Union chose to rely upon the use of instruments in all four contexts which comprised the relationship. The greatest emphasis, though, was placed on instruments in the personal and institutional contexts.

Stalin demanded that key East European party and state positions be filled by "communists with an extensive Soviet or Comintern background, frequently with experience in the NKVD networks."[73] For example, the Polish Premier Boleslaw Bierut had been a member of the NKVD, and the Bulgarian Premier Georgi Dimitrov had been the head of the Comintern as well as a Soviet citizen. Like the other East European party leaders, they had spent the war years in Moscow where they had been groomed by the Soviets for their new roles.[74] Perhaps the most blatant example of this practice at lower levels, although it did not occur until late 1949, was the appointment of Marshall Konstantin Rokossovski as the Polish Minister of National Defense. Rokossovski was a Polish national who had served in the Russian army since 1914 and had risen to the rank of Marshall in it. As Khrushchev acknowledged in his memoirs, "Rokossovski would never raise his hand against the Soviet Union, nor would he lead the Polish Army against the Soviet army. In short, he may have been a Polish marshal, but he was also a Soviet marshal -- and no one had better forget it."[75] Thus, the leaders of the East European states were predominately men and women loyal to the Soviet Union who were often unknown in their own countries. They were thoroughly indoctrinated and dependent on the Soviet Union for their positions.

In the institutional context, the Soviets were building their ties through the presence of Soviet advisers who were helping the East Europeans to rebuild their police forces, armies, intelligence forces, planning commissions, etc. on the model of their Soviet counterparts. Special attention was paid to "those governmental institutions which were particularly important as instruments of power: usually the secret police and the armed forces."[76] For example, Soviet military advisers arrived in Hungary in November 1948, and according to a former Hungarian general, "an adviser was assigned to each branch of the army, to the infantry officers' school and to the staff officers course." The number of advisers continued to increase, and before it reached its peak in 1953, the Soviet advisers at the officers' Academy alone "included one general, one high-ranking political officer and 13 colonels."[77]

There were also "Soviet advisors in the [CMEA] member countries who played a top-level role in their national economies -- in the ministries of economy, in the offices of cabinet ministers and their deputies, in some of the central headquarters and key factories."[78] After 1945, all high economic functionaries in East Germany had their 'partner' in the Soviet embassy whom they consulted for every important move.[79] And, "Soviet instructors in the [Bulgarian] Ministry of Agriculture advised Minister Titko Chernokolev to issue orders regarding the number of cooperatives to be set up, the number of members to be included and the area to belong to them."[80] Thus, the presence of their advisers allowed the Soviets to participate directly in the decision-making process in the East European states and gave them access to detailed information about all aspects of life in Eastern Europe.

The Soviets not only sent advisers, but they also obtained a share of key industries in Bulgaria, Romania, and Hungary through the creation of joint stock companies. In 1945 Romania and the Soviet Union signed conventions which set up these companies in the oil, river and marine transportation, air transportation, and banking industries. In 1949 and 1952 additional joint stock companies were formed in the metal, coal, oil machinery, tractor, chemical, gas, lumber, and construction industries.

> The Soviet Union paid the companies mainly by supplying modern equipment and materials necessary for the work of the companies' enterprises. [These were usually German assets seized locally.] Technical assistance was also rendered by the Soviet Union by giving blueprints, sending specialists, compiling plans for construction and reconstruction of enterprises and helping to train skilled cadres of Rumanian citizens.[81]

These companies typically had monopolies in their respective industries and were exempt from taxes, assessments, customs or duties as well as receiving preferential treatment with regard to supplies and labor. Generally, the chairman of the board of directors was a Romanian, and the deputy chairman was a Soviet while the general manager was a Soviet and the assistant general manager was a Romanian.[82] Since the executive functions were entrusted to the general manager, the Soviets were able to control the exploitation of key Romanian natural resources as well as to virtually exclude the Romanians from the management of their airfields, harbors, and other important sectors of their economy.

There were fewer joint stock companies in Bulgaria and Hungary, but they also represented key industries. In 1948 there were eight Soviet-Hungarian companies in the river transport, civil aviation, oil, mining, and construction industries.[83] Four joint stock companies were established in Bulgaria in the mining, civil aviation, shipbuilding, and construction industries. These operated under the same conditions as the Soviet-Romanian joint stock companies.

The control was even more direct in East Germany. In December 1945, the Soviet Military Administration transferred to Soviet ownership and management 200 German-owned enterprises which were some of the largest and most important in the Soviet zone. By the end of 1949, 89 of these had been sold back to the Germans although some had been partially or wholly dismantled. No German could hold a position higher than the sub-directorate function known in Germany as *Prokurist*, and the SAG, as these enterprises were called, were given priority in raw material, labor, and fuel supplies.[84]

The Soviet Union did not neglect to create more traditional instruments of control in the national and international contexts either. At the end of World War II, the Soviet Union was in military control of Eastern Europe, and in 1949 there were still 31 Soviet divisions stationed in Bulgaria, Romania, Poland, Hungary, and East Germany. All of the East European states (except East Germany) were bound to the Soviet Union and to each other by treaties of friendship, collaboration, and mutual aid.[85] Also, the Czechoslovak coup in 1948 had completed the process of consolidating communist party rule in the region.

In the multilateral context, the Cominform, heir to the Comintern, was formed in 1947 and charged "'with the organization of interchange of experience and, if need be, coordination of the activities of the Communist Parties on the basis of mutual agreement.'"[86] This multilateral organization provided a means whereby the Soviet Union could once again direct the activities of the European communist parties, and the expulsion and universal condemnation of Yugoslavia for nationalist deviations in 1948 demonstrated what the consequences of following an independent course would be.

Conclusion

Since the Soviet Union was clearly hegemonic within its sphere of influence, it ultimately determined the choice of a trading system. Although ideas about other forms of economic cooperation based on specialization were present which could have satisfied its economic and security interests, it chose to create a trading system based on economic autarky and bilateral state-controlled trade. It also chose to create a weak institutional structure for CMEA and to rely chiefly upon instruments in the personal and institutional contexts to insure that CMEA decisions were in the Soviet Union's interest. In the short-term, these choices did allow the Soviet Union to satisfy its interests: reorientation of East European trade from the West to the East, coordination of East European demands on the Soviet economy, and an emphasis on the production of capital goods by the East Europeans.

At the Sofia meeting of the Council Session, a resolution was passed which recommended a "rapid and maximal expansion of multilateral trade among the member countries and a maximal and immediate limitation of trade with the capitalist world" through the negotiation of long term trade agreements among the members.[87] As Table 2.2 shows, East European trade was rapidly redirected to the East.

Table 2.2: Percentage of Foreign Trade With the Socialist Camp

	1948	1949	1950	1951	1952
Poland	41	43	59	58	67
Czechoslovakia	32	46	55	61	71
Hungary	34	46	61	67	71
Rumania	71	82	83	80	85
Bulgaria	78	82	89	92	89

Source: A. Chistyakov, "Growth in Economic Cooperation Among Countries of the Socialist Camp," *Kommunist*, October 1954 in *CDSP* 6 (January 19, 1955), p. 6.

Also, the CMEA members agreed to stop all loans, restrict deliveries, and cease offering technical assistance to Yugoslavia.[88] As a result of this trade with Yugoslavia virtually ceased.

The reduction in trade with the West and Yugoslavia made the East Europeans more dependent on Soviet markets, raw materials, and equipment, and long-term bilateral trade agreements became the means by which the East European economies were restructured. The Soviets pressured the East Europeans to increase their production of heavy industrial products. For example, they refused to accept traditional Czech exports and requested instead what Mikoyan termed "'very sophisticated equipment which was being produced by perhaps only two or three other countries in the world.'"[89] About 45 percent of the volume of Czechoslovak machinery exported to the Soviet Union consisted of products not previously manufactured in Czechoslovakia.[90] Production of these goods required extensive retooling of Czech factories and a 1.5 million increase in manpower which meant adding adolescents, housewives, and farmers to the work force. As a result of similar pressures, the production and export of heavy industrial products in the region increased dramatically. The percentage of machinery and means of production in Czechoslovakia's exports increased from 6.1 percent in 1937 to 42.3 percent in 1953.[91] Similar increases occurred in the exports of other East European states. For example, Poland's exports of machinery, industrial equipment, and transportation equipment increased from three percent in 1949 to twelve percent in 1953, and Romania's exports of industrial items increased from 1.79 percent in 1938 to 17.8 percent in 1953.[92]

Finally, the Soviets encouraged the East European states to exploit their own raw material resources to reduce demand for Soviet resources. For example, the Soviets refused to supply Czechoslovakia with the necessary quantities of iron ore thereby forcing the Czechs to develop their own large but low quality ore deposits. When the Czechs protested, the Soviets replied, "'An economy is much more stable if it develops all its own resources, even if this requires certain investments.'"[93]

Although the Soviet decision to base regional development on the autarkic development of each state and to rely on informal instruments of control to ensure that CMEA decisions corresponded with its interests was initially successful, it contained the seeds of future difficulties. The economic costs associated with autarky soon became apparent, and as Brzezinski observed, "Soviet supremacy, stressed ideologically, was thus not given a formal basis and could not, in the future, justify itself by any reliance on formal arrangements."[94] Once there was a change in the informal instruments of Soviet control, the egalitarian forms of CMEA could begin to exert some influence of their own.

Notes

1. See Brabant, "On the Origins and Tasks" for a review of the literature on this topic.

2. Siluyanov, "Brotherly Collaboration," p. 15.

3. Faddeev, *Sovet Ekonomicheskoi Vzaimopomoshchi*.

4. See Lukin, "Pervoe Desiatiletie" and Loshchakov, "35 Let SEV."

5. See, for example, one of the most authoritative sources on the creation of CMEA: Kaser, *Comecon*. Jozef van Brabant's work is an exception to this generalization.

6. Brabant, *Adjustment, Structural Change and Economic Efficiency*.

7. Wandycz, "Recent Traditions," p. 43. The following account draws heavily upon this source.

8. Wandycz, "Recent Traditions," p. 56.

9. Brzezinski, *The Soviet Bloc*, p. 57.

10. Berend, "The Problem of Eastern European Economic Integration," p. 11.

11. Interest in a Balkan federation dates back to 1910 so this was the latest in a long history of attempts to unify the region.

12. Wandycz, "Recent Traditions," p. 89.

13. Wandycz, "Recent Traditions," p. 81.

14. Quoted in Wandycz, "Recent Traditions," p. 85.

15. Djilas, *Conversations with Stalin*, p. 185. Djilas was a participant in these meetings.

16. "Remarks by the Honorable George C. Marshall," in Department of State, *Foreign Relations of the United States, 1947*, Vol. 3, p. 239.

17. Campbell, *The United States in World Affairs, 1947-1948*, p. 427. The reasons for the Soviet refusal are discussed below.

18. "The Soviet Foreign Minister, Vyacheslav Molotov, to the Soviet Charge d'Affaires in Czechoslovakia," July 5, 1947, 8:15 a.m. and July 8, 1947, 0:50 a.m. in Takhnenko, "Anatomy of a Political Decision," pp. 123, 124. Tait, "Pole in London," p. 11. See also the cable traffic from the U.S. embassy in Poland in Department of State, *Foreign Relations of the United States, 1947*, Vol. 3, pp. 320-22.

Recent historiography also points to the role of the U.S. and contrasting economic policies in limiting possible economic cooperation between Eastern Europe and the West. See Anderson, "A Dollar to Poland is a Dollar to Russia" and Nelson, "Czechoslovak Political Economy."

19. Quoted in Fierlinger, "The Truth About Czechoslovakia's Attitude," p. 19.

For a participant's account of the discussions in Czechoslovakia, see Ripka, *Czechoslovakia Enslaved*. Ripka, a National Socialist, was the Czechoslovak Minister of Foreign Trade. See also the cable traffic in Department of State, *Foreign Relations of the United States, 1947*, Vol. 3, pp. 318-20, 327.

20. Kaplan, "The Council for Mutual Economic Aid," pp. 2-3.

The assertion that Romania played a role in the creation of CMEA is supported by another Czechoslovak source: Cizkovsky, *Mezinarodni Planovani*, p. 54. The U.S. embassy in Moscow also noted that the visit of a high-level Czech delegation in mid-December of 1948 might have been connected with the creation of CMEA. Kohler, Moscow EMBTEL 293 to Secretary of State, February 5, 1949, 640.6131/2-549, National Archives, Washington, D.C.

The document referred to may be one obtained by the U.S. embassy in Bucharest. C. Montagu Pigott, "Purported Text of Agreement Signed at Moscow Setting up Council of Mutual Economic Assistance," Despatch 654 from the American Legation, Bucharest, Romania, to Secretary of State, February 28, 1942, 640.6131/22849, National Archives, Washington, D.C. The U.S. Government decided not to publish the full text of this agreement, which differs significantly from the *Pravda* communique, because it "might jeopardize source which has been useful in past and is desirable to maintain." Acheson, Telegram to American Embassy, Paris, April 7, 1949, 640.6131/4-749, National Archives, Washington, D.C.

21. Brabant, *Adjustment, Structural Change and Economic Efficiency*, p. 31.

22. Quoted in "The Work of Comecon," p. 3.

23. Gallman, Warsaw EMBTEL 123 to Secretary of State, January 27, 1949, 640.6131/1-2749, National Archives, Washington, D.C.

24. Ausch, *Theory and Practice of CMEA Cooperation*, p. 44.

25. See Table 1 in the Appendix for a description of how I obtained these figures.

26. Department of State, *Treaties and Other International Agreements of the United States of America, 1931-1945*, Vol. 3 *Multilateral*, p. 1255.

27. *The Statesman's Yearbook, 1950*, p. 1052. For a more detailed discussion of the East German police see Nettl, *The Eastern Zone*, pp. 137-38.

28. The peace treaties are included in Department of State, *Treaties and Other International Agreements of the United States of America, 1946-1949*, Vol. 4 *Multilateral*, pp. 403-79.

29. See Table 1 in the Appendix for a discussion of the problems with the military data for this period and the sources.

30. The data in this paragraph are from Bureau of Mines, *Minerals Yearbook*. See Table 2 in the Appendix for a comparison of the production of coal, iron ore, and crude petroleum in these countries.

31. However, the Joint Hungarian-Soviet Bauxite Aluminum Company controlled more than 90 percent of Hungary's bauxite resources. Marshall, Telegram from the Department of State to the American Embassy, Belgrade, August 1, 1948, 640.6131/8-148, National Archives, Washington, D.C.

The joint stock companies in other East European states also controlled key natural resources. For a discussion of the joint stock companies, see below.

32. Campbell, *The United States in World Affairs, 1947-1948*, p. 427.

33. "The Soviet Foreign Minister, Vyacheslav Molotov, to the Soviet Charge d'Affaires in Czechoslovakia, Mikhail Bodrov," July 5, 1947, 6:40 a.m. in Takhnenko, "Anatomy of a Political Decision," p. 122.

34. Berend, "The Problem of Eastern European Economic Integration," pp. 11-12.

35. Campbell, *The United States in World Affairs, 1947-1948*, p. 67.

36. Yur. Zhukov, "Aiding or Undermining the Reconstruction of Europe?" p. 162.

37. Pryor, *The Communist Foreign Trade System*, p. 166.

38. Herman, "The New Soviet Posture," p. 11.

39. "Establishment of the Council of Mutual Economic Aid," p. 11.

40. Brabant, *Socialist Economic Integration*, pp. 28-9.

41. See Melnikov, "Western Europe and the Marshall Plan."

42. Zamora, "Voting in International Economic Organizations," pp. 574, 576-80.

43. See Nove, *An Economic History of the USSR*, Chapter One for a comparison of the Russian economy to those of the other European powers.

44. Brabant, *Socialist Economic Integration*, p. 60.

45. Ausch, *Theory and Practice of CMEA Cooperation*, p. 42. For figures on the proportions of these goods within total industrial production, see Voznesenskii, *Voennaia Ekonomika SSR*, p. 76.

46. Herman, "The Promise of Economic Self-Sufficiency," p. 81.

47. See, for example, a contemporary work on foreign trade: Mishustin, ed., *Vneshniaia Torgovlia Sovetskogo Soiuza SSR*, p. 10, quoted in Holzman, *Foreign Trade Under Central Planning*, p. 54, n. 20.

48. Quoted in Kaser, *Comecon*, p. 18.

49. Voznesenskii, *Voennaia Ekonomika SSR*, pp. 144, 178.

50. Voznesenskii, *Voennaia Ekonomika SSR*, p. 147.

51. Stalin, *Ekonomicheskie Problemy*, p. 3. Stalin's criticisms of Voznesenskii were published during the preparations for the publication of a new textbook on political economy. A more specific criticism of Voznesenskii's book can be found in Suslov, "Po povodu statei," p. 2.

52. Stalin, *Ekonomicheskie Problemy*, pp. 20, 52.

53. Stalin, *Ekonomicheskie Problemy*, p. 25.

54. Kaser, *Comecon*, p. 35.

55. Voznesenskii was shot in 1950, and discussion of value planning did not receive official approval again until 1962 when a series of articles on the topic was published by the economist Evsei Liberman. See, for example, his "Plan, Pribyl', Premiia," p. 3. For Khrushchev's account of Voznesenskii's final days, see *Khrushchev Remembers*, pp. 250-57.

56. P. Haas, "Introduction," p. 28.

57. "Establishment of the Council for Mutual Economic Aid," p. 11.

58. Pryor, *The Communist Foreign Trade System*, p. 174.

59. Loshchakov, "35 Let SEV," p. 34.

60. "Establishment of the Council for Mutual Economic Aid," p. 11.

61. Ken Jowitt also concludes that "the Soviet bloc was an international political organization based on political replication of the Soviet 'sacred center.'" "Moscow 'Centre,'" p. 310.

62. Schapiro, *The Communist Party of the Soviet Union*, p. 220.

63. I. D. Levin, "On the Essence and Significance," p. 6.

64. Brzezinski, *The Soviet Bloc*, p. 111.

65. Quoted in Schapiro, *The Communist Party of the Soviet Union*, p. 222.

66. I. D. Levin, "On the Essence and Significance," pp. 6, 4.

67. Liu Shao-Chi, "Internationalism and Nationalism," p. 434.

68. Zamora, "Voting in International Economic Organizations," p. 571.

69. Fainsod, *How Russia is Ruled*, p. 174.

70. Kaplan, "The Council for Mutual Economic Aid," p. 42. Anastas Ivanovich Mikoyan was also the Soviet Minister of Foreign Trade.

71. Rostow, *The Dynamics of Soviet Society*, p. 60.

72. *Khrushchev Remembers*, p. 614. The text of this speech was not made public at the time, but U.S. intelligence sources acquired copies of it. The Department of State released a text on June 4, 1956.

73. Brzezinski, *The Soviet Bloc*, p. 119. The NKVD was the predecessor of the KGB.

74. See Leonhard, *Child of the Revolution* for a description of the Comintern school and the preparation of Ulbricht's group for the return to Germany.

75. *Khrushchev Remembers: The Last Testament*, p. 201.

76. Brzezinski, *The Soviet Bloc*, p. 120.

77. Kiraly, "Hungary's Army Under the Soviets," pp. 12, 14.

78. Kaplan, "The Council for Mutual Economic Aid," p. 48.

79. Pryor, *The Communist Foreign Trade System*, p. 201.

80. Karaivanov, "Unequal Relations," p. 18.

81. "Soviet-Rumanian Communique," p. 16.

82. For the texts of the agreements creating the Soviet-Romanian oil company and the Soviet-Romanian bank, see Spulber, *The Economics of Communist East Europe*, pp. 217-23.

83. For a detailed description of these companies see Spulber, *The Economics of Communist East Europe*.

84. For an analysis of the SAG and their influence on the German economy see Nettl, *The Eastern Zone*, pp. 219-25, 233-38.

85. The East Germans were not included in the network of treaties until after the German Democratic Republic was formed in October 1949.

86. Quoted in Brzezinski, *The Soviet Bloc*, p. 60.

87. Kaplan, "The Council for Mutual Economic Aid," p. 12. See also J. K. Penfield, "Long-term Trade Agreements in Eastern Europe," Despatch No. 654 from American Embassy, Praha, Czechoslovakia to Secretary of State, October 25, 1949, 640.6131/10-2549, National Archives, Washington, D.C.

88. Kaplan, "The Council for Mutual Economic Aid," p. 11.

89. Quoted in Kaplan, "The Council for Mutual Economic Aid," p. 25.

90. Sebesta, "USSR's Second Largest Trading Partner," p. 8.

91. Amort, "The Development and Structure," p. 5.

92. Chistyakov, "Growth in Economic Cooperation," p. 7.

93. Quoted in Kaplan, "The Council for Mutual Economic Aid," p. 16.

94. Brzezinski, *The Soviet Bloc*, p. 111.

Chapter Three

The Issue of Supranational Planning

> "The basic structure of CEMA -- where an elephant and small mice are shut up in one cage, and they try to define their relationship to one another in a comradely manner -- cannot work, because even in the most comradely atmosphere, the elephant sooner or later will have to tread on one of the small mice."[1]

The autarkic model of development which had been so successful for the Soviet Union was not well suited to the small and, in some cases, highly developed East European states. After the death of Stalin, the economic strains caused by high investment and low consumption with little economic advantage coupled with the political strains of deStalinization led to a series of political disruptions in Eastern Europe. In May and June of 1953 there were riots over economic grievances in Bulgaria, Czechoslovakia, and the GDR.[2] These were contained fairly easily, but more serious challenges to communist party rule and Soviet domination arose in Poland and Hungary in 1956. The Polish crisis was resolved peacefully when the Soviets consented to the appointment of Wladyslaw Gomulka, a national communist who advocated a Polish road to socialism, as First Secretary of the Communist party. However, Soviet troops invaded Hungary in November 1956 to stop the restoration of a multiparty system and its withdrawal from the Warsaw Pact.[3]

In response to the growing economic problems within the socialist bloc, the CMEA Council Session was reconvened in 1954, and it began meeting regularly after its four year hiatus. The first three Council Sessions advocated the voluntary coordination of national economic plans and increased specialization among the East European states. This represented a recognition that a planning system based upon the premise of autarky was not leading to rational allocation of investment resources and that CMEA could better benefit from economies of scale. However, no real progress was made until the Seventh Session in 1956 when twelve standing industrial commissions were created to facilitate the negotiation of bilateral specialization agreements. Attention was first focused on the machine building industry and later extended to the chemical industry. Progress was slow, and it was soon recognized that these agreements must be based on the coordination of longer-term (10-15 year) plans and extended to the field of investments in order to be successful. Therefore in June 1962, a conference of representatives of the Communist and Workers' Parties of the CMEA participants (members and observers) "approved the 'Basic Principles of the International Socialist Division of Labor' that had been worked out by the 15th session of the Council and recommended them as a basis for drawing up a long-range program of economic cooperation."[4]

The approval of the Basic Principles in July 1962 was intended to signal a renunciation of the principle of autarkic development. Autarky was criticized for leading "to reduced efficiency and slower rates of economic development both in individual countries and in the entire system." However, the formula for the development of the international socialist division of labor which was adopted represented a compromise between the positions of the Soviet Union and Romania which remained wedded to an autarkic development strategy. Therefore, no clear criteria for specialization were articulated. For example, specialization was to be based on calculations of economic effectiveness, but the document acknowledged that it was also necessary to consider "the need for ensuring full employment of the labor force, an even balance of payments, the role of a given industry in increasing the productivity of social labor in the whole of the national economy and in attaining an equal level of economic development for all countries, the strengthening of defence capabilities, and other factors."[5] Given the difficulty of calculating economic effectiveness and the multiplicity of factors to be considered with regard to specialization, it is not surprising that this principle was not translated into norms of behavior strong enough to restrain the members' actions.

Several months later Khrushchev proposed the next logical step. He noted that "the world socialist system has approached the point at which it is no longer possible to chart its development correctly simply by mechanically adding together the respective national economies," and he recommended that CMEA be granted supranational authority with regard to planning and investment.[6] In the ensuing debate, the Soviets placed their emphasis on the development of the bloc as a whole and recommended that CMEA's role in planning and investment increase. The Romanians, on the other hand, placed their emphasis on the development of the individual states and protested that the "'the planned management of the national economy is one of the fundamental, essential and inalienable attributes of the sovereignty of the socialist states'" and that transmitting this "'to the competence of superstate or extrastate bodies would make of sovereignty an idea without any content.'"[7] At a Council Session in July 1963, Romania succeeded in blocking the creation of supranational authority within the framework of CMEA thereby ensuring that each member was free to develop its economy as it saw fit.[8]

Structural factors cannot explain this decision. The Soviet Union wanted to reform CMEA to better reflect its interests, and it was unable to do so although it remained the regional hegemon. I argue that the Soviet failure can be explained by three other factors. The decision rule of CMEA required unanimous approval so the Soviet Union had to achieve Romanian approval of its proposal either by force or persuasion. The Soviet Union was unable to force Romania to change its position because deStalinization had led to changes in the informal instruments of Soviet control in Eastern Europe. The Soviet Union was also unable to persuade Romania to accept an increase in CMEA's authority over planning and investment because of a lack of technical information about the relative costs and benefits of the competing models of socialist economic development.

Structural Factors: *Power and Interests*

Soviet Interests

As Khrushchev acknowledged, the Soviet Union's desire to reform CMEA ensued "first of all from the inner requirements of the development of world socialism, and also from the need to ensure our superiority in the competition with capitalism."[9] Thus, both economic and security interests led to the Soviet proposal.

The pattern of trade between the Soviet Union and Eastern Europe which had developed in the Stalin period had gradually become unfavorable to the Soviet Union. Commodities traded within CMEA could be classified in terms of their hardness or softness. Hard goods were in short supply in the bloc and could be easily sold on world markets. For the most part, they were raw materials. In contrast, there was little demand for soft goods in either the socialist or capitalist market. These were generally manufactured products. In their bilateral trade with each other, the East European states balanced hard goods with hard goods and soft goods with soft goods. However, the Soviet Union was a net exporter of hard goods and a net importer of soft goods in its trade with Eastern Europe.[10] This pattern of trade was economically disadvantageous to the Soviet Union for several reasons.

Although there is little differentiation in the quality of raw materials, there is a great deal of differentiation in the quality of manufactured goods. By the 1960s it was obvious that East European manufactured goods, although often of higher quality than Soviet products, were rapidly falling behind those produced in the West in terms of quality and technological level. Because of their autarkic development strategy and their small domestic markets, the East Europeans were unable to take advantage of "the growth of serial production and the resulting possibility of using more advanced technology and organization of production."[11] As the West's trade embargo was relaxed, alternative suppliers became available to the Soviet Union, and the Soviet criteria of comparison for East European imports changed.[12]

At the same time, the Soviet Union's terms of trade with Eastern Europe were deteriorating. Prices in intra-bloc trade were not based on the costs of production or on relative demand, rather they were negotiated bilaterally by government agencies. In an attempt to bring some rationality to the system, a CMEA Price Clause was adopted at the 9th Session in June 1958. The Price Clause was a multilateral agreement on rules for the bilateral negotiations, and it represented "a first attempt to institutionalize and de-politicize intra-CMEA pricing."[13] Under its terms, the parties would choose a basic world market, document the world market price for the commodity on that market, and then make certain broadly specified adjustments to obtain a CMEA foreign trade price. (Prices still had to be negotiated bilaterally since the currencies were not convertible.) This was intended to make prices on the socialist world market more uniform and to bring them closer to those on the capitalist world market. However, a detailed study of foreign trade prices on the socialist world market by the Conference of Varna (Bulgaria) in 1962 revealed that there were variations in pricing levels among commodity groups. According to one of the economists who participated in the study, "intra-CMEA contractual prices exceeded those of the capitalist world market by 25.9 per cent in the group of machines, by 15.4 per cent in the case of raw materials and by 1.7 per cent in the group of agricultural products." He also observed that since the prices of machines were not adjusted for quality, "the price difference of 26 per cent obtained by us may be considered as the *lowest* measure of the really existing price deviations."[14]

There are several possible explanations for this anomaly in pricing that worked to the detriment of the Soviet Union. Western economists often note that there is a wider variation in prices for machinery on world markets than for raw materials so under the new price rules it was possible to document very high prices for machinery. Prices on the socialist world market then tended to gravitate toward the upper end of the range because of the shortages of hard currency.[15] Also, there was a greater incentive for the East Europeans to spend the time necessary to document prices in their negotiations with the Soviet Union because of the asymmetry of interest. Trade with the Soviet Union formed the bulk of their foreign trade whereas the Soviet Union's trade with each East European state individually was relatively unimportant.[16] However, a Hungarian economist, Sandor Ausch, links the anomaly to the domestic pricing systems in Soviet-style economies which were based on a "prime-cost-type pricing system." In this system, "the price level of raw materials is relatively the lowest because they are subject but to few phases of processing." Also, the domestic prices of raw materials were often subsidized by the state. Ausch suggests that CMEA foreign trade prices for machinery were not based on capitalist world market prices, as the pricing rules mandated, but on domestic prices. He then presents evidence that Hungarian prices for machines were based on domestic prices converted to rubles.[17] Whatever the reason, the end result was that the prices of the products imported by the Soviet Union from Eastern Europe were overvalued relative to the prices obtained by the Soviet Union for its exports to Eastern Europe.

This occurred at a time when East European demand for Soviet raw materials was growing rapidly. The raw material, fuel and power base was lagging behind the needs of the manufacturing branches in Eastern Europe. For example, it was estimated that "the anticipated requirements in power in the Comecon countries, with the exception of the USSR, after 1970 will exceed the resources by about one fifth."[18] Since approximately 95 percent of all sources of energy in the CMEA member states were in the Soviet Union, the responsibility for meeting this deficit would largely fall to the Soviet Union.[19] A similar situation existed with regard to other raw materials. "In 1957 the share of the USSR in the total imports of member-nations of the Council of Mutual Economic Assistance was: in petroleum -- over 90%, in iron ore -- about 80%, in copper -- 75%, in rolled products -- 57%, in cotton -- 67%, and in grain -- the bulk of all imports."[20] East European import requirements in these goods were also increasing rapidly. For example, it was estimated that "the delivery of iron ore from the Soviet Union to those countries rose from 3.2 million tons in 1950 to 13 million tons in 1959 and will rise to 24 million tons in 1965."[21] The Soviet Union was reluctant to increase its investment in raw material extraction to meet this increased demand because it required a larger initial investment and had a longer recoupment period than investment in processing or other industries. Therefore, the Soviet Union was very interested in reducing this drain on its economy, and much attention was focused on ways to increase production and to decrease demand at the CMEA Council Sessions.

Several of the obvious solutions to the Soviet Union's problems in its trade with Eastern Europe were not attractive. First, even though the pricing rules were not working in the Soviet Union's favor, it was difficult to change them quickly. The amount of time involved in renegotiating all the prices with each of the CMEA members would be enormous. Also, since the currencies were not convertible, every attempt was made to balance trade bilaterally. Major price revisions could play havoc with this. Finally, the Soviet Union was unwilling to make major cuts in supplies of raw materials to Eastern Europe. As I noted earlier, the Soviet Union was the major supplier of raw materials to Eastern Europe. Since these states lacked the hard currency to purchase them elsewhere, maintaining the supply of needed raw materials was a necessary component of their domestic political stability, which was also a Soviet interest.[22]

Specialization of production achieved through granting CMEA supranational authority over planning and investment provided a means to improve the Soviet Union's terms of trade with Eastern Europe without any major economic disruptions in the region. The Soviet proposal to coordinate capital construction programs in order to achieve a "more even distribution of the efforts of the countries in the sphere of the capital expenditures" sought to alleviate the burden of major Soviet investments in raw materials extraction.[23] Specialization in production could help reduce demand for power and raw materials by increasing efficiency.[24] It could also improve the Soviet Union's terms of trade without any major price revisions by increasing the quality and technical level of East European production. As Khrushchev observed, "it is specialization and production cooperation that will make it possible to build larger and more profitable enterprises of a modern technological level."[25]

Moreover, granting CMEA supranational authority would allow the Soviets to achieve the desired changes in the East European economies in a way less likely to arouse national sentiments. As Joseph Nye observes, if a state "can support institutions that make other states wish to channel or limit their activities in ways the dominant state prefers, it may be spared the costly exercise of coercive or hard power."[26] Also, the size of the Soviet economy made it highly unlikely that any specialization agreements would have a major impact on its structure. A Soviet economist asserted that

> big countries with vast territory and a large population, plus a more or less full supply of natural wealth, develop primarily on the basis of an integral economic complex. They have especially favorable opportunities for making the most of all the advantages of specialization and cooperation within the country.[27]

Khrushchev later retreated from that position somewhat stating that "the Soviet Union is prepared even to cut down production of some kinds of manufactures if it proves more expedient to produce them in other countries."[28] However, in reality, specialization would have an enormous impact on the small East European economies and little on the Soviet economy. Thus, Khrushchev hoped that "improvement of the system of cooperation and mutual aid [would] create favorable soil for drawing the socialist nations closer in every way" without any substantial cost to the Soviet Union.[29]

Finally, granting CMEA supranational authority over planning and investment provided a way to parry the threat to Soviet economic and security interests posed by the creation of the European Economic Community (EEC) on March 24, 1957.[30] The lowering of internal tariffs and the implementation of a common external tariff by the EEC raised Soviet and East European fears about the loss of markets in Western Europe.[31] This would reduce their hard currency earnings and affect vital imports such as capital goods. Although the Soviet Union was less likely to be directly affected by the tariffs because it primarily exported commodities for which the EEC tariffs would be negligible (mainly raw materials), the East Europeans who exported primarily agricultural and industrial products which were subject to high tariffs feared an adverse affect on their trade. Changes in the pattern of East European exports and perhaps even production resulting from the EEC tariffs could have a disruptive effect on planning in the entire bloc, including the Soviet Union. They could also threaten the Soviet desires for modernization of the East European industrial plant.

The creation of the EEC threatened Soviet security interests because it raised the stakes in the economic competition between socialism and capitalism. Khrushchev believed that war between capitalism and socialism was no longer inevitable due to the destructiveness of nuclear weapons and the strength of the socialist bloc. He had announced a policy of peaceful coexistence.[32] However, this did not mean that competition between the two systems had ended: the arena had only shifted. According to Khrushchev, "peaceful coexistence can and should develop into peaceful competition for the purpose of satisfying man's needs in the best possible way."[33] The Soviet and East European economies had been growing more rapidly than those of Western Europe, but as Table 3.1 demonstrates, growth rates in the socialist states were slowing.

Table 3.1: Annual Increase of National Income, 1958-1962 (in %)

	1958	1959	1960	1961	1962
Bulgaria	7.0	21.0	7.0	2.9	--
Czechoslovakia	8.0	6.0	8.0	7.0	0.5
GDR	10.9	8.5	4.5	4.2	3.5
Hungary	6.2	8.0	7.3	5.8	5.0
Poland	5.6	5.3	4.5	8.0	2.5
Romania	3.4	13.0	10.8	10.9	--
USSR	12.0	8.0	9.0	7.0	6.0

Source: Adam Zwass, "The Economy of the Comecon Countries in 1962," *Zycie Gospodarcze*, March 17, 1963 in *Polish Press Survey* No. 1505, Radio Free Europe Research, p. 3.

Soviet economists noted that at the same time "industrial production in the Common Market countries rose by 30% and the volume of exports by 50%. The rates of growth in 'integrated' Europe were 50% to 100% higher than in the capitalist world as a whole." Thus, integration was allowing the West European states to take advantage of an objective tendency toward the internationalization of production "in order to increase their superprofits."[34] If the Soviet Union was to meet its goal of surpassing the economic level of the most developed capitalist countries and move into first place for production per capita within 20 years, a goal which had been proclaimed at the 22nd Party Congress, it also needed to take advantage of the economic fruits of integration.[35] Therefore, Khrushchev concluded that "the necessity of more active cooperation among the countries of socialism is dictated likewise by the interests of gaining the most time for victory in the economic competition with capitalism."[36]

East European Interests

All of the East European states, except Romania, publicly supported Khrushchev's proposal to increase CMEA's authority over planning and investment. As a Czech author phrased it, "the exploitation of the advantages of the *international socialist division of work* is a necessity dictated by our *vital interests*."[37] Like the Soviet Union, the East Europeans hoped that specialization could help them overcome decreases in their growth rates, the problems resulting from the uneven distribution of natural resources in the region, and the challenge presented by the formation of the EEC. However, specialization was not without cost to the East Europeans, and they expressed concerns about the loss of control over their domestic economies which would result from granting CMEA supranational authority over planning and investment.

In the 1950s the East European economies had achieved very high growth rates through an extensive growth strategy. "By attracting labor into production, especially from rural areas, by increasingly introducing work in two and even three shifts, and by building a number of new factories, we achieved annually both a big increase in production and an increase in total social labor productivity."[38] However, as shown in Table 3.1, growth rates had begun to drop by 1960, particularly in the most developed states, had begun to drop, and labor and capital reserves had been exhausted.

A further increase in the growth rate would require an increase in productivity, which was low. For example, Czechoslovakia and the GDR had the highest productivity in Eastern Europe yet an East German source estimated that their "labor productivity [lagged] 25 per cent behind that of West Germany."[39] Many East European economists linked low productivity to the autarkic development strategy which encouraged these states to produce a wide assortment of products. For example, "Czechoslovakia [made] some 70 per cent and the GDR some 90 per cent of all types of engineering products in existence."[40] This led to the unnecessary duplication of capacities in the region and the predominance of small series production. The duplication of capacities caused balance of trade problems in intrabloc trade as the less developed states began to produce domestically and even to export products they had once imported from the more developed states, in particular Czechoslovakia. Small series production was less efficient so it raised the costs of production. Moreover, technical innovation and quality control had been neglected so East European manufactured goods generally sold at low prices on foreign markets. In fact, the Bulgarian Minister of Foreign Trade Lachezar Avramov estimated that in 1961 only 35 percent of the domestic value of exported goods was achieved on foreign markets.[41]

To overcome the problems of low productivity and low quality, the East Europeans needed to introduce new technology. However, "modern, mechanized, automatic production demands the production of goods [in such large quantities] that in almost every branch of production they are above the supply needed by a small country."[42] Therefore, the East European states needed to specialize and participate in a division of labor in order to reap the benefits of modern technology. They also hoped that specialization would allow them to reduce funds spent on research and development and to concentrate their scarce capital on a limited number of projects.

The East European states were also interested in supranational planning as a solution to the problems resulting from the uneven distribution of natural resources within the bloc. Hungary, a major supplier of bauxite, and Poland, a major supplier of hard coal, shared the Soviet interest in obtaining investment in their extraction industries.[43] The consumers of raw materials wanted to guarantee secure sources of supply without expending scarce hard currency so the majority were willing to invest in extraction plants in other member states.[44]

East European economic interests were also threatened by the creation of the EEC in 1957. A reduction in trade with Western Europe could cause serious problems for the East European economies because as Table 3.2 shows, it represented the bulk of their trade with capitalist states which in most cases accounted for over one-fourth of their total foreign trade.

Table 3.2: Proportion of the Capitalist Sector in the Foreign Trade of the Comecon Countries

	1956	1957	1958	1959	1960
Bulgaria	14.5	15.3	14.0	17.7	16.1
Czechoslovakia	24.4	32.5	29.7	27.8	28.5
GDR	26.6	26.6	20.5	23.9	25.1
Hungary	37.1	29.2	28.1	28.8	29.2
Poland	37.6	39.2	41.6	37.5	37.4
Romania	21.9	25.5	22.1	20.3	27.0

Source: "Hungarian Anxieties About European Economic Integration," *Background Report* (Hungarian Unit), July 10, 1962, Radio Free Europe Research and Evaluation Section, p. 2.

Any resulting hard currency loss would also make it more difficult to buy the equipment needed to modernize production. The East European states were particularly concerned about the reduction of internal tariffs and the institution of a common external tariff by the EEC.

All the East European states would suffer from the reduction of internal tariffs within the EEC. Theoretically, the institution of a common external tariff by the EEC would have had mixed effects on the East Europeans since the new tariff was to be the arithmetic mean of national tariff rates from 1957. However, the Federal Republic of Germany, the major European trading partner of most of the East European states, had been one of the members with the lowest national tariff rates so the overall effect was a deterioration in the competitiveness of East European exports. The East Europeans also believed that they were being further discriminated against because they were not granted most favored nation status by the EEC.

> Although the 'most-favoured-nation' clause applies to most CMEA countries in their trade relations with the EEC countries, we have not been given the benefit of reductions in the rates of duty that the EEC has granted to outside countries (the United States, Great Britain, Switzerland, etc.). Thus, the EEC customs policy undermines the competitiveness of our products not only in comparison with the products of the 'Six' but also in relation to products exported by other Western European and North American countries.[45]

A further problem was the expectation that future negotiations about the level of the tariffs would be conducted with the community as a whole rather than with the individual members which would decrease the bargaining power of the individual East European states.

Those who primarily exported agricultural products to Western Europe were particularly hurt by two additional measures. The first measure was the agricultural produce charge which required that imported agricultural products be sold at a price higher than the price on the free market of the EEC with the difference going into the Agricultural Development fund. According to a Polish economist, "[s]ince the equalization charges, . . ., are, as a rule, higher than the previous rates of duty, the export of agricultural products is now subject to such strong discrimination that in many cases it becomes unprofitable."[46] The second was a policy of setting overall import quotas for the non-member states regarding imports to the whole common market area at a time when quotas for members were being raised automatically and were finally to be eliminated altogether.[47] The economic impact of these measures was felt immediately. For example, "West German statistics for the August-October 1962 period reveal the setback already incurred by Poland in the German market alone; poultry exports fell to 64 tons from 900 tons and pigs to 14,800 from 58,000."[48] As Table 3.3 indicates, the states most affected were Hungary, Poland, and Bulgaria.

Table 3.3: Proportion of Agricultural Produce in Exports to OECC Countries

	1959	1960
Bulgaria	76.3	58.5
Czechoslovakia	18.0	11.5
GDR	6.4	11.0
Hungary	51.5	50.5
Poland	45.0	43.0
Romania	11.6	28.5

Source: "Hungarian Anxieties About European Economic Integration," Background Report (Hungarian Unit), July 10, 1962, Radio Free Europe Research and Evaluation Section, p. 2.

Although Romania was the only state to publicly oppose the proposal to increase CMEA's authority over planning and investment, it was not the only state to express reservations about specialization. This was due to the fact that specialization was not without cost to the East Europeans. Articles in the East European presses sought to explain the benefits of specialization to skeptical publics. There were three major areas of concern: concerns about the quality, timely supply, and the availability of spare parts for goods produced in other socialist states; concerns about disruption of domestic production; and concerns about a loss of control over the management of the national economy.

Changing paths after pursuing autarky for over a decade would be difficult because in that time organizations "with a stake in the existing constraints" had been created.[49] Specialization would necessitate eliminating some production lines and replacing them with others. As a Hungarian analyst observed, "[i]t is evident that, to switch over to a new, complicated task and solutions, to abandon the old routine, and to exchange an area under development for long years for another, are coupled with great difficulties, much study and with eventual 'tuition fees.'"[50] One of the great difficulties was the emergence of structural unemployment. A Czech commentator acknowledged

> that in order gradually to remove disproportions, it has become necessary to slow down production in some branches and that it has been difficult thus far to win people for work in those branches and factories where production is to rise steeply this year and where there is a shortage of workers.[51]

Workers not only resisted changing their place of employment; they, along with management, also resisted changing the product line in their enterprises for fear that it would lead to a drop in their incomes. A large portion of wages in Eastern Europe were derived from fulfilling or over-fulfilling plan targets. Since there were always problems with introducing new product lines, plan targets were rarely met, and workers' wages suffered.

The concern about the quality, timely supply and the availability of spare parts was not new. For example, a Slovak publication cited the lack of spare parts for Soviet combines as the biggest problem in the 1963 harvest:

> Many of the Soviet combines were damaged en route to our country -- some arrived without radiators, with ruined sieves, without any spare parts whatsoever. The latter are not available up to this very day (although their supply is part of the contract), in spite of every possible step having been taken.[52]

Such stories were common, but if the East Europeans began to abandon certain production lines and became more dependent on imports, the problem was sure to be magnified. As a Polish commentator observed,

> It is possible, of course, to safeguard the interests of the customer in the contract, by defining the financial responsibility of the specialized producer of the given goods for non-observance of the guaranteed parameters. However, the heart of the matter lies in the fact that the enterprises of the manufacturers who in a far-reaching specialization of the production of a given article is its sole producer determine the maintenance of the technical standard and the quality of the goods.[53]

The problem of uncertain supply was crucial because of the planning process in Eastern Europe. As Paul Marer notes, "Under central planning all movement of goods and factors across national borders requires an explicit action by the governments involved."[54] Therefore, it was difficult to locate alternative suppliers in the short term. Because plans were taut, any problem with supply could reverberate through whole production processes. As a member of the Czechoslovak State Planning Commission observed, "We must not forget that the times of delivery of our products tie in with other time schedules governing the construction of works and production and that every day of delay means a loss of production, failure to fulfill plans."[55]

Concerns about quality were also intensified because specialization often meant transferring some production to the less developed states. For example, Hungarian consumers were concerned that the transfer of their radio production to Bulgaria would result in lower quality. A letter to the editor inquired, "'Is the country which is to start the manufacture of an article produced before by Hungary, able to come out with the same quality?'"[56] Similar concerns were expressed by Czechoslovak consumers about the transfer of production to Hungary.[57]

Finally, the East Europeans were concerned about the loss of control over the management of their national economies. The Soviet solution required the balancing of two sets of competing interests: overall bloc economic development versus national economic development and national sovereignty versus economic development.

The less developed states in Eastern Europe were particularly concerned about the outcome of the balancing of bloc development versus national economic development.[58] The history of prior attempts at specialization supported this concern. For example, "out of 613 products chosen for international specialization, the Berlin Session of CMEA [in 1956] recommended the production in the GDR, of 73% of the entire nomenclature, in Czechoslovakia -- 60%, in Poland -- 45%, in Hungary -- 22%, in Romania -- 9%, and in Bulgaria -- 7%."[59] Statements like this from the 12th Session: "the most favorable conditions for cultivating fruit, grapes, and vegetables obtain in Albania, Bulgaria, Hungary and Rumania" also fueled fears that the socialist international division of labor would ensure that these states remained less developed and more agrarian.[60] Therefore, Romania repeatedly insisted that "building Communism on a world-wide scale is incompatible with the notion of dividing countries into industrial states and agrarian states, into developed countries and underdeveloped countries."[61] This view was also shared by Bulgaria.[62]

Furthermore, the economic problems of the less developed states were somewhat different from those of the more developed. As shown in Table 3.1, their economies were growing at a faster rate than most of the more developed CMEA members, and instead of being faced with a labor shortage, they were faced with the need to "provide new employment for the forces of labor now working in agriculture, but which will become increasingly idle with the rise of labor productivity."[63] For example, two-thirds of Romania's economically active population was still engaged in agriculture.[64] The Romanians feared that if the criterion of economic efficiency were the sole criterion of specialization, they were unlikely to be granted the profitable, heavy industrial tasks. Therefore, they argued that other criteria should be taken into consideration.

> Pointing to such factors as the natural conditions and resources of the given country, technical know-how, production traditions, highly skilled technicians, labor productivity, production costs at a given moment, etc., he [Moldovan] said that these should not be analyzed statistically, by a non-historical method.
>
> First, he said, no single one of these factors could be an essential criterion, but in company with other factors, including also political factors, they should be regarded as important elements of a comprehensive analysis. Second, these factors should be examined historically, i.e., not from the angle of today's level, but, above all, of a possible future level.[65]

Romania was particularly concerned about the future of its machine building industry because of the lack of Soviet support for the development of its steel industry, namely the construction of the Galati steel works.[66]

The East European states also expressed more general fears about the possible outcome of any balancing of interests between themselves and the Soviet Union. A Hungarian party daily complained "that many people even though well disposed had doubts that 'can one talk of full equality and mutuality between the USSR, with 200 million inhabitants, power resources, and all kinds of raw material, and between Hungary, with a population of less than 10 million.'"[67] Therefore, they were also unwilling to place bloc development above national development. A Polish analyst expressed this common sentiment when he stated:

> It must be said openly that, indeed, there does exist a vital problem of combining the interests of various countries with the interests of the community and that the problem cannot be solved simply through assigning absolute priority to the interests of the whole to the detriment (even a temporary and limited one) of a single country.[68]

Even the Czechoslovaks, who were the most supportive of supranational planning and saw the contradiction of interests which existed to be a nonantagonistic one,[69] noted that "[o]n the other hand one cannot ad infinitum sanction a relatively larger contribution by certain countries [i.e. the more developed] and regard it as a permanent institution."[70] Therefore, even those who supported specialization had reason to be wary of transferring control over their national economic development to CMEA.

For these reasons, it is possible that Romania received tacit support from others although it was the only East European state to publicly oppose the Soviet proposal to grant CMEA supranational authority over planning and investment. According to Adam Zwass, a Polish economist who was serving in the CMEA Secretariat at the time, the other East European members "wanted neither supranational nor international executive authorities because they knew quite well that with the present CMEA membership, the existing proportionalities would inevitably prevail in determining economic policies, despite all the solemn declarations."[71]

Soviet and East European Power Capabilities

The failure of the Soviet Union to reform CMEA to better reflect its interests, even in the face of East European skepticism, cannot be explained by a decline in Soviet power capabilities relative to the other members. There was no such decline in the period 1950-65, and the Soviet Union was still clearly the regional hegemon. The area of all the countries was the same for the whole period. Soviet population and GDP remained approximately twice that of Eastern Europe. Soviet military capability also remained over twice that of Eastern Europe. Naturally, there were no changes in the relative resource endowment either. (See Tables 1-8 in the Appendix).

Soviet power capabilities just did not prove to be very useful in the Soviet attempts to bring Romania into line. An invasion was the only way that military force could be applied since Soviet troops had been withdrawn from Romania. However, as Nye observes, "the direct use of force for economic gain is generally too costly and dangerous for modern great powers."[72] The Soviet Union did try to apply some economic pressure. "Romania either did not receive access to Soviet fuel, raw materials, and other goods important to its national economy, or received it only under relatively strict conditions."[73] However, the Romanians were largely self-sufficient in their domestic power production, and they began to seek alternative suppliers of other raw materials. As Michael Montias observes,

> the threat to curb the delivery of raw materials for manufactures is one of the last economic trumps that Moscow has left to keep the Rumanians from going astray. If this threat can be parried and if Western markets can be found for the products of Rumania's new industries, the Rumanians will be safe to pursue their independent economic policy.[74]

Also, there was not much East European support for economic sanctions being used against other socialist states.[75] However, it was necessary for the Soviet Union to secure Romania's agreement because of the egalitarian structure of CMEA, in particular the unanimity rule.

The Institutional Structure of CMEA

As a consequence of its increased importance and role, CMEA had undergone a process of institutionalization in this period which culminated in the signing of a charter in 1960. The Council Session remained the highest organ, but many new bodies were created. An Executive Committee composed of deputy heads of the members' governments was established to manage "all CMEA organs which are related to the execution of the Session's directives" and to supervise "the member countries fulfillment of responsibilities resulting from the recommendations they have adopted" between Council Sessions.[76] Permanent Commissions were established which corresponded to the various branches of the members' economies. They were empowered to "adopt recommendations and decisions in accordance with this Charter. The Commissions may also submit proposals for examination by the Session of the Council."[77] The permanent chairmanships of these Commissions were distributed among the members. Committees, conferences, and institutes were also created, and the Secretariat was reorganized and expanded.

Despite the organizational changes, CMEA was not granted additional authority, and the egalitarian features of the organization were not changed. The principle of national sovereignty was constantly referred to in the communiques of the Council Sessions and was reaffirmed in the Charter which stated that "the Council of Mutual Economic Aid shall be based on the principles of the sovereign equality of the member countries of the Council."[78] There had been some changes in the conception of national sovereignty though. The Soviet invasion of Hungary in 1956 forcibly demonstrated that national sovereignty was still limited by the interests of the proletariat defined as socialism, but the interests of international socialism were no longer defined as the interests of the Soviet Union. The Soviets had recognized that "as action gives rise to counter action, so did Stalin's great-power policy revive and intensify nationalist prejudices."[79] Therefore, they began to "speak about the need for the socialist countries to agree upon actions and to coordinate policy, that is, about the skillful combination of national and international interests" which of course required a recognition "that these interests have not always fully coincided in every respect."[80] Thus, the interests of international socialism was no longer a well-defined limitation of national sovereignty.

Also, there was no change in the decision rule. In the main policy-making organ, the Council Session, each member had one vote, and decisions had to be unanimous. The Charter stated that "all recommendations and decisions shall be adopted only with the concurrence of the member countries of the Council concerned, and each country shall have the right to declare its interest in any question being considered in the Council." In contrast to the 1949 communique though, the Charter continued

> Recommendations and decisions shall not extend to countries that have expressed their disinterest in the given question. However, any of these countries may subsequently subscribe to the recommendations and decisions adopted by the other members of the Council.[81]

Although this formulation rule would later provide the grounds for a reinterpretation of the decision rule, the consensus in 1963 was that unanimity was required for CMEA decisions. Therefore, the Soviet Union was in a position where it needed to either force Romania to agree to the adoption of the proposal to grant CMEA supranational authority over planning and investment or to persuade it to agree.

Soviet Instruments

The Soviet Union was unable to force Romania to agree to the adoption of Khrushchev's proposal because the instruments by which the Soviets exercised their control in Eastern Europe had undergone a major transformation by 1962. The uprisings in Poland, East Germany, and Hungary caused the Soviets to recognize that it was counterproductive to treat the East Europeans as subjects rather than as allies. "Because of the lingering hard feelings and even antagonisms on the part of our allies," Khrushchev explained, "we found it difficult to achieve the desired degree of monolithism in the Socialist camp."[82] In October 1956, the Soviet government issued a declaration on relations between the Soviet Union and other socialist states in which it admitted that there had "been many difficulties, unresolved problems and downright mistakes, including mistakes in the mutual relations among socialist countries -- violations and errors which demeaned the principle of equality in relations among the socialist states."[83] The Soviets realized that excessive reliance on instruments in the institutional and personal contexts during the Stalin period had aroused nationalist sentiments in Eastern Europe and was therefore counterproductive. They began to restructure their instruments of control and to place their emphasis on instruments in the multilateral context.

Although the Soviets continued to cultivate personal ties and loyalties by educating and training large numbers of East Europeans in the Soviet Union, Soviet personal contacts at the highest levels in Eastern Europe had been reduced. By 1957 East Germany's Walter Ulbricht was the only East European party leader from the Stalin period who was still in power. Poland's Bierut and Czechoslovakia's Gottwald had died, and the others had, for the most part, been victims of the de-Stalinization campaigns in Eastern Europe. Also, many of the most obvious Muscovites at lower levels, like the Polish Defense Minister Marshall Rokossovski, had been removed from their posts.

In Romania this process occurred as the result of an internal power struggle. The General Secretary of the Romanian Communist Party, Gheorghiu-Dej, was a "home" communist (one who had remained in the country during World War II) who purged the party's Muscovites in order to consolidate his own position.[84] During the confrontation with the Soviet Union over Khrushchev's proposal, the Romanian leaders recognized that the Soviet Union would try to find alternative leaders who might be more amenable to Soviet desires. Therefore, they, "held a series of closed meetings throughout the country to explain their new policy" in order to further forestall this possibility.[85] Thus, the men and women who replaced the Muscovites of the Stalin period as the leaders of Eastern Europe differed from them in that they had a domestic political base they could appeal to for support, and like Tito they would not necessarily fall at the whim of the Soviet Union.[86]

Perhaps the most significant changes occurred in the institutional context. In the 1956 Declaration, the Soviet Union stated that

> in view of the fact that by this time the people's democracies have formed their own qualified national cadres in all spheres of economic and military affairs, the Soviet government

> considers it urgent to review, together with the other socialist states, the question of the expediency of the further presence of USSR advisors in these countries.[87]

Although the Soviets were able to maintain the presence of many of their military advisors in Eastern Europe under the auspices of the Warsaw Pact,[88] they began to dismantle or substantially reduce the remaining networks of Soviet advisors which had given them a direct link with East European institutions and access to decision-making. Khrushchev also recognized that "Stalin had created bad feeling in Czechoslovakia, the German Democratic Republic, Rumania, Hungary, China, and Austria as well as Poland by setting up international organizations to exploit our allies natural resources."[89] Therefore, the Soviet Union relinquished its control over key industries in Bulgaria, Romania, and Hungary through the sale and transfer of the Soviet share in the joint stock companies to the respective national governments.

In the national context, there was an equalization and extension of formal ties. Treaties were signed in Poland and East Germany which defined for the first time the terms and conditions under which Soviet troops were stationed on their territory, and the Soviet military presence in most East Europeans states was either withdrawn, as in Romania, or reduced, as in Poland and East Germany.[90] There were economic reasons (it was more expensive to have troops stationed abroad) as well as what Khrushchev referred to as "compelling political reasons" for this action. The East Europeans "would take it as a sign of political trust if we removed our forces," and "[w]e wanted to give the lie to the enemy's insinuation that the Hungarian, Polish, Rumanian and other fraternal peoples were being prodded along the path of socialism at bayonet-point by Soviet soldiers."[91] Khrushchev also recognized that the "unequal commercial treaties forced on Cyrankiewicz by Stalin had helped turn Poland into a resentful neighbor and nearly set off a political explosion."[92] Therefore, the trade treaties signed after 1957 stipulated "the right of *each* party to have its trade delegation on the territory of the other contracting party," a right which had formerly been granted only to the Soviet Union. And, the trade delegations of both parties were "given all the usual rights and privileges granted earlier to the USSR trade delegations."[93]

Although the Cominform was formally dissolved in April 1956, there was a general proliferation of instruments in the multilateral context during this period. A Czech commentator observed that it was necessary to dissolve "such international organizations as Comintern and Cominform whose organizational structure and activity had come into conflict with the objective requirements of the Communist movement and which were too closely connected with the era of the personality cult."[94] Because of its inactivity in the Stalin period, CMEA was free of this taint so it was reactivated in 1954 and underwent a process of increased institutionalization. In 1955 the Warsaw Pact was created as a response to West Germany's admission to the North Atlantic Treaty Organization (NATO).[95] The creation of many more multilateral organizations, such as the Organization for International Railway Cooperation and the Organization for the Cooperation of Socialist Countries in Telecommunication and Posts, soon followed.[96] However, in their economic relationship with Eastern Europe, the Soviets were not able to consolidate their control at this level because the egalitarian form of CMEA was not altered despite its increased institutionalization.

Because they were unable to use instruments in the four contexts to pressure the Romanians into approving the Soviet proposal, the Soviets needed to convince them that a division of labor would profit them economically and that it would allow for greater economic growth than autarky. However, as cognitive theories of regime change suggest, this proved to be difficult because contending models of socialist economic development had emerged, but there was a lack of technical information about the costs and benefits associated with the various models. Ernst Haas defines consensual knowledge as "the sum of both technical information and of theories about it that command sufficient agreement among interested actors at a given time to serve as a guide to public policy." He also observes that "before the claims to knowledge become truly consensual, the interplay will take the form of an ideological debate."[97] This occurred in CMEA.

Cognitive Factors

The socialist bloc was united by its adherence to Marxist-Leninist theory (Stalin had generally been removed from the pantheon) and the ultimate goal of building communism. However, cracks had appeared in the monolithic unity which had characterized doctrine until the death of Stalin. The Soviet Union still held an honored position as the first socialist state, but it was no longer the sole purveyor of experience in building socialism nor the chief interpreter of Marx and Lenin. China under Mao Zedong was challenging the Soviet Union's ideological leadership of the socialist bloc,[98] and the socialist bloc now offered three tested alternative methods of economic development. The Chinese Great Leap Forward had some appeal for the less developed states because of "the ideology of the immediate transition to communism and the belief in the practicability of an unprecedented mobilization of resources."[99] Bulgaria had even gone so far as to elaborate a plan for such a leap in 1958.[100] The normalization of relations with Yugoslavia after Khrushchev's Secret Speech in 1956 also provided another alternative, worker self-management. Finally, there was the autarkic model that the Soviet Union had followed, and although the experiences of the past ten years had eroded some of the East Europeans' confidence in the applicability of this model of development to their own economies, it was still generating successes in the less developed states. Therefore, the Soviets had to convince the skeptics, mainly Romania, that a socialist division of labor was theoretically justified and that this untested alternative offered better prospects for growth than the other, tested alternatives.

The autarkic model of development had been associated with the Soviet Union's economic development and rise to power, but it was no longer generating such success in the Soviet Union. The Soviet growth rate, which had been considered the model's hallmark of success, showed signs of slowing, and there were also problems with quality control and technical innovation. A search began for some objective, scientific method of economic decision-making. For example, a renewed debate on the operation of the law of value under socialism was stimulated by a September 1962 article in *Pravda.* In this article, the Soviet economist Evsei Liberman called for less reliance on planned targets and greater use of the profit motive to stimulate economic growth.[101] A Czech writer cited Liberman's proposals as "evidence of the effort of Marxist economists to overcome the dogmatic and canonized conception of the model of the planned economy."[102] This same effort extended to economic relations within the socialist bloc.

The Soviets argued that the bilateral economic relations characteristic of the Stalin period were "a kind of period of transition from the old system of foreign economic relations typical of capitalism to the formation of the new-type international ties."[103] Changes in the objective situation required a new type of relations (multilateral) and a new law of economic development. At the 21st Party Congress Khrushchev made a dramatic pronouncement: "by successfully employing the potentialities inherent in socialism, the socialist countries will enter the higher phase of communist society more or less simultaneously."[104] This was possible because "with the victory of socialism in a number of countries and the establishment of a world socialist system there arose a completely new law in their development," the law of planned, proportional development.[105] According to Khrushchev, this law "operates in the socialist economic system with the result that formerly economically backward countries rapidly make up for lost time and raise their economic and cultural levels by drawing on the experience of other socialist countries and on cooperation and mutual assistance."[106] The Soviets quoted Lenin in support of this law and the division of labor it was intended to encourage. For example, the economist Bogomolov argued that

> the tendency noted by V. I. Lenin 'of setting up a single world economy as a whole, regulated by the proletariat of all nations according to a general plan, a tendency which is quite clearly discernable under capitalism and which unquestionably should be developed further and fully completed under socialism,' is becoming ever clearer.[107]

The heart of the Soviet position was that since all the members of CMEA had developed the material-technical base of socialism, it was necessary to focus on achieving the proper proportions on an international scale, to end the unnecessary duplication of capacities. Khrushchev asserted that "the law of planned and proportional development, operating within the framework of the whole system, requires observance of planning and definite proportions both in the socialist countries individually and on the scale of the entire commonwealth."[108] This would then lead to increased growth for all.

The Romanians supported the idea that one of the characteristics of the international socialist system is the gradual leveling off of the economic development of all socialist states. However, they argued that to achieve this it was necessary for *each* state to establish the material-technical base of socialism, "introducing socialist industrialization by concentrating on the production of the means of production with its main branch, the machine building industry."[109] At the November-December 1961 central committee plenum, the Romanian planning chief, Gaston-Marin, stated his party's position that it was important to maintain the priority development of heavy industry within each country.

> Our party has always resolutely opposed and has always combated from a Marxist-Leninist standpoint those erroneous 'theories' which, while defending the keeping of proportions between the branches of the national economy and the priority development of heavy industry on the scale of the whole socialist camp rather than within the framework of the individual socialist country, in fact deny the necessity of creating the technical and material base of socialism and present in a distorted manner the principles of specialization and cooperation within the framework of the socialist international division of labour.[110]

The Romanians also questioned whether they could catch up with the more developed socialist states if they were relegated to the role of a raw material producer. A Romanian economist noted that "[t]he latest international surveys showed clearly that the countries confining themselves to the production of basic raw materials not only do not succeed in overcoming their backwardness, but are in a position in which their situation becomes worse."[111]

Winning this ideological debate would have been an uphill battle for the Soviet Union given the difference in interests with Romania.

However, the lack of technical information which could have served as a guide to implement a policy of specialization ensured that the Soviet Union would lose. Economists were unable to develop any objective standard for determining which country should specialize in producing what because both wages and prices were set arbitrarily in socialist states. A Soviet economist expressed the problem in this manner:

> The maximum reduction of expenditure of human labor and materials on the production and transport of goods . . . must be the criterion . . . of division of labor between the socialist countries. The question arises as to how we are to calculate this reduction of expenditure under conditions in which it is expressed in various countries in different monetary units [which are not convertible]. I shall not even speak of the difficulty of establishing the real cost of production within individual countries, given the individual characteristics of the national price systems.[112]

Value planning at the domestic level could have produced the information necessary to evaluate specialization proposals, but as George Breslauer observes, "Khrushchev remained in power too short a period of time, and was too absorbed in the short-term pressures generated by his authority crisis, to either absorb fully or act upon the ideas presented by Liberman."[113] The failure to solve these technical problems made it impossible for the Soviet Union to demonstrate convincingly that a division of labor would be profitable or that it would not hinder the development of the less developed states.

Conclusion

The Soviet Union was unable to attain the adoption of its proposed reform of CMEA at Council Sessions or in extensive bilateral discussions with Romania although its relative power capabilities had not declined. It discovered that the path originally chosen created impediments to reform. First, the rules of CMEA required that decisions be unanimous. Second, achieving unanimity had become problematic given the changes in the Soviet instruments of control in the institutional and personal contexts. And third as cognitive theories of regime change suggest, the lack of technical information about the relative costs and benefits associated with the alternative models of socialist economic development made it impossible for the Soviets to persuade the Romanians to abandon autarky.

The Soviet Union recognized the role that the unanimity rule had played in making it possible for Romania to block acceptance of Khrushchev's proposal to grant CMEA supranational authority over planning and investment. Since the underlying economic problems had not been solved, the Soviet Union began to explore possible reinterpretations of the decision rule based on the new Charter. As one Soviet economist concluded,

> [i]t would be wrong to strike from the agenda the proposals for extending collaboration that for the time being not all the Council participants, but only a few interested countries are prepared to accept . . . . It is advisable to meet these demands through the efforts of the interested countries, leaving room for the remaining countries to join later."[114]

Notes

1. "Nyers, Bogomolov Discuss Socialist Economics," p. 18.

2. Rothschild, *Return to Diversity*, p. 150.

3. For a detailed discussion of these events, see Brzezinski, *The Soviet Bloc*, Chapters 10 and 11.

4. "Basic Principles," p. 3.

The importance of this meeting is underscored by two facts. The delegations were headed by the Party leaders rather than the permanent representatives, and it was held in Moscow out of the rota. This meeting also marked changes in CMEA's membership. Mongolia, the first non-European member, was admitted, and Albania did not attend. Albania withdrew its representative from the Secretariat and stopped paying dues in late 1961. It did not resume participation although it never formally withdrew from CMEA.

5. "Basic Principles," p. 7.

According to Randall Stone, "under CMEA rules, any country could introduce a section of text to any document as its own 'particular opinion,' and those sections could not be eliminated by majority vote." *Satellites and Commissars*, p. 131.

6. Khrushchev, "Vital Questions," Part 1, p. 4.

Randall Stone claims that Khrushchev's proposal "for a dramatic push for East European integration based on joint planning of the whole region by a single Gosplan" was "never a serious proposal." He continues that a Central Committee investigation found that "the document had been written by a nonspecialist without going through the proper channels. Khrushchev had read it but had not been committed to the idea, and the specialists on Eastern Europe had done their best to bury it." Stone, *Satellites and Commissars*, p. 34. Although there is no reason to doubt Stone's account of the origins of this particular article, it is also clear that a serious debate on the nature of a socialist international division of labor and the role of CMEA in this was occurring.

7. Quoted in "A Rumanian Manifesto," p. 28.

8. "Communique on Conference of First Secretaries."

9. Khrushchev, "Vital Questions," Part 1, p. 3.

10. A chart on the balance of hard versus soft goods in Soviet and East European foreign trade can be found in Ausch, *Theory and Practice of CMEA Cooperation*, p. 100.

11. Vinogradov, "Collaboration of Socialist Countries," p. 53.

For a more complete discussion of East European economic problems, see below.

12. An article in *Pravda* noted that the Soviet Union had traded with 29 capitalist countries in 1950, but by 1961 the number had increased to 60. Podklyuchnikov, "Mezhdunarodnoe Obozrenie," p. 4.

For a discussion of the liberalization of Western export controls in this period, see Mastanduno, *Economic Containment*, pp. 93-105.

13. Hewett, *Foreign Trade Prices*, p. 105. This work contains a detailed discussion of the Price Clause.

14. Ausch, *Theory and Practice of CMEA Cooperation*, pp. 85, 86, emphasis in the original.

For some Western measures of the price deviations which attempt to include quality adjustments, see Marrese and Vanous, *Soviet Subsidization of Trade* and Marer, "The Political Economy."

15. See Marer, "The Political Economy" and Marrese and Vanous, *Soviet Subsidization of Trade*.

16. In 1960, six percent of Soviet foreign trade was with Bulgaria, eleven with Czechoslovakia, 18 with the GDR, five with Hungary, eight with Poland, and five with Romania. In contrast, 53 percent of Bulgaria's foreign trade was with the Soviet Union, 34 of Czechoslovakia's, 43 of the GDR's, 30 of Hungary's, 30 of Poland's, and 40 of Romania's. Calculated from data in Marer, *Soviet and East European Foreign Trade*. Also, foreign trade represented only about 2-3 percent of the Soviet national income while it represented 30-40 percent of the East European national incomes. Gyulai, "The Socialist Program for Economic Integration," p. 2.

17. Ausch, *Theory and Practice of CMEA Cooperation*, pp. 96, 95.

18. Kosnar, "Does the Economic Cooperation," p. 3.

19. Albinowski, "Fuel -- A Bottleneck," p. 4.

20. Gertzovitch, "The Economic Development," p. 80.

21. Oleinik, "The Equalization of the Economic Development Level," p. 4.

22. Reisinger concludes that "short-term economic gain seems to have been a secondary guideline for Soviet energy exports to its allies." *Energy and the Soviet Bloc*, p. 110.

For interviews and archival sources which support this conclusion, although they refer to later events, see Stone, *Satellites and Commissars*, pp. 59, 232.

23. Khrushchev, "Vital Questions," Part 1, p. 7.

24. For example, a Soviet radio broadcast to Romania claimed, "in practice this policy [of relying on one's own forces, or autarky] leads to an unwise squandering of manpower and material resources." "Unity Essential to Socialist Economies," p. BB7.

25. Khrushchev, "Vital Questions," Part 2, p. 3.

26. Nye, "Soft Power," p. 167.

27. Bogomolov, "The International Socialist Division of Labor," p. 44.

28. Khrushchev, "Vital Questions," Part 2, pp. 3-4.

29. Khrushchev, "Vital Questions," Part 1, p. 4.

30. For an account of the evolution of Soviet policy toward the EEC, see Forte, "The Response of Soviet Foreign Policy." Binns, "From USE to EEC" examines the theoretical roots of the Soviet analysis of European integration.

31. An analysis of the possible economic impact can be found in Zdziechowski, "The Impact of the Common Market." A more extensive analysis of the economic impact on Eastern Europe can be found below.

32. "Declaration of Conference" and "Communique on Conference of Representatives."

33. Khrushchev, "On Peaceful Coexistence," p. 4.

34. "Concerning Imperialist 'Integration,'" pp. 10, 9.

35. Khrushchev, "On the Program," Part 1, p. 9.

36. Khrushchev, "Vital Questions," Part 1, p. 5.

37. Sekera, "In the Spirit of the Progressive Tradition," p. 6, emphasis in the original.

38. "Report on 1st Session of PZPR Plenum," p. GG 13.

39. W. Berger, "Socialist Economy and International Cooperation," p. 34.

40. Kosnar, "Prices and International Socialist Division of Work," p. 4. Thus, they produced a greater variety of products than were produced in larger capitalist states such as France and Italy.

41. Avramov, "Our Foreign Trade," p. 7.

The more developed states, such as Czechoslovakia, were not immune from this either. In fact they were probably more affected because a larger percentage of their exports was composed of manufactured goods. See Burks, "The Decline of Communism in Czechoslovakia," p. 25, n. 11.

42. E. Apro, "On the Economic Cooperation," p. 4.

43. See E. Apro, "On the Economic Cooperation."

44. For a Czech statement of this position, see Stransky, "Toward Further Progress."

45. Albinowski, *Commercial Policy of EEC*, p. 151.

46. Albinowski, *Commercial Policy of EEC*, pp. 153-54.

47. For Hungarian, Polish, and Bulgarian discussions of these difficulties see: Szilagyi, "The Policy of Europe's Division;" Wirski, "Poland's Commerce;" and Penev, "Trade Between the People's Republic of Bulgaria and the German Federal."

48. Zdziechowski, "The Impact of the Common Market," p. 55. For an estimate of Hungarian losses, see Hedri, "Changes in the West European Closed Economic Groups," p. 8.

49. North, *Institutions*, p. 99.

50. Foldes, "Economic Cooperation and Internationalism," p. 3.

51. Kouril, "Division of Work," p. 6.

52. "New Machinery -- New Problems," p. 11.

53. Keh, "The International Specialization of Production," p. 3.

54. Marer, "The Political Economy," p. 161.

55. Maryska, "For the Closest Cooperation," p. 4.

56. Quoted in Foldes, "On Cooperation and Nationalism," p. 9.

57. See Maryska, "For the Closest Cooperation," and Kouril, "Division of Work."

58. The East European states can be placed in three groups by the level of development. Czechoslovakia and the GDR were the most developed; Romania and Bulgaria were the least developed; and Poland and Hungary were in the middle although closer to the least developed.

59. Bogomolov, "Problems in Production Specialization," p. 71.

60. Oleinik, "Forms of International Division of Labor," p. 60.

61. Rachmuth, "The Importance of Establishing a Rate of Development," p. 3.

62. Filipov, "The Main Economic Task," p. 3.

63. Rachmuth, "The Importance of Establishing a Rate of Development," p. 9.

64. Montias, *Economic Development in Communist Rumania*, p. 207.

65. Moldovan, "The Socialist International Division of Labor," p. 74. For a Hungarian statement echoing this position, see E. Apro, "On the Economic Cooperation," p. 6.

66. Khrushchev justified the lack of support by stressing the need for efficient production of steel. "In view of the uneven distribution of ore and coking coal deposits, great importance attaches to the question of more rational location of iron and steel enterprises with the least expenditure of time, means, and labor." Khrushchev, "Vital Questions," Part 2, p. 5. For a description of Soviet-Romanian interaction on this issue, see Montias, *Economic Development in Communist Rumania*, Chapter 4.

The Bulgarian steel industry was under no similar threat, despite a similar shortage of natural resources, and the Soviets had granted a 650 million ruble credit to expand the Kremikovtsi steel works. On the Bulgarian steel industry and Soviet support of it, see Palairet, "'Lenin' and 'Brezhnev.'" This variation may help to explain the variation between the Romanian and Bulgarian public positions on the proposed reforms of CMEA.

67. Fazekas, "Traditions in Fetters," p. 2.

68. Kuzinski, "About the International Socialist Division of Work," p. 4.

69. Novozamsky, "A United Economy," p. 4.

70. Krylova and Rohan, "The Development of the Socialist System," p. 8, emphasis removed.

71. Zwass, *The Council for Mutual Economic Assistance*, p. 32. This statement is also supported by a Romanian who worked at the CMEA headquarters. Nicolae, "CMEA in Theory and Practice," p. 57.

72. Nye, "Soft Power," p. 159. See also the discussion on p. 162.

73. Nicolae, "CMEA in Theory and Practice," p. 60.

74. Montias, *Economic Development of Communist Rumania*, p. 230.

75. See, for example, Krylova & Rohan, "The Development of the Socialist System," p. 8.

76. Nicolae, "CMEA in Theory and Practice," p. 9. This contains organization charts and detailed descriptions of various bodies.

77. "Charter of the Council on Mutual Economic Aid," Article VIII(3).

It is interesting to note that a Soviet analyst asserts that the new institutional structure of CMEA was "copied from the Gosplan of the USSR at that time." Rybakov, "The Economic Platform of Interaction," p. 79.

78. "Charter of the Council on Mutual Economic Aid," p. 9.

79. "On the Nature of Relations," p. 3.

80. "Combine National and International Interests," p. 4.

81. "Charter of the Council on Mutual Economic Aid," Article IV (3).

82. *Khrushchev Remembers: The Last Testament*, p. 253.

83. "On the Principles," p. 10.

This declaration was published between the first and the second Soviet interventions in Hungary. According to Brzezinski, it "was obviously designed to prevent a Hungarian defection from the Soviet bloc and to define the new conditions created by the events in Poland and Hungary." *The Soviet Bloc*, p. 229.

84. See Fischer-Galati, *The New Rumania* and Levy, "The 'Right Deviation' of Ana Pauker," for discussions of Gheorghiu-Dej's power struggle.

85. Gross, "Rumania," pp. 18-19.

86. One exception to this generalization is Janos Kadar of Hungary who came to power after the Soviet invasion in 1956.

87. "On the Principles," p. 11.

88. A discussion of Romania's evolving relationship with the Warsaw Pact can be found in Jones, *Soviet Influence in Eastern Europe*.

89. *Khrushchev Remembers: The Last Testament*, pp. 238-39.

90. The Soviet troops were withdrawn from Romania in 1958 at Gheorghiu-Dej's request. The justification for their presence had been the terms of the Romanian Peace Treaty which guaranteed "the right of the Soviet Union to keep on Roumanian territory such armed forces as it may need for the maintenance of the lines of communication of the Soviet Army with the Soviet zone of occupation in Austria." "Treaty of Peace with Romania," Article 21 in Department of State, *Treaties and Other International Agreements of the United States of America, 1946-1949*, Vol 4. The signing of the Austrian State Treaty in 1955 and the subsequent withdrawal of Soviet troops from Austria removed that justification. For a detailed analysis of the Soviet troop withdrawal from Romania, see Verona, *Military Occupation and Diplomacy*.

91. *Khrushchev Remembers: The Last Testament*, pp. 261, 252.

92. *Khrushchev Remembers: The Last Testament*, p. 237. Jozef Cyrankiewicz was the Polish Prime Minister 1947-52.

93. Medvedev, "Soviet Trade Agreements," p. 55, emphasis in the original.

94. Kotyk, "Some Aspects of the History of Relations," p. 17.

95. For a discussion of the origins of the Warsaw Pact, see Mackintosh, "The Warsaw Treaty Organization."

96. Texts of the agreements can be found in Szawlowski, *The System of the International Organizations*.

97. E. Haas, *When Knowledge is Power*, pp. 74, 31.

98. For an account of the dispute between China and the Soviet Union, see Griffith, *The Sino-Soviet Rift*.

99. Kaser, *Comecon*, p. 86.

100. This is the explanation for the 21 percent growth rate in 1959. A description of the Bulgarian great leap can be found in Grigorov, "New Problems and Accelerated Socialist Advance."

101. Liberman, "Plan, Pribyl', Premiia," p. 3.

102. Selucky, "The Dynamic Force of Socialist Advance," p. 3.

103. Khrushchev, "Vital Questions," Part 1, p. 4. The sense that the abandonment of the multilateral forms of cooperation favored by the East Europeans in 1949 for bilateral forms was a mistake permeates Soviet histories of CMEA. In fact, the initial period of CMEA's history is generally ignored in Soviet accounts. See Lukin, "Pervoe Desiatiletie," and Loshchakov, "35 Let SEV."

104. Khrushchev, "On Control Figures," Part 4, p. 17.

105. Oleinik, "A Law of Development," p. 62.

106. Khrushchev, "On Control Figures," Part 4, p. 17.

107. Bogomolov, "The International Socialist Division of Labor," p. 45. This same quote was later used in the *Kommunist* article, and it is perhaps the quote most commonly used to support the socialist international division of labor.

108. Khrushchev, "Vital Questions," Part 1, p. 4.

109. Quoted in Rachmuth, "The Importance of Establishing a Rate of Development," p. 5. Like the Soviets, they also quoted Lenin in support of their position. "Setting out to build the socialist state, the Rumanian Workers' Party took as the cornerstone of its economic policy Lenin's words: 'The only real factor in the consolidation of resources, in the establishment of socialist societies, is found in large-scale industry.'"

110. Quoted in Brown, "Rumania Steps out of Line," pp. 22-3.

111. Murgescu, "Rumania's Industrialization," p. 5.

112. Quoted in Gamarnikow, "The Future of Comecon," p. 5. See also Albinowski, "There is Still no Conception . . .," p. 2.

113. Breslauer, "Soviet Economic Reforms Since Stalin," p. 269.

114. Bogomolov, "Strengthening of Cooperation," p. 27.

Chapter Four

The Elaboration of the Interested-Party Principle

> But can the boundary on the Elbe truly become an irreversible frontier of the socialist camp if we fail to achieve, gradually, carefully, but with determination a radical change in the methods of economic cooperation?[1]

Conflict over the decision rule of CMEA erupted when some members continued to press for socialist economic integration as a solution to their economic problems despite Romanian objections. Acting on the basis of Article 4 of the CMEA Charter, interested-parties created international organizations to promote specialization in branches of industry. In April 1964 an agreement on the establishment of the Organization for Cooperation in the Ball-Bearing Industry (OCBI) was signed by Bulgaria, Hungary, the GDR, Poland, and Czechoslovakia. It was also signed by the Soviet Union in 1965.[2] The Organization for Cooperation in Ferrous Metallurgy (Intermetall) was established by Czechoslovakia, Hungary, and Poland in July 1964.[3] By the end of the year, Bulgaria, the GDR, and the Soviet Union had also joined. According to a Soviet economist the functions of the OCBI and Intermetall were

> defining categories and a single nomenclature of goods, the output of which is being cooperatively arranged, preparing suggestions for expanding the product mix, unifying standards and conditions of reciprocal deliveries and making full use of productive capacities, and finally, coordinating scientific research, experimentation and designing.[4]

The results in specialization obtained by these organizations were evaluated positively by the participants.[5] Therefore, plans were made to expand the competence of the existing organizations and to create new ones. For example, Intermetall was to begin "performing more fundamental functions such as coordinating capital investments, production plans and implementing further specialization."[6] At the 28th Session of the CMEA Executive Committee in February 1967 a proposal was made to set up a similar organization in the field of chemistry.[7]

Romania, although it did not participate in these organizations, became concerned about the progress that was being made towards integration. The interested-party principle as stated in the Charter did not specifically exclude members from voting on questions in which they were not interested. The Romanians took full advantage of this lack of clarity to veto proposals which they felt were "aimed at orienting the activity of Comecon in directions which do not tally with the principles of collaboration agreed upon between socialist countries and with the provisions of the statutes of that organization."[8] For example, Romania insisted that an Intermetall plan for joint investment be removed from the agenda of the January 1967 meeting of the CMEA Ferrous Metals Commission.[9] The result of Romania's actions was a period of stagnation in the activities of CMEA as the other members were prevented from pursuing multilateral cooperation programs.

Discussion of the principle of interest was apparently on the agenda of the Executive Committee meeting in October 1966. The other members asserted that the CMEA Charter required "unanimity only among those countries which are interested in a concrete question and in definite forms of cooperation," and they began to complain openly about Romania's obstructionist tactics.[10] The Soviets in particular were determined to overcome the problem of Romanian vetoes. In a 1968 *International Affairs* article, Yuri Belayev stated:

> --in the coming period, the principle of *interestedness* will be applied within the framework of CMEA to a considerably greater extent than formerly.
>
> This will mean that important questions of economic cooperation will be discussed and resolved by a definite number of countries, namely those interested in their solution. Moreover, the countries will not insist on discussion of each question by all CMEA countries, that is, by those which are not directly interested in them. As a result, many problems which were formerly shelved owing to some CMEA countries taking different positions may find a positive solution in the coming five-year period.[11]

The breakthrough on the issue of interestedness came at the 23rd Council Session held in April 1969. The communique called for "the creation by the interested countries of international scientific-technical and other organizations,"[12] and shortly afterwards the long-awaited Organization for Cooperation in Small-Tonnage Chemical Products (Interkhim) was established. Over the next two years a compromise on the decision rule gradually emerged which was codified in the August 1971 "Comprehensive Program for the Intensification and Improvement of Cooperation and the Development of Socialist Economic Integration of Comecon Member Countries" (the Comprehensive Program). Under the terms of the compromise, non-interested parties could not prevent interested parties from pursuing cooperation. However, the interested parties could not compel non-interested parties to participate in cooperation either, although they were free to join later. This clarification of the decision rule made it possible for CMEA members to establish six new international economic organizations over the next three years.

As in the previous case, structural factors are a necessary, but not a sufficient, explanation for the Soviet success in achieving a change in interpretation of the CMEA decision rule. Soviet interest in reforming CMEA to better reflect its interests remained high, and the Soviet Union's power capabilities remained unchanged. However, the interest of CMEA members in the economic benefits which could be derived from specialization continued to increase because the underlying economic problems which had led to the first attempt to reform CMEA had not been resolved. By 1970 even Romania had begun to evaluate specialization positively. Cognitive factors were also a significant component of the Soviet success. This time the Soviet Union was able to effectively argue that the proposed reform was based on the language of the Charter and that it did not violate the national sovereignty of the members.

Structural Factors: Power and Interest

Soviet Interests

The Soviet Union's economic and security interests continued to lead it to desire increased economic integration within CMEA. Integration could help resolve problems with the growth rate, labor productivity, and the effectiveness of capital investment both domestically and in the bloc as a whole. In particular, the Soviet Union was interested in organizing multilateral investment in its extraction industries to relieve the burden of the additional investments necessary to meet increased East European demand for raw materials. Economic integration could also improve Soviet security by enabling the socialist states to better compete economically with the capitalist states and by once again drawing the socialist states closer together. Romanian obstructionism made a change in the decision rule a necessary precondition for achieving any of the Soviet interests.

At the 23rd Party Congress in 1966, Leonid Brezhnev, who had replaced Khrushchev, observed that "in recent years negative phenomena have appeared such as a slowing down of the rates of growth of production and labor productivity and a reduction in the effectiveness of the utilization of production assets and capital investments."[13] Therefore, it was declared that

> the *chief economic task* of the five-year plan is to ensure -- on the basis of the comprehensive utilization of the achievements of science and technology, the industrial development of all social production and a rise in its effectiveness and in the productivity of labor -- a significant growth in industrial production.[14]

The role that the division of labor among the socialist countries could play in accelerating technical progress and increasing the effectiveness of social production in all countries, including the Soviet Union, was also acknowledged. The Soviet Union was particularly interested in reaping the benefits of the scientific-technical revolution. A Soviet analyst claimed that "the application of the latest scientific and technological achievements in production increases the national income by no less than 50 per cent" and that it was "almost four times more effective than ordinary investments."[15] Moreover, it was acknowledged that "large-scale research without co-operation with other countries has become quite difficult even for large states with vast territories and resources."[16] Therefore, the Soviet Union was interested in increased economic integration within CMEA.

The Soviet Union was also interested in organizing multilateral investments in its extraction industries to relieve the burden of additional investments necessary to meet East European demand for imports of Soviet raw materials which continued to increase as industrial production in the region grew.[17] Although the Soviets hoped that "as the socialist countries assimilate the fruits of the scientific-technical revolution, imports of industrial raw materials will grow at a less rapid rate than industrial production,"[18] as shown in Table 4.1, the planned growth in Soviet deliveries of fuels and raw materials to Eastern Europe for 1971-75 was considerable.

Table 4.1: Soviet Exports to CMEA Countries

	1966-70	1971-75	% Growth
Oil (mln tons)	138	243	176
Gas (1,000 mln cubic m.)	8	33	412
Electric power (1,000 mln kWh)	14	42	300
Iron ore (in terms of metal, mln tons)	72	94	130

Source: N. Shiryayev, "USSR Trade with CMEA Countries in the Ninth Five-Year Period," *International Affairs* [Moscow], October 1971, p. 113.

The problems in exporting raw materials under the CMEA price system which were discussed in the previous chapter still existed and were even exacerbated by price trends in the world market. The Soviet Union had become the only net exporter of raw materials among the European members of CMEA even though it had increased the share of machinery and equipment in its exports to the CMEA members.[19] This pattern of trade continued to be disadvantageous for the Soviet Union because the prices of machinery and equipment in intra-CMEA trade continued to be overvalued relative to the prices of raw materials.[20] The problem was further exacerbated in 1966 when the price base of intra-

CMEA trade was changed from the average of world market prices in 1957-58 to the average of 1960-64 because world market prices for industrial products had risen while prices for raw materials and fuels had dropped.[21]

In addition, the Soviets believed that "the actual conditions of raw materials and fuel production in the CMEA countries [were] often less favorable for objective reasons than average conditions on the world market."[22] To meet growing demand, both domestically and in Eastern Europe, the Soviet Union began to exploit the vast reserves in its eastern regions. However, prospecting and exploitation of deposits in these regions were more expensive than in already developed regions because of the often unfavorable climatic conditions and the need to develop infrastructure such as roads and housing. The increased cost of transportation to Eastern Europe would also be borne by the Soviet Union since the actual costs incurred in shipping raw materials to the border of the exporting country were not covered under the CMEA price system.[23]

The Soviets were also concerned because investment in raw material extraction was less effective than investment in manufacturing. It was widely argued that "in order to gain 1 foreign exchange ruble on the world socialist market, one has to invest in the production of iron ore, raw materials for fertilizers, and coal -- all destined for export -- 5 to 8 times more means than when exporting machines." Also, investment in extraction has a longer recoupment period than investment in manufacturing. As a Soviet economist concluded,

> therefore, the production of raw materials for export is connected, as a rule, with an enormous burden of capital investment on the part of the exporting country. In conditions of shortage of capital, this restrains the realization of programs to raise living standards for the working people.[24]

An obvious solution to these problems, which was proposed by many Soviet economists, was to switch from prices based on world market prices to prices based on the costs of production within CMEA.[25] However, as another Soviet economist observed, "the study of this question for ten years has not enabled the [Standing CMEA]

Commission [on Economic Problems] to draw any definite conclusion about the possible ways of transition by socialist countries, specifically CMEA members, to a price basis of their own in reciprocal trade." The Soviets recognized this was not only because revising the price structure would be a difficult, time consuming task, but also because "a redistribution of the national income created in individual fraternal countries is possible through the mechanism of prices."[26]

Another possible solution was to further increase the percentage of machinery and equipment in Soviet exports to Eastern Europe, and the Soviets planned to increase it to about 33 percent by 1975.[27] However, there were limits to this solution. The East Europeans lacked sufficient raw material resources to cover their needs, and it was often more efficient to exploit Soviet resources than East European ones. Therefore, the Soviets concluded that "deliveries of Soviet oil, gas, and electric power, as hitherto, will be indispensable for ensuring the stability and improving the pattern of the fuel and power balance of the fraternal countries."[28]

The solution selected by the Soviet Union was to require East European investment in Soviet raw material extraction in order to secure additional future deliveries. This decision was announced at the 23rd Party Congress in 1966. Czechoslovakia had begun to invest in Soviet raw material extraction as early as 1959-60. The first credit of $330 million, "which was earmarked for the development and processing of iron and non-ferrous mineral ores, was repaid later by Soviet deliveries of raw materials." In September 1966, Czechoslovakia granted a second credit of $550 million to the Soviet Union for the development of crude oil extraction in the Tiumen Taiga. A third credit was granted in 1968 for "the development of natural gas extraction processes."[29] Although the credits granted were substantial, Czechoslovakia was the only East European state to participate heavily in this type of cooperation. Bilateral investment also had shortcomings. Credits were granted in the form of increased deliveries of goods so the investing state might not always be able to supply the range of goods or services needed by the Soviet Union to develop a particular site. Also, some sites would require more investment than could be supplied by a single investor. Therefore, the Soviet Union was interested in the initiation of multilateral investment projects.

The improved climate of East-West relations affected both Soviet security and economic interests. On the one hand, the Soviet Union's security was increased because it had achieved rough nuclear parity with the United States by the end of the 1960s, and the process of arms control had begun. The nuclear non-proliferation treaty was signed in 1968, and the strategic arms control talks between the United States and the Soviet Union, which would culminate in the signing of SALT I in 1972, were also under way. Western recognition of the post-war borders in Europe, which Leonid Brezhnev had declared was the key to creating "an atmosphere of genuine security for everyone in Europe,"[30] had also been achieved. On August 12, 1970 a formal agreement between the FRG and the Soviet Union was signed which recognized the inviolability of the territorial status quo in Central Europe,[31] and in November a similar agreement was signed with Poland. Thus, by the end of 1970 the foundations for detente had been laid.

The Soviet Union expected that the improvements in East-West relations would also lead to economic benefits through an expansion of East-West trade.[32] Trade with the West did expand as Western trade restrictions were eased, long term credits became available, and Western companies invested in the Soviet economy. The easing of restrictions occurred most rapidly in trade with Western Europe and Japan.[33] By 1964 the CoCom lists of goods which required a license for export to Eastern bloc countries contained only ten percent of internationally traded goods.[34] The Soviets were confident that this trend of liberalization would continue. Barriers to Soviet exports were also being lifted. A Soviet analyst noted that "some Western countries, for example France and Italy, have committed themselves under trade agreements now in operation, to lift all quantitative restrictions on imports from socialist states in the near future."[35]

Western states had begun to grant long-term credits which made it possible for the Soviet Union to import more Western technology. In

1964-69 the Soviet Union signed agreements for the receipt of long-term credits from France, Italy, Britain, and Austria totaling about 1.2 billion rubles.[36] Intergovernmental agreements and protocols on scientific and technical cooperation were signed with these countries as well as Finland, Sweden, and Belgium.[37] The Soviets then began to buy both licenses and plants in the West.

Western investment in Soviet raw material extraction also occurred. In 1968 the Japanese signed an agreement to deliver equipment and materials for developing the timber industry to the Soviet Union on credit in return for lumber. The Soviets hoped that further Japanese investment in the development of Soviet deposits of petroleum, gas, coking coal, iron ore and nonferrous metals would be forthcoming.[38] In 1960-70 bilateral agreements were also signed with Italy, France, and the FRG "to deliver large amounts of natural gas in exchange for equipment and steel pipes needed for pipeline construction and operation."[39]

The lessening of tensions in East-West relations improved the security of the Soviet Union and opened new opportunities for the Soviet Union to acquire the advanced technology and capital investment it needed more advantageously than it could within CMEA. However, there were also developments in the EEC and in relations between Eastern Europe and the West which could adversely affect the security of the Soviet Union, and these developments led the Soviet Union to favor increased economic cooperation with Eastern Europe.

After a period of stagnation in the development of the EEC, progress was again being made towards integration. The last EEC internal customs tariffs were abolished on June 30, 1968. Agricultural tariff barriers were to be lifted in December 1969, and a common foreign trade policy was scheduled to be implemented on January 1, 1970.[40] Expansion of the membership was also on the agenda. Great Britain, Ireland, Denmark, and Norway had applied for admission. This increased integration threatened Soviet security interests because a 'united Europe' could alter the alignment of forces by becoming a third power in the world, and it also raised the stakes in the economic competition with capitalism. Therefore, increased integration within the EEC led the Soviet Union to favor increased integration within CMEA. As a Soviet analyst concluded, "the further economic cooperation of the socialist states is dictated not only by the internal conditions of their development, but also by the international situation -- the need to resist imperialist integration."[41]

Soviet security interests were also threatened by the improved relationship between Eastern Europe and the West which was also a product of detente. East European trade with the West was growing faster than both their total trade and trade with other socialist states.[42] The FRG, which was traditionally a major trading partner of the East Europeans, had been particularly aggressive in expanding this trade. By 1969 it had accumulated a 2,479 million DM surplus in its trade with the socialist countries, and the surplus was growing.[43] The Soviets were concerned that this would translate into increased West German influence in their sphere of influence. For example, one reason given for the Soviet invasion of Czechoslovakia was the fear that "peaceful penetration" of that country by the West would undermine "the ideological and political foundations of the socialist system so as to consolidate imperialist positions in the campaign against socialism and the change the balance of power in favor of imperialism."[44] Soviet analysts also complained that "socialist countries which hold special views on certain international issues quickly find 'understanding' in Bonn, and the barriers raised to their exports to West Germany are lowered or even completely removed."[45] Thus, the Soviet Union's economic and security interests led it to favor increased economic integration within CMEA.

Soviet and East European Power Capabilities

The Soviet success in achieving a reform of CMEA cannot be explained by an increase in Soviet power capabilities relative to Eastern Europe though because there was no significant change in 1965-75. The Soviet Union had been the regional hegemon, and it continued to be. The area of all the countries was the same. Soviet population, GDP, and military capability remained over twice as much as those of Eastern Europe. There were no changes in the relative resource endowment either. (See Tables 7-12 in the Appendix.)

The Warsaw Pact invasion of Czechoslovakia in August 1968 to stop the political and economic liberalization associated with the Prague Spring had once again demonstrated the willingness of the Soviet Union to use its military capability to obtain an objective in Eastern Europe. However, it had also demonstrated some of the difficulties of using force to obtain political objectives even though the Czechoslovak government did not resist militarily. As Christopher Jones observed, "the Soviets found that although their soldiers had seized all their military objectives, they were not able to install in power a group of Communists with the legitimacy to govern."[46] It took eight months after the invasion before a pro-Soviet faction, under the leadership of Gustav Husak, gained control of the Czechoslovak Communist party. Also, the Romanian response to the Soviet use of force in another East European state was quick and decisive. The next day Nicolae Ceausescu announced that "the Romanian people will not permit anyone to violate the territory of our fatherland," and he mobilized components of Romania's territorial defense system to demonstrate that Romania could and would make an invasion very costly.[47]

The Soviet capability which was becoming more relevant in this period was its resource endowment. As industrial production in Eastern Europe continued to rise so did demand for raw materials. In the early 1970s even Romania moved from being self sufficient in power production to being an energy importing state. Therefore, the Soviets had an economic trump card in their ability to trade raw materials for manufactured goods.[48] However, as was noted in the previous chapter, the ultimate success of this card depended upon Romania's ability to find alternative markets for its exports.

East European Interests[49]

Although Soviet power capabilities had not increased, the interest of all the East European states, including Romania, in economic integration had grown in response to the demands of the scientific-technical revolution, difficulties in trade with the West, and increased demand for raw materials. However, the risks of integration continued to be greater for the East Europeans than for the Soviet Union. In particular, the East Europeans remained concerned about the loss of control over the management of their national economies which could result from increased economic integration.

Like the Soviet Union, the East Europeans were interested in economic integration as a means to increase their growth rates, labor productivity, and effectiveness of capital investment.[50] They recognized that their domestic markets were too small to support the production of high quality goods at low costs, and they were particularly alarmed by the "tempestuous development of science and technology."[51] As a Polish analyst observed, "the modern technological solutions concerning production of the same goods are born quicker than the physical wear and tear of the installed machinery."[52] Therefore, the East Europeans concluded that "small countries are faced with an alternative -- either to unite their efforts or to face relative impoverishment."[53] Although Romania continued to deny that "there may be a conflict between the level to which the forces of production develop and national limits on production,"[54] it too began to acknowledge that the demands of the scientific-technical revolution required greater cooperation. In Ceausescu's electoral speech on February 28, 1969, he noted,

> We start from the incontestable reality that, in view of today's enormous technical and scientific progress, the progress of every country is dependent on its active participation in the international division of labor. Isolation results only in stagnation, in lagging behind, with serious consequences for the whole economic and social development of the country in question.[55]

Spurred by East European interest in acquiring advanced technology, foreign trade between Eastern Europe and the capitalist countries grew dramatically in the late 1960s. As was the case with the Soviet Union, this rise in trade was facilitated by "the improved international situation and easing of the earlier embargo policy of Western countries as well as the growing interest of the latter in exports to socialist markets."[56]

Despite the positive developments, there were barriers to the further expansion of East European trade with the West. The East European states were generally denied most-favored-nation (MFN) status, and quantitative restrictions were imposed on their export of some commodities. They sought to overcome these barriers by participating in the GATT. Poland had acceded to full membership in 1967. Romania and Hungary had applied for accession in 1968 and 1969, and Bulgaria had been granted observer status in 1967.[57] As a Hungarian official stated, "the only reason for our request to join was to protect the foreign trade interests of our country and, furthermore, to fight for complete observance of the principle of the most-favored-nation-clause -- meaning equality."[58] Membership in the GATT had become particularly important since the Kennedy Round of tariff negotiations had "resulted in an agreement to reduce by an average of 33-35% the import duties on a number of industrial and agricultural products representing some 80% of the volume of world trade." However, as Czechoslovakia and Poland had discovered, membership in the GATT did not mean automatic MFN status.[59] Also despite some liberalization of quantitative restrictions on imports from socialist countries, a Hungarian analyst concluded that "this has not gone so far as to abolish totally the import license and import quota systems."[60]

The EEC also posed barriers to East European exports.[61] The East Europeans feared that the EEC's abolition of internal customs tariffs and imposition of a common external tariff "will act as a brake to imports or will cause their prices to rise, which will be detrimental to them competitively."[62] They also continued to be concerned about the EEC agricultural policy. A Romanian economist complained that the policy "adversely reflects upon the imports of agricultural and food products from Rumania"[63] Moreover, the East Europeans felt that they were disproportionately affected by EEC tariffs because "the number of items falling under import quotas in the case of CMEA-exports is a multiple of those affecting imports from developed capitalist countries."[64] The East Europeans were also concerned about the proposed expansion of the EEC to include Denmark, Ireland, and the United Kingdom because it would increase the concentration of their foreign trade with the EEC. Hungary, for example, estimated that after the expansion "65 per cent of all Hungarian exports to developed capitalist countries will have a Common Market country as their destination."[65]

One of the major barriers to the expansion of East European trade with the West though was the commodity composition of their exports. Over 70 percent of East European exports to the West was composed of raw materials and food products, and the East Europeans realized that it was impossible to base a major expansion of trade on the export of these commodities.[66] Therefore, they concluded that it was necessary "to give first place to trade in industrial finished goods, machinery, instruments, and equipment" in order to guarantee a continuous and rapid increase in foreign trade with the West.[67] However, they continued to have difficulty exporting finished goods to the West. For example, Table 4.2 compares the share of machinery and transportation equipment in exports to advanced capitalist countries with their share in total exports. The major reason for this disparity was the low quality of East European manufactured products.

Table 4.2: Proportion of Machinery and Transportation Equipment Exports, 1966

	Within Total Exports	Within Exports to Advanced Capitalist Countries	Difference
Bulgaria	25.3	2.5	22.8
CSSR	49.7	17.5	32.2
GDR	--	22.8	--
Hungary	31.3	6.5	24.8
Poland	35.3	7.9	27.4
Rumania	17.3	1.3	16.0

Source: Al. Puiu and C. Cuilea, "The Development of Trade Exchanges Between Socialist and Advanced Capitalist Countries," *Probleme Economice*, 1968, no. 5 in *Rumanian Press Survey* No. 767, Radio Free Europe Research, p. 5.

These problems in trade with the West led all the East Europeans, including Romania, to favor closer cooperation within CMEA. A Polish analyst offered this rather pessimistic assessment:

> obviously these barriers [to trade with the West] should be overcome, but experience shows that our chance in this respect is rather limited. This fact explains, to a considerable extent, why the main solution for the socialist countries consists . . . in mutual relations within the framework of the socialist system.[68]

Other East European analysts offered more positive reasons for increased intra-CMEA cooperation. For example, a Hungarian economist asserted that "development of cooperation within the CMEA is the sole realistic possibility for a broad scale fruitful use of the import of technology from the developed capitalist countries."[69] In particular, the East Europeans hoped that increased intra-CMEA cooperation would create "favorable conditions to overcome the difficulties encountered in trade [with the West] on a bilateral basis."[70] There were also other more prosaic reasons to increase intra-CMEA cooperation. As a Romanian noted, "interest on credits granted by Western companies is, in most cases, much higher than that on credits granted by the socialist countries."[71]

The East European states were also concerned about their growing demand for raw materials. As industrial production grew, their ability to cover their demand through domestic output declined. Table 4.3 demonstrates this trend for iron ore and metallurgical coke production.[72] Even Romania, which had previously been an energy exporting country, had become an energy importing country. In 1971 it imported 2.85 million tons of crude oil, although domestic production had been increased at great cost, and imports were expected to rise to about 6.0 million tons by 1975. Romania also expressed an interest in imports of natural gas.[73]

Table 4.3: Needs Covered by Domestic Output (in %)

	Iron ore (processed)				Metallurgical Coke		
	1960	**1971**	**Change**		**1960**	**1971**	**Change**
Bulgaria	100.00	56.11	-43.89		3.57	75.60	+72.03
CSSR	20.62	6.36	-14.26		113.61	124.86	+11.25
GDR	57.46	14.65	-42.81		80.59	73.33	-7.26
Hungary	20.38	11.84	-8.54		48.05	47.15	-0.90
Poland	18.03	9.28	-8.75		108.73	116.90	+8.17
Romania	60.09	21.62	-38.47		57.79	32.97	-24.82

Source: Radu Constantinescu, "Economic Collaboration and Co-operation in Material Production Among the Socialist Countries," *Viata Economica*, March 9, 1973 in *Rumanian Press Survey* No. 946, Radio Free Europe Research, p. 2.

The East Europeans could not meet their own needs for raw materials because of insufficient deposits or prohibitively expensive exploitation. Therefore, they needed to expand their imports of raw materials and fuels. One possible source of additional imports was the West, and some agreements were signed to expand this trade. Romania and Czechoslovakia signed long-term agreements in 1965 and 1966 to deliver investment equipment to Iran in exchange for crude oil. Hungary was also reported to be considering the purchase of crude oil from Algeria.[74] However, doubts were expressed by East Europeans about their ability to pay for extensive imports of raw materials from hard currency areas. A Hungarian economist stated bluntly: "we would not be able to purchase this quantity of [raw] material in the capitalist countries, because we would be unable to produce annually the needed dollar funds."[75] A section head at the Czechoslovak Planning Commission was equally blunt:

> If it is realized that the exports of machinery to the capitalist countries have increased in the past five years by some 50 million convertible Kcs yearly, while the increase of crude oil imports represents 100 million yearly, it becomes absolutely clear that any transfer of imports of crude oil to the capitalist countries is sheer utopia.[76]

Some concerns were also raised about the political implications of becoming dependent on the West for raw materials. An article in a Czechoslovak Communist Party publication referred to the "danger of subsequent conditions being demanded by the capitalist countries involved, or of cancellation and refusal to continue the supply of raw materials, fuel, and power in the case of political tensions in the world."[77]

Moreover, it was generally conceded that when transportation costs and the overall effectiveness of trade were considered, it was economically advantageous for the East Europeans to import raw materials from the Soviet Union.[78] Because of the way that shipping costs were calculated in CMEA pricing and the proximity of the East European states to the Soviet Union, transportation costs were generally lower for raw materials imported from the Soviet Union. Also, the "reproduction value" of the ruble was higher than that of the dollar for most East European states. For example, in Czechoslovakia it was estimated that "to earn a dollar we must export Czechoslovak goods costing about 32 kcs, while to earn a ruble we only have to export goods costing about 18 kcs."[79] This disparity arose because the East Europeans were able to sell their industrial products to the Soviet Union at world market prices whereas they were often forced to discount these products in order to sell them in the West. As the Hungarian Minister of Foreign Trade acknowledged, "in some of our export branches, the Soviet market is a permanent safety valve for the sale of products which it is difficult to sell or can only be sold under unfavorable circumstances."[80]

Finally, there was also increasing competition for Soviet raw materials, particularly from Western Europe and Japan. A Hungarian observed that "by exporting raw materials to the advanced capitalist countries, however, the Soviet Union is able to obtain up-to-date machinery and technical know-how that contribute to a more rapid advancement of its own industry's technical level."[81] A Czech writer concluded, "for these reasons, this trade is of big advantage for the Soviet Union and is very competitive for our crude oil contracts with the USSR." The author then stated that "the Soviet Union makes good use of this fact for obtaining excellent credit terms for its oil extraction."[82] Thus, all the East European states, including Romania, expressed interest in "collaboration for the countries concerned regarding the setting up on Soviet territory of additional capacities for the extraction and transportation of crude oil and gas."[83]

Despite this strong interest by the East Europeans in participating in economic integration, the reservations expressed earlier about the risks of integration continued. Concerns were again expressed about the quality, timely supply and the availability of spare parts for goods produced in other socialist states and about the disruption of domestic production which could result from increased specialization.[84] However, the major concern of the East Europeans remained the loss of control over the management of their national economies which could result from increased economic integration.

This loss of control was a concern because of the continuing conflicts of interest about the distribution of benefits. The less developed members of CMEA, primarily Bulgaria and Romania, continued to be concerned that integration would be conducted at their expense although the gap between the most developed and least developed members of CMEA was closing. The gap in per capita national income had shrunk from 3:1 in 1950 to about 2:1 in 1970, and it was continuing to shrink.[85] More importantly the gap in per capita industrial production was also closing. It declined from 4:1 in 1960 to 3:1 in 1965.[86] This was reflected in the increased share of Romanian machinery and equipment exports to socialist states -- from 4.7 percent in 1950, to 19.8 percent in 1960, and to 28.4 percent in 1967.[87] However, as Romanian analysts were quick to point out, "although nowadays the economic gaps among these countries are smaller than at the beginning of the period under consideration, nevertheless they are still fairly large."[88] Therefore, the Romanians and the Bulgarians continued to press for assistance and temporary preferences arguing that it was to everyone's benefit to equalize the levels of development within CMEA.[89] However, as a Hungarian economist noted, "labor productivity and technological structures in the manufacturing industries of different countries had not

yet converged."[90] Therefore, the more developed members of CMEA feared that preferential treatment for Romania and Bulgaria "may bring about a slow-down in the development of the most advanced countries, sectors and enterprises of the region, as well as losing touch with the international technical and economic development."[91]

The East Europeans were also concerned about the distribution of benefits between the Soviet Union and themselves. A Hungarian analyst observed that "a large country due to the different relative importance of the mutual contacts, may use her bigger bargaining power and accelerate her own national development at the expense of the smaller country."[92] The East Europeans were particularly concerned about the distribution of multilateral investment credits since it was "known that the investment plans of Comecon member countries are very much extended, that many areas of the economy are under-financed and that there are continuous shortages in this field."[93] Therefore, they were interested in gaining investment for the conversion or expansion of their own industrial structures. The Czechoslovaks implied that the Soviet Union was not entitled to special treatment when they pointed out that in the past other CMEA members had made investments for the good of the community which were not particularly efficient economically.[94]

Also, in the past investment credits had flowed from the more developed to the less developed members of CMEA. "During the past quarter century, for example, the long-term Soviet credits constituted about one-quarter of *all* investments in Bulgaria's utilized investment structure. In Romania, the same index is approximately 6%, in Hungary -- 4%, in Poland -- 2%."[95] Since the investments requested by the Soviet Union were large and long term, a Yugoslav commentator asked, "Can such investments be borne by the economies of the less developed countries? Can they bear them without this having a serious effect on the further intensive development of their own natural forces?"[96]

Thus, the East Europeans saw increased economic integration as the most feasible solution to their economic problems although they continued to be concerned about the possible repercussions for their

sovereignty. However, over time the economic arguments had become more compelling, and the East Europeans were afraid that if they did not participate in the division of labor they "would remain outside the circle, or, if you prefer, the 'club' of producers making goods necessary to our economy."[97] Even the Romanians conceded that

> the dialectics between national sovereignty and international economic collaboration should not be interpreted rigidly; it should mean that whenever a state considers that one form of co-operation or another meets its own interest of economic development and does not affect its basic sovereignty, it has full latitude to adopt any form of economic collaboration without any outside coercion, on a reciprocal basis.[98]

This provided the grounds for a possible compromise. If the Soviets could find a description of the proposed model of development which was acceptable to Romania and a formula for the decision rule that respected Romania's concern for its sovereignty, it would be possible to proceed with plans for increased economic integration.

Cognitive Factors

The cracks which had appeared in the monolithic unity of doctrine in the early 1960s had widened by the late 1960s. The Soviet Union was forced to recognize that the international Communist movement had

> assumed such a scale, so many experienced Marxist leaders steeled in the great school of struggle have grown up in its ranks, its detachments are operating in such varied conditions and the importance of reckoning with the specific national conditions has become so great in their policy that it is impossible to lead the movement within the old framework and guide it from a single center.[99]

However, the Soviet Union felt that its position "as authenticating center and leader of the Leninist world"[100] was threatened by alternate models of economic development based on different national experiences which continued to emerge. Soviet analysts identified two erroneous tendencies -- left-wing revisionism (China and Romania) and right-wing

revisionism (Yugoslavia and Czechoslovakia).[101] Proponents of these models questioned the universal validity of Russian experience and even of Leninism. According to Mikhail Suslov, "[s]ome of them have been saying that the path of October is the path of economically backward countries and that Leninism is a particular interpretation of Marxism applicable to conditions of backwardness. Others contend that the socialist path of development of the U.S.S.R. is a strictly 'European' phenomenon and that therefore Leninism is presumably unsuitable for the countries of Asia, Africa and Latin America."[102] Although the Soviets acknowledged the "necessity for creative application of the general laws of socialist construction to different countries with due regard for their actual conditions," they also argued that "Lenin discovered and scientifically substantiated the general laws governing the transition period from capitalism to socialism and the subsequent construction of a new society, and proved that these operate in all countries regardless of their historical, national and other specific features."[103]

The Soviet invasion of Czechoslovakia in August 1968 to stop that country's political and economic reforms led to a concerted attack on the model of "market socialism" proposed by the Czech economist Ota Sik even though it was "hardly more than Libermanism with a vengeance."[104] However, it also revealed splits within the world Communist movement. For example, Romania, Yugoslavia, China, Albania, and eighteen non-ruling West European Communist Parties publicly condemned the invasion.[105] The Soviet Union sought to consolidate and strengthen the unity of the movement by supporting the organization of a new international conference of Communist and Workers' Parties which could work out a common viewpoint on the wide range of questions confronting the entire movement. A conference was finally convened in June 1969 with representatives of 75 parties, including the Romanian, in attendance. However, the conference did not succeed in working out a common viewpoint on socialist construction. A number of the speeches at the conference condemned the Chinese, leading Romania to protest, but as Ceausescu observed, the final

document did not "criticize or condemn any fraternal party."[106] Nonetheless, it was not accepted unanimously. As Ceausescu observed, the conference did not serve to strengthen the unity of the world communist movement because it was recognized that "each party has a right to accept or not accept the document, fully or partially, as well as to take part in the International conference or not to take part in it."[107]

Likewise in CMEA, the Soviet Union was unable to achieve agreement on a new model of economic development so it settled for a vague statement that was acceptable to Romania. The rejection of autarkic development proclaimed in the Basic Principles was reaffirmed in the 1971 Comprehensive Program. The Comprehensive Program even went a step further by promoting the goal of socialist economic integration rather than just an international socialist division of labor. However, the uneasy tension between somewhat contradictory objectives which characterized the Basic Principles also characterized the Comprehensive Program. Neither the tension between the goals of greater efficiency and equalization of the levels of economic development nor the tension between national and international interests was resolved. As a Polish analyst observed, the term integration was not even defined in the Comprehensive Program, "presumably because the members of Comecon interpret the process in varying ways, and in some cases even deny its existence and oppose its introduction among the socialist countries."[108] Therefore, the principle was still not translated into generally accepted norms of behavior.

Institutional Structure of CMEA

There were no major changes in the institutional structure of CMEA nor was it granted any additional authority. The controversy revolved around the interpretation of the decision rule which was stated in Article IV, Section 3 of the Charter:

> All recommendations and decisions of the Council shall be adopted only with the concurrence of the member countries of the Council concerned, and each shall have the right

> to declare its interest in any question being considered in the Council.
>
> The recommendations and decisions shall not extend to countries that have expressed their disinterest in the given question. However, any of these countries may subsequently subscribe to the recommendations and decisions adopted by the other member countries of the Council.[109]

The concept of "interest" can be traced back to the original communique announcing the formation of CMEA which stated that decisions were adopted "only with the consent of the interested countries."[110] However, it had never been clarified whether unanimity was required among all members or only among those interested in a proposal. In their arguments, both sides drew upon the language of the charter and other CMEA documents for support for their positions.

Romania argued that

> the adoption by the bodies of the Council of only those recommendations and decisions which preserve the objects, character, and content of CMEA activities without distorting them, and which show concern for the strict observance of the provisions of the statutes and other Comecon regulations is a binding obligation on every member of this organization.[111]

In particular, Romania reserved the right to veto proposals which, in its view, threatened the national sovereignty of the members which it stressed was recognized in both the CMEA Charter and the "Basic Principles." Romania interpreted national sovereignty in a traditional, legalistic manner as "the supremacy of state power, within the limits of the territorial borders, supremacy which must be complete and exclusive in all matters."[112] Therefore, it publicly stated that the invasion of Czechoslovakia was "a flagrant violation of the national sovereignty of a fraternal, socialist, free and independent state, of the principles on which the relations between socialist countries are based, of the unanimously recognized norms of international law."[113] Romania consistently asserted that

> only the Communist Party of each country is responsible to the working class to the people of the relevant country for its political, tactical and strategic course, for its policy of constructing socialism and Communism; this responsibility cannot be taken over by any other Party outside the country, or by any group of parties.[114]

Thus, Romania asserted that neither the interests of the proletariat nor the interests of international socialism could justify the limitation of national sovereignty.[115]

Romania also argued that economic collaboration and the national sovereignty of the socialist states should not be set in opposition to each other. Intensification of regard for national sovereignty "implies providing not for abstract situations, which disregard realities and the reasons for collaboration, and encroach upon unanimously accepted practices; on the contrary, it implies efforts to find and promote forms and methods fully in keeping with these practices."[116]

On the other hand, the Soviet Union and some of the other East European states argued for a strict interpretation of the Charter. In stating their position on the decision rule, they generally quoted Article IV, Section 3 straight from the Charter.[117] Under their interpretation unanimity was required "'only among those countries which are interested in a concrete question and in definite forms of cooperation.'"[118] They stated that this was "the original interpretation of the basic charter,"[119] thereby implying that Romania was the one arguing for a reinterpretation of the charter. Moreover, they argued that this interpretation did not violate the national sovereignty of the members because "CMEA recommendations and decisions do not apply to countries which have stated their lack of interest in the given question."[120] Indeed it was argued that Romania's "unlimited interpretation of sovereignty would impair the chances of cooperation between other countries within the community, and in this sense infringe on their own sovereignty."[121]

The Soviet position was also based on a very different understanding of national sovereignty. Although the Soviets had acknowledged that there was a dialectical relationship between national and international interests, the events in Czechoslovakia raised the issue of the correct combination of these interests. The Soviet Union continued to follow a class-based analysis of national sovereignty which emphasized the international obligations of socialist states. It maintained that the invasion of Czechoslovakia was "aimed at defending the fundamental interests of the socialist commonwealth and primarily at defending Czechoslovakia's independence and sovereignty *as a socialist state.*" It was argued that Czechoslovakia's sovereignty was threatened not by "the assistance given to the working people of the C.S.R. by the other socialist countries" but by "those who would like to deprive it of this sovereignty by delivering the country to the imperialists."[122] Lenin was cited in support of this proposition:

> in defining policy in relations between nations, between states, Marxist-Leninist parties are guided above all by the class interests of the working people, the task of preserving revolutionary gains and strengthening socialism. "Which should be put first, the right of nations to self determination or socialism?" Lenin asked and right there replied: "Socialism should."[123]

As stated earlier, the breakthrough on the issue of interestedness came at the 23rd Council Session held in April 1969. The communique acknowledged Romania's continued concern with protecting its sovereignty by including the formula that mutual ties are based on the principles of "socialist internationalism, full equality, respect for sovereignty and national interest, and mutual advantage and comradely mutual aid." However, it also called for "the creation by the interested countries of international scientific-technical and other organizations, insofar as is necessary."[124]

Shortly after the Council Session, Interkhim was established with the participation of all CMEA members except Mongolia and Romania. The agreement on its establishment contained the obligatory phrase about respect for equality and sovereignty, and each member was given one vote. However, the agreement contained a formulation of the interested-party principle which was more specific than the formulation in the CMEA Charter. It stated that

> Resolutions of the Council of 'Interkhim' shall be adopted only with the agreement of the Contracting Parties, which express their interest in the solution of a given problem.
>
> The Contracting Parties which have not expressed their interest in a given problem shall not take part in the preparation of a resolution. Resolutions of the Council shall not extend to Contracting Parties which are not interested in the given problem. However, each of these Contracting Parties may later join the resolutions passed by the remaining Contracting Parties.[125]

In acquiescing to the creation of Interkhim, although it did not initially join, Romania accepted the principle that "on nonorganizational questions an 'interested' party might object but could be overridden by others, who would then be free to participate without it."[126] The 24th Council Session in May 1970 then approved "the possible organizational forms and function of international organizations that might be created by interested C.M.E.A. member-countries."[127]

The greatest challenge to the Romanian position on the decision rule was provided by the International Investment Bank (IIB). The Articles of Agreement on the establishment of the IIB were signed in July 1970 by all of the members of CMEA except Romania. The Articles once again stated that the organization would operate "on the basis of full equality and respect of the sovereignty of all member countries of the Bank." However, Article XIX stated: "Major decisions must be taken by the Council [of the Bank] unanimously, while for other questions a majority of at least three-quarters is sufficient."[128] Article 22 (2) of the statutes of the IIB then defined which matters the Bank must decide unanimously.[129] As a Polish commentator observed, the "departure from the rule of unanimity heretofore in force in Comecon as well as the impossibility of one partner imposing a veto" was a real innovation which could offer "smoother working conditions."[130] However, "it evidently had not been decided just what obligations a minority would have to the majority once a project had been decided upon over the former's objections."[131] This issue was at the heart of Romania's negotiations with CMEA over the possibility of joining the new bank.

In an article published shortly after the 23rd Council Session, Romania had stated that it would participate in international economic organizations "to the extent in which it is interested in such collaboration, and depending upon the organization, management, functions, and prerogatives of the organization in question."[132] On February 3, 1970 the Romanian foreign trade enterprise Metallimport concluded a cooperation agreement with Intermetall "on the basis of the principles of full equality, respect for sovereignty and national interests, mutual advantage, and comradely mutual assistance in the spirit of the Twenty-Third [Special] Session."[133] Romania then signed the Interkhim Convention in December 1970 "bearing in mind the fact that this organization makes a major contribution to the strengthening and continuous improvement of collaboration among Comecon member countries, and taking the interests of our country into account." The analysis also stressed that decisions "will not be binding upon parties which are not interested in a given problem."[134]

The decision to join the IIB was more difficult because by doing so Romania would be assenting to an even greater departure from unanimity. However, the costs of not participating were potentially very high. As Henry Schaefer phrased it,

> [i]f [Romania] did not join the bank, it not only could not exercise its veto on (potentially precedent-setting) questions of principle or try to prevent a three-fourths majority on projects to which it objected, but it would be ill-informed on what was going on in areas affecting its vital interests and would find itself excluded from multilateral investment projects of potential interest, some of which were to include joint efforts to obtain economic help from the West.[135]

Romania did join the IIB in January 1971 in order to "expand economic and technical-scientific collaboration among the socialist countries and, implicitly, to increase and strengthen the potential of its own economy."[136] However, this decision seems to have been justifiable in terms of Romania's principles because the real meaning of the majority vote was left obscure, probably deliberately. For example, an article published in a Romanian economics journal shortly after Romania joined the IIB asserted that only in "certain cases which necessitate prompt handling" could a three-quarters majority prevail.[137] This was a very different interpretation from that of the other members. An article in *International Affairs* published several months earlier stated that "decisions in the Council [of the IIB] are taken unanimously on fundamental questions specified by the Charter and on all other questions by a majority of no less than three-fourths of the votes."[138] However by joining the bank, Romania accepted the principle that under certain conditions (which were not specifically defined) unanimity need not be required.

The Comprehensive Program which was published in August 1971 further codified these changes in the decision rules. As a concession to the Romanian position, Section 3 stated that international economic organizations created by CMEA members "should not have the character of supranational organs and should not concern themselves with questions of internal planning." However, the paragraph on the decision rules of inter-state economic organizations codified all the inroads into Romania's position that had already been made. On the model of Interkhim, it stated that "decrees of the plenary organ on key issues on which depend the existence and basic orientations of activity of the inter-state economic organization . . . are adopted on the basis of the principle of unanimity of the representatives of participating countries." It also included the more explicit definition of the interested-party principle. Finally, it acknowledged that on issues other than those specified above majority decision rules were permissible, as in the case of the IIB.[139]

Conclusion

The Soviet Union was able to achieve a reinterpretation of the CMEA decision rule because the interest of all the members, including Romania, in increased economic cooperation had grown, and because it was able to successfully argue that this would not violate Romanian sovereignty. Under the terms of the compromise on the decision rule, "interested parties" could pursue cooperation programs, but non-interested parties could not be forced to participate against their will, and the door was left open for their participation in the future.

Although this compromise did allow CMEA to move ahead with increased economic cooperation, it was not enough to effect a radical change in the methods of economic cooperation. Fundamental disagreements on the goals of economic cooperation were unresolved. Without a shared vision of the future and without the means to impose that vision on the dissenters, it proved impossible to do more than tinker with the existing forms of cooperation. The Soviet Union received the multilateral investments in its extraction industries that it desired, but it was unable to effect dramatic improvements in the economic performance of either its own economy or the economies of the East European states. Trade continued to be largely bilateral, barter arrangements, and little progress was made towards specialization or economic integration. These economic problems played a role in the collapse of communism in Eastern Europe in 1989, and in the final analysis, the quote with which I began this chapter proved to be prophetic.

Notes

1. Kruczkowski, "The Whys and Wherefores of Integration," p. 10. The Elbe river formed the boundary between the FRG and the GDR.

2. For the text of the agreement, see Szawlowski, *The System of International Organizations.*

3. The texts of the agreement and the charter can be found in Butler, *A Source Book.*

4. Bogomolov, "Problems in Production Specialization," p. 84.

5. See, for example, Sokolov and Shirayev, "Important Trend," p. 42.

6. Bogomolov, "Problems in Production Specialization," pp. 84-5.

7. Faddeyev, "CMEA," p. 11 and Drewnowski, "The Problem with Problems," p. 5.

8. Negru, "Development of Rumania's Economic Relations," p. 2.

9. Kaser, *Comecon,* p. 128. Trend, "Rumanian Favors Even More Limited Comecon Council." The Polish reaction to this can be found in Jakubowicz, "After the 20th Comecon Session," p. 3.

10. "Polish Comments on Comecon Meetings," p. 5. See, "Stagnation in Comecon," p. 1 and Jakubowicz, "After the 20th Comecon Session," p. 3.

11. Belayev, "CMEA Cooperation Today," p. 8.

12. "Communique on 23rd Special Session," p. 19.

Again the importance of this meeting was underscored by two facts. The delegations were headed by the Party leaders rather than the permanent representatives, and the meeting was held in Moscow out of rota.

13. "Report of the C.P.S.U. Central Committee," p. 15. For a more detailed discussion of these problems, see Mikulsky, "Economic Efficiency."

14. "The Directives of the 23rd C.P.S.U. Congress," p. 5. See also, Ikonnikov, "CMEA's Role in Cooperation," p. 69.

15. Mikulsky, "New Scientific and Technological Horizons," pp. 39-40.

16. Bykov, "CMEA," p. 16.

17. For the annual average industrial growth in the CMEA countries 1966-70, see Ikonnikov, "The CMEA Countries in 1966-1970," p. 28.

18. Medvedkov, "The Scientific-Technical Revolution," pp. 37-8. However, the evidence on this point was mixed. See above and Szabo, "Hungarian Foreign Trade," p. 215.

19. In 1955 Poland, Romania, and Czechoslovakia had also been net exporters of raw materials and fuels. Dobozy, "Raw Materials Supply," p. 3. Zotova, "Improving the Structure of Foreign Trade," p. 36.

20. For a Soviet analysis of the reasons for this discrepancy, see Kormnov and Cheburakov, "Improving the Management of Branch Integration."

There are various estimates of the size of the implicit subsidies granted to Eastern Europe by the Soviet Union as a result of the pricing levels. Marrese and Vanous estimate that the subsidy rose from 368.7 million current dollars in 1965 to 1036.7 in 1970. *Soviet Subsidization of Trade,* p. 43. However, Marer believes that they have introduced a "significant upward bias into their calculations."

He concludes that "while Marrese and Vanous are probably correct that as a net importer of manufactures the USSR provides some subsidy to the exporters, there is simply not enough statistically meaningful information to attach a dollar price tag to the amounts that might be involved." Marer, "The Political Economy," pp. 77-9.

21. Tarnovskii, "Price Formation," p. 44.

22. Dudinskii, "The Problem of Fuels and Raw Materials," p. 28.

23. For a description of the adjustments made to the base prices to cover shipping costs, see Hewett, *Foreign Trade Prices*, pp. 33-4.

24. Dudinskii, "The Problem of Fuels and Raw Materials," p. 31.

25. See, for example, Bautina, "International Socialist Production Relations;" D'iachenko, "Main Trends in Improving Prices;" and Kormnov, "Economic Stimulation."

26. Zolotarev, "Integration of CMEA Countries," p. 19.

27. Zolotarev, "Integration of CMEA Countries," p. 20.

28. Sokolov, "Socialist Countries," p. 19.

29. "Facts About the Economic Links," p. 4. "Cooperation in the Development of Crude Oil Extraction," p. 7.

30. "Speech by Comrade L. I. Brezhnev," p. 10.

31. For the text, see "Treaty Between the Union of Soviet Socialist Republics and the Federal Republic of Germany."

32. Patolichev, "The Present Day and Problems of European Security," p. 7.

33. Trade between the Soviet Union and the U.S. also began to improve, but progress was slower. See Holzman, *Foreign Trade Under Central Planning* and Friesen, *The Political Economy of East-West Trade*.

34. Koves, *The CMEA Countries in the World Economy*, p. 58. For a more detailed discussion of CoCom, see Mastanduno, *Economic Containment*.

35. Vetrov, "Economic Ties," p. 7.

36. Voinov, "Ekonomicheskie otnosheniia," p. 115.

37. Gvishiani, "Soviet Scientific and Technical Cooperation," p. 49.

38. Voinov, "Ekonomicheskie otnosheniia," p. 116.

39. Vetrov, "Economic Ties," p. 8.

40. Andreyev and Makov, "The Common Market After Eleven Years." The common trade policy, however, did not actually come into force until January 1975. John, "The Soviet Response to Western European Integration," p. 48.

41. Dudinsky, "Economic Integration," p. 10. See also Petrov, "Political Integration in Western Europe."

42. Ciulea and Rudareanu, "The Development of Rumanian Foreign Trade," p. 9.

43. Tyszko, "The Development and the Prospects of Trade Exchange," p. 3.

44. Sanakoev and Kapchenko, "Triumph of the Principles of Proletarian Internationalism," p. 35.

45. Andreyev and Makov, "The Common Market After Eleven Years," p. 48. This was a reference to Romania which had established diplomatic relations with the FRG in January 1967, several years before the Soviet Union. Larrabee, "Soviet Crisis Management," p. 121.

46. Jones, *Soviet Influence in Eastern Europe*, pp. 102-3. For a discussion of the attempts to form a pro-Soviet government, see Valenta, *Soviet Intervention in Czechoslovakia, 1968*, pp. 148-53.

47. "Balcony Speech by Nicolae Ceausescu on Czechoslovakia," in Remington, ed., *Winter in Prague*, p. 360. Jones, *Soviet Influence in Eastern Europe*, p. 83. Ceausescu assumed the leadership of Romania in March 1965 upon Gheorghiu-Dej's death.

48. For a discussion of the Soviet use of this trump, see Reisinger, *Energy and the Soviet Bloc*, Chapter 4.

49. It is important to realize that the Prague Spring and the Soviet invasion of Czechoslovakia occurred during the period discussed in this chapter. Although some changes in Czechoslovak policy toward CMEA can be identified in the three periods (Novotny, Dubcek, and post-invasion), there were also continuities throughout. Perhaps the most significant change relevant to CMEA is that for several years after the invasion Czechoslovakia became a much less important actor in CMEA debates. For a similar characterization based on interviews with Czechoslovak officials, see Stone, *Satellites and Commissars*, pp. 121-22.

I will point out the discontinuities in policy that are relevant to the issues discussed in this chapter as they arise. In the meantime, the important dates to remember are: January 1968 --Alexander Dubcek replaces Antonin Novotny as General Secretary initiating the Prague Spring and August 1968 -- the Warsaw Pact invasion of Czechoslovakia.

50. See "The Reserves Have Been Exhausted," p. 1 and Popisakov, "Successes and the Future of Economic Cooperation," p. 11.

51. Wysocinski, "The Urgent Need for New Forms of Cooperation," p. 3. See also Kohlmey, "World Economic Structures," p. 43. This is one of several articles advocating specialization that was censored in the Romanian language edition of *World Marxist Review*.

52. Fikus, "The Change," p. 4.

53. Reutt, "Comecon," p. 1.

54. Moisiuc, "National vs. World Economy," p. 1.

55. Quoted in Schaefer, *Comecon and the Politics of Integration*, p. 46.

56. Szabo, "Hungarian Foreign Trade," p. 219.

57. For a description of the accession negotiations, see Haus, *Globalizing the GATT*, Chapter 3. Romania and Hungary acceded to full membership in 1971.

58. Nyerges, "Hungary and GATT," p. 3.

59. "US Poses Czech Trade Obstacles," p. 1. Czechoslovakia was an original signatory of the GATT in 1947 and continued to remain a member after it adopted a centrally planned economy. However, the U.S. canceled Czechoslovakia's MFN status in 1951.

A Polish rebuttal to Western arguments against granting the socialist states MFN status can be found in Toczek, "Most-Favoured-Nation Treatment."

60. Szita, "On Intra-European Economic Cooperation," p. 288.

61. The GDR was an exception to this. According to EEC rules, it was considered to be part of the FRG for trade purposes. See Miller, "East Germany" for a description of some of the trade that resulted from this policy.

62. Stanescu, "Common Market Autarky," p. 5. See also Soldaczuk, "Regional Integration and East-West Trade."

63. Puiu, "The Federal Republic of Germany," p. 2. For a similar statement by a Hungarian, see Szita, "On Intra-European Economic Cooperation," p. 290.

64. Szita, "On Intra-European Economic Cooperation," p. 288. There is a chart on this page that demonstrates the point.

65. Valyi, "Hungary and International Integrations," p. 23.

66. Soldaczuk, "Regional Integration and East-West Trade," pp. 13-14, 16-17. Similar statements can be found in Bognar, "Principles of Foreign Trade," p. 169.

67. Benedek, "Relations Between Hungary and the Common Market," p. 2.

68. Iskra, "Economic Integration," p. 11.

69. Kozma, "The Effects of the International Division of Labour," p. 356. For similar statements by an East German and a Romanian, see Kohlmey, "World Economic Structures," p. 47 and Economic Research Institute, "New Stage in International Economic Interdependence," p. 38.

70. Zarev, "Forms of Socialist Integration," pp. 74-5. See also T. Kiss, "Integration of CMEA Countries' National Markets," p. 233.

71. Murgu and Barbu, "Rumania's Economic Cooperation," p. 7.

72. Since this table is from a Romanian source, it reflects the two raw materials in which Romania was particularly deficient. It is apparent that deposits of metallurgical coke were generally plentiful in Eastern Europe although they were not spread evenly.

73. R. Constantinescu, "Collaboration and Cooperation in Material Production," pp. 7-9.

Romania was the only East European country which was not receiving imports of Soviet oil in this period. This was a punishment for its continuing recalcitrance in its relations with the Soviet Union.

74. Albinowski, "Where to Get Petroleum," p. 5. Further details of the Czechoslovak agreement and the reasoning behind it can be found in Plechac, "Iranian Oil in Addition to Soviet Oil."

75. A. Apro, "International Economic Cooperation," p. 4.

76. Vintera, "The Facts About an Orientation," p. 8.

The Czechoslovak position on the difficulty of a major expansion of raw material imports from the West seems to have remained relatively constant during this period despite the upheavals of the Prague Spring and the subsequent Soviet invasion.

77. Sojak and Riha, "Cooperation with the Socialist Countries," p. 3. Note that this was published just before Dubcek took office. See also Fazekas, "Socialist Economic Integration," p. 2. However, this concern was not universally shared. See, for example, Albinowski, "Where to Get Petroleum," p. 4.

78. The East Europeans would sometimes find themselves paying above world market prices for Soviet raw materials due to price fluctuations. Therefore,this was a heated topic of discussion in Eastern Europe, particularly in Czechoslovakia where there were strong popular sentiments that the Soviet Union was exploiting Czechoslovakia economically. See "Notes."

For detailed examinations of the prices which Czechoslovakia would have paid in each market, see "Soviet Crude Oil," and Brozik, "The Truth About Czechoslovak-Soviet Trade." For a similar analysis by a Hungarian, see "A Report on Antal Apro's Lecture," p. 8.

79. Brozik, "The Truth About Czechoslovak-Soviet Trade," p. 6. Ota Sik, a liberal Czech economist who was closely associated with the Prague Spring, estimates that in 1967 it took 31 kcs to earn a dollar of foreign exchange. "Prague's Spring," p. 7.

80. Biro, "The Development of Hungarian-Soviet Economic Relationships," p. 4. See also Dobozy, "Raw Materials Supply," p. 3 and Brozik, "The Truth About Czechoslovak-Soviet Trade," p. 5.

It was recognized, particularly by Polish economists, that foreign and domestic pricing systems which encouraged the continued existence of unprofitable enterprises were double-edged swords. This led to "a lack of incentive to introduce technological progress and -- as a further consequence -- the inability to adjust to the production of new goods of higher quality which could be offered on foreign markets." (Pawlicki, "The Starting Point," p. 6.) Thus, it could be argued that while prices in trade with the Soviet Union were beneficial in the short-term, the long-term result would be costly if the savings to the East European economies were not invested wisely in raising the technical level and quality of their manufactured goods.

81. Dobozy, "Raw Materials Supply," p. 3.

82. "Facts About the Economic Links," p. 4.

83. R. Constantinescu, "Collaboration and Cooperation in Material Production," p. 9.

84. See, for example, Soldaczuk and Giezgala, "Economic Integration of Comecon Countries," pp. 7-8. A more detailed discussion of these issues can be found in the previous chapter.

85. Belli, "Equalizing the Economic Development Levels," p. 7.

86. Wasilkowski, "Comecon Countries," p. 3.

87. Ciulea and Rudareanu, "The Development of Rumanian Foreign Trade," p. 6.

88. Belli, "Equalizing the Development Levels," p. 8.

For example, the maximum gap in per capita industrial production within the EEC was 1.9:1. Belyaev, "Economic Ties Between the Socialist Countries," p. 19.

89. Moldovan, "Equalizing the Levels of Economic Development," p. 18. Avramov, "On the Frontiers of Integration," p. 14.

90. Kozma, "Dialectics of Equalizing Development Levels," p. 43.

91. Kadar, "Small-Sized Developing Countries," p. 222. This very interesting article does not refer directly to CMEA. The specific examples in it are drawn from other regional organizations such as the Latin American Free Trade Association (LAFTA), but the parallels are obvious.

92. Kadar, "Small-Sized Developing Countries," p. 222.

93. Reutt, "Comecon," p. 6.

94. Selucky, "The Impact of the Economic Reforms," pp. 81-2.

95. Iskra, "The Mechanisms of Integration," p. 125, emphasis added.

96. B. Bogdanovic quoted in Harry Trend, "Comecon Confronted by Hard Economic Facts," p. 3. Yugoslavia had been granted observer status in CMEA in 1964 so it was privy to the discussions.

The solution that Bulgaria adopted to this dilemma is interesting. Their contribution to Soviet investments was generally labor which was an excess commodity in their own economy.

97. Drewnowski, "The Problem with Problems," p. 3.

98. Paraluta, "Setting International Economic Relations on New Bases," pp. 5-6.

99. "On the Eve," p. 10.

100. Jowitt, "Moscow 'Centre,'" p. 303.

101. Kuzminov, "Lenin and Problems of the Economic Theory of Socialism," p. 13. For a Soviet critique of worker self-management, see Georgiyev, "Yugoslavia: 'New Variant of Socialism'?" For a critique of Czechoslovakia, see Pomelov, "Common Principles and National Characteristics."

102. Suslov, "Leninism and the Revolutionary Transformation of the World," p. 3. Suslov was a member of the Politburo and the Secretariat who was known as "principal Defender of the ideological Faith." Gelman, *The Brezhnev Politburo*, p. 72.

103. Oleinik, "Leninism and the International Significance," p. 28.

104. Shaffer, "An Economic Model in Eclipse," p. 54.

105. Valenta, *Soviet Intervention in Czechoslovakia, 1968*, p. 151. Some of the statements made are included in Remington, ed., *Winter in Prague*.

106. "At the International Conference," (June 18), p. 18.

For speeches condemning China, see Todor Zhivkov's speech in "At the International Conference," (June 11), pp. 4-5; Wladyslaw Gomulka's speech in "At the International Conference," (June 8), pp. 5-6; and Brezhnev's speech "For Strengthening the Solidarity of Communists," pp. 10-12.

The fact that Romania raised a point of order was mentioned in *Pravda*'s coverage ["At the International Conference," (June 7), p. 4], but the details were only given in Ceausescu's speech ["At the International Conference," (June 10), p. 6].

107. "At the International Conference," (June 18), p. 18.

108. Gyulai, "The Socialist Program for Economic Integration," p. 1. An interesting exchange between Romanian scholars and scholars from other socialist states can be found in "Laws Governing the Development of World Socialist System," esp. pp. 29-33.

109. "Charter of the Council on Mutual Economic Aid."

110. "Establishment of the Council of Mutual Economic Aid," p. 11.

111. Negru, "Development of Rumania's Economic Relations," p. 3.

112. "The Nation in the Contemporary World" p. 6.

113. "Official Rumanian Communique on the Military Occupation of Czechoslovakia," in Remington, ed., *Winter in Prague*, p. 358.

114. "The Nation in the Contemporary World," p. 8. For similar statements made after the invasion of Czechoslovakia, see "Balcony Speech," in Remington, ed., *Winter in Prague*, p. 360 and Duculescu, "The Sovereign State in International Relations," p. 3.

115. For an interesting exchange between Romanian scholars and scholars from other socialist states on this point, see "Dialectics of National and International," pp. 29-34.

116. Gh. Constantinescu, "The Historical Function of the Relations Between the Socialist Countries," pp. 5-6.

117. For example, see Zavolzhsky and Lukin, "Bourgeois Criticism," p. 9.

Similar East European statements can be found in Smilek, "Coordination of the Economic Development," p. 7; "A Report on Antal Apro's Lecture," pp. 3-4; and "Progress and Difficulties in Comecon," pp. 3-4.

118. Quoted in "Polish Comments," p. 5.

119. "A Report on Antal Apro's Lecture," p. 3.

120. Bykov, "CMEA," p. 17.

121. Kuzinski, "Integrating Eastern Europe," p. 12.

122. Kovalev, "Sovereignty and the Internationalist Obligations," pp. 10, 12, and 11, emphasis added.

This article is generally regarded as the first statement of what became known as the Brezhnev Doctrine of limited sovereignty. However, as the discussions in the previous two chapters demonstrate, the Brezhnev Doctrine did not represent a departure from previous definitions of national sovereignty. In Soviet theory, sovereignty had always been limited.

123. Sanakoyev, "Proletarian Internationalism," p. 14.

124. "Communique on 23rd Special Session," pp. 19, 20.

125. "Agreement Concerning the Establishment of an International Branch Organization for Cooperation in the Sphere of Small Tonnage Chemical Production, 'Interkhim'" in Szawlowski, *The System of International Organizations*, Articles II (2), VIII (1), and VIII (4).

126. Schaefer, *Comecon and the Politics of Integration*, p. 62.

127. "Communique on the 24th Session," p. 17.

128. "Articles of Agreement of the Establishment of the International Investment Bank," in Szawlowski, *The System of International Organizations*, Articles I and XIX.

129. "Statutes of the International Investment Bank," in Szawlowski, *The System of International Organizations*.

130. Solska, "A Joint Bank," p. 4.

131. Schaefer, *Comecon and the Politics of Integration*, p. 108.

132. R. Constantinescu, "The Development and Improvement of Collaboration," p. 3.

133. "Agreement of Cooperation Between Intermetall, the Organization for Cooperation in Ferrous Metallurgy, and Metallimport, the State Enterprise of Foreign Trade of the Rumanian Socialist Republic," in Butler, *A Source Book*.

134. Comanici, "Interchim," pp. 2, 3.

135. Schaefer, *Comecon and the Politics of Integration*, pp. 107-8.

136. Eremia, "The International Investment Bank," p. 4.

137. Eremia, "The International Investment Bank," p. 3.

138. Karpich, "CMEA Countries' Plan to Develop Integration," p. 12.

139. "Comprehensive Program for the Intensification and Improvement of Cooperation and the Development of Socialist Economic Integration of Comecon Member Countries," in Butler, *A Source Book*, Sections 3 (2) and 8 (3.1).

Chapter Five

The Collapse of CMEA

> The profound changes in the public and political life of the East European countries and the implementation of fundamental economic reforms in many member-states of the Council for Mutual Economic Aid are putting on the agenda the need to accelerate the restructuring of the mechanism for their multilateral interaction and to work out fundamental decisions regarding a changeover to new conditions of cooperation in the CMEA.[1]

Neither the 1971 Comprehensive Program nor the Multilateral Concerted Plan for Integration Measures which was adopted in 1975 succeeded in bringing the economic efficiency of the CMEA members up to world standards or in redressing the decline in growth rates. In their quest for greater economic efficiency, the East Europeans imported Western high technology in the 1970s using hard currency loans which they then found themselves unable to repay. By the early 1980s they were faced with payments difficulties, a continuing decline in economic growth, and stagnating specialization measures. Once again the idea of increased cooperation within CMEA as a solution to economic problems grew. Talks were delayed by the rise of Solidarity in 1980 and the imposition of martial law in Poland in 1981 and the deaths of Leonid Brezhnev and his successor Yuri Andropov, but a CMEA Council Session with the General Secretaries leading the delegations was held in June 1984, the first meeting at that level since 1969. However, this was nine months before Mikhail Gorbachev took office so little resulted from it.

After Gorbachev assumed the Soviet leadership in 1985, there were further attempts to revive CMEA. He sought to switch "international cooperation between socialist countries to an intensive track, as well, making it deeper and more productive and renovating the machinery of political and economic cooperation."[2] At the 41st

Extraordinary Council Session in December 1985 a new Comprehensive Program was adopted, and at the 43rd Extraordinary Council Session in October 1987 a proposal was made to pursue mutual convertibility of national currencies. However, due to the opposition of the more conservative members -- the GDR, Romania, and Vietnam -- an official agreement was not signed.[3]

The East European revolutions in 1989 changed the course of events decisively. In order to repay their hard currency debts, the East European states had to cut imports. This led to a decline in the standard of living and popular discontent. Poland and Hungary turned to negotiations with the opposition in the winter of 1989 in an effort to gain legitimacy for desperately needed economic reforms. In August 1989, a non-Communist government was formed in Poland after Solidarity's stunning success in the June parliamentary elections. The lack of Soviet interference in Poland's domestic affairs made possible the abandonment of communist party rule and the Stalinist model of economic development throughout the bloc. For the first time since the creation of CMEA, the role of the state in the economy began to be systematically reduced by several states.

For this reason, it was not surprising that the future of CMEA itself was at issue prior to the 45th Council Session which was held in Sofia January 9-10, 1990. In an interview published on January 4, Czechoslovakia's Finance Minister Vaclav Klaus responded to a question about the future of the organization with the statement that "Czechoslovakia has decided to apply for CEMA's dissolution."[4] Federal Premier Marian Calfa later moderated this stance in another interview stating that "neither the Czechoslovak Government nor any of its members have proposed or will propose the dissolution of CMEA." However, he continued, "naturally, we are going there [Sofia] with very fundamental proposals for changing the function and activity of CEMA."[5] This view was also shared by members of the other delegations. The head of the Soviet delegation, Prime Minister Nikolai Ryzhkov, phrased it thus: "'Either we will actually lose the CMEA, or we will build a sound economic organization based on new principles.'"[6]

At the 45th Council Session it was apparent that the members held very different views on how CMEA should be reformed. However, according to *Pravda*, the consensus of the meeting was that the members were "interested in principle in seeing the CMEA continue and, at the same time, wished to see it fundamentally restructured."[7] A special commission was formed to draft a new charter as soon as possible. As Hungarian Premier Miklos Nemeth observed, "the devil is in the details."[8]

During the course of consultations on the restructuring of CMEA, it was decided to create an entirely new organization instead. Draft statutes for the Organization for International Economic Cooperation (OIEC) were prepared and then signed at a meeting of the CMEA Executive Committee in January 1991.[9] The Prime Ministers of the member states were expected to meet in Budapest in February to disband CMEA and sign an agreement creating its successor. However, the meeting was postponed when it became clear that Poland and Czechoslovakia would not sign the statutes of the OIEC in their original form.[10] Then on June 28, 1991 the members met without fanfare to formally disband the oldest multilateral organization in the socialist bloc. There were no speeches or addresses at what was called "the shortest sitting in the entire history of CEMA's existence."[11]

These events pose two interesting questions. First, why did this particular attempt to reform CMEA result in its collapse? As the preceding chapters demonstrate, this was not the first attempt to reform CMEA, and the criticisms of its performance were not new. Second, why was no definite successor organization created at that time despite a very real need for some mechanism to coordinate trade among the former members?

I argue that these puzzles can best be explained by the interaction of structural and cognitive factors. Although there was continuing interest in reforming CMEA, there was also interest in maintaining some form of regional cooperation. However, it proved impossible to create a successor organization for several reasons. The Soviet Union did not provide the leadership necessary to create a new economic infrastructure. Reform of the existing organization was no longer sufficient because, for the first time, the Soviet Union had allowed the East European states the freedom to transform the role of the state in the management of their economies. This transformation meant that the old pattern of transactions flows was incompatible with the domestic economic structures that were emerging.[12] However, the changes in the domestic economic structures were not occurring at an even pace so it was difficult to reach a new consensus on what role the state should play in managing the economies in the region. Finally, the decision rule of CMEA was based on the equality of all the members and required unanimity. As mentioned earlier, one of the drawbacks of a unanimity decision rule is that it tends to lead to least common denominator solutions. In this case, the least common denominator was no cooperation.

Structural Factors: *Power and Interests*

Soviet Interests

The Soviet Union continued to be dissatisfied with its terms of trade with Eastern Europe so it was interested in fundamentally restructuring CMEA. Moreover, its interest in joining the world economy had increased. However, the Soviet Union recognized that its entry into the world economy, and particularly into the new European economic space, was likely to be slower than that of most of the East European states. Maintaining trade ties with Eastern Europe was one way for the Soviet Union to gain an easier entry into the European market than it could achieve on its own. Also, in the wake of the failure to create a pan-European security structure and the collapse of its alliance ties with Eastern Europe, the Soviet Union faced the possibility of becoming isolated in Europe. Economic cooperation within the region could reduce the possibility of isolation.

Despite some reforms in the pricing structure, the Soviet Union's pattern of trade with Eastern Europe continued to be a drain on its economy. The major source of this drain was the exports of crude oil which provided 80 percent of the bloc's requirements.[13] The oil shocks of the 1970s had greatly increased the amount of the implicit subsidies granted to Eastern Europe because prices in the bloc were only changed every five years.[14] A new pricing formula adopted in 1975 attempted to reduce this drain by basing prices on a five year moving average of world market prices. Although this allowed oil prices to rise more quickly than the previous pricing formula, it did represent a significant Soviet concession.[15] Also, the Soviet Union further cushioned the impact of the change by allowing the East Europeans to run deficits in their trade and by increasing the quantity of its fuel exports.[16] At the same time, a drop in the quality of East European exports to the Soviet Union, which was a by product of their attempts to pay back enormous hard currency debts, further eroded Soviet terms of trade.

Although these problems were not new, the Soviet economy was increasingly unable to bear the burden, and a change in the Soviet leadership led to a reevaluation of the importance of Eastern Europe. It became more difficult for the Soviet Union to maintain the subsidies to Eastern Europe because output of the economy was dropping, and oil production was plummeting. Although the terms of trade improved somewhat in the 1980s when the world market price of oil dropped faster than the intrabloc price, the Soviet Union's opportunity costs rose because it needed to export more merely to purchase the same quantities of imports from hard currency areas.[17] This put further pressure on Soviet fuel supplies because it had become apparent that hard currency earnings could only be increased by increasing energy exports. An economist pointed out that "in 1988, the entire ambitious campaign to promote nonenergy exports yielded a mere .7% increase in the share of machinery and equipment in our export structure. And the lion's share of these increased exports went to the socialist countries, so we did not obtain any freely convertible currency."[18]

As discussed in the previous chapters, the Soviet Union had rejected several possible solutions to its trade problems with Eastern Europe because of concern about the possible impact on political stability and communist party rule in the region. However, it was clear that under Gorbachev the ranking of Soviet preferences had changed.[19] The Soviet Union did nothing to prevent the collapse of communist party rule in Eastern Europe, and it began to fundamentally restructure its economic relationship with Eastern Europe in ways that it had previously rejected. For example, the Soviet Union unilaterally cut its oil exports to Eastern Europe by 30 percent in July 1990, and it maintained a tough stance in negotiations on the volume of deliveries for 1991. It also demanded that beginning in 1991 CMEA trade accounts be settled in hard currency at current world prices.

At the same time that its interest in Eastern Europe declined, the Soviet Union became more interested in joining the world economy and more able to do so. It feared that if it did not, it was "bound to be pushed to the sidelines of world technological and economic progress and [might] become a backyard of the world economy in the 21st century."[20] Increased trade with the West had become possible as Western barriers to trade fell. The CoCom export controls were eased, and barriers to trade with the U.S., which had been the most restrictive, were relaxed.[21]

The Soviet Union slowly began to join world economic organizations. It first joined the European Bank for Reconstruction and Development (EBRD) which is intended to aid in the reconstruction of Eastern Europe by acting as a source of loans. The Soviet Union joined despite the fact that it was displeased with several aspects of the original proposal to create the EBRD. First, it objected because "We are seen as a donor rather than a borrower. Some don't want to grant us the right to take out loans. Naturally, we cannot agree to this. We favor equal rights and obligations." The Soviets were also displeased because Western countries, particularly the U.S., emphasized that the EBRD "should promote the development solely of private enterprise. Others advocated that credits should be linked with party pluralism and the holding of free elections."[22]

The charter and statues of the EBRD which were signed in Paris in May 1990 recognized some of the Soviet Union's concerns. The Soviet Union won a victory because only 60 percent of the bank's funds were reserved for the private sector. However, the charter also stated that the purpose of the EBRD is to "'promote private and entrepreneurial initiative in the central and eastern European countries committed to and applying the principles of multi-party democracy, pluralism and market economics.'"[23] Finally, during a three year transition period, the Soviet Union was granted access to a limited number of the bank's services. For example, it would be able to borrow an amount equivalent to its six percent share of the bank's capital.[24] Nonetheless, participation in the EBRD was important for the Soviet Union because it "could provide a forum to bring the USSR gradually into the international financial community as a preparation for IMF and World Bank membership."[25]

The Soviet Union was also pursuing membership in the GATT, the IMF, and the World Bank. It first expressed interest in participating in the GATT in 1986 "to secure the country's trade and political interests abroad on a multilateral basis."[26] The U.S. and the EU blocked all Soviet attempts to participate until after the Malta summit in December 1989, and the Soviet Union was only granted observer status in May 1990. As Leah Haus concludes, "attaining observer status at the GATT was an important symbolic step toward integration into the global economy."[27]

The Soviet Union expressed interest in membership in the IMF and the World Bank because this "would result in our country's more complete and real integration into the world economy, and consequently in strengthened political and economic positions for the Soviet Union."[28] As an intermediate step President Bush proposed that the Soviet Union be granted a special association. According to the President, this would "'give the U.S.S.R. access to the considerable financial and economic expertise of these institutions.'"[29] However, the Soviet Union was unlikely to receive major financial support from these organizations because in December 1990 they had recommended "that the West should hold back financial aid, other than credits for food, until a comprehensive reform program is in place."[30] The Soviet Union also faced the same problem in the IMF and the World Bank that it did in the EBRD; it could be treated as a potential donor rather than as a recipient of aid.

In particular, the Soviet Union had expressed interest in rejoining Europe, or as Gorbachev phrased it, in the creation of a "common European home." Some progress had been made toward this goal. In June 1989 the Soviet Union, Hungary, Poland, and Yugoslavia were granted special guest status in the Council of Europe "because of the dramatic improvement in their human rights records and the Council's desire to strengthen ties between the two halves of Europe."[31] The Soviets hoped that the Council of Europe would "become one of the supports of [a common European] home and the venue of joint elaboration of European initiatives."[32]

However, the Soviet Union realized that there were limitations on its ability to satisfy its economic and security interests through cooperation with the West. Soviet security interests were threatened by the failure of the Conference on Security and Cooperation in Europe (CSCE) to institutionalize a new Europe security structure. Some military leaders felt especially vulnerable since the Warsaw Pact was being dissolved and Soviet troops were rapidly being withdrawn from Eastern Europe while NATO remained intact.[33] The overtures to NATO by the East Europeans in the spring and summer of 1991 did nothing to diminish these concerns. The Soviet Union was trying to create a set of bilateral security ties to replace the Warsaw Pact, but it had only been able to sign a new treaty with Romania. Negotiations with the other East European states were stalemated over a clause contained in the Romanian treaty in which the parties pledged not to join organizations directed against the other party.[34] It was in the Soviet Union's security interest to maintain some form of regional cooperation because, as Ronald Linden notes, "great powers care about what happens on their doorstep; they care even more when they fear becoming not-so-great powers."[35]

Also, although the Soviet Union had signed a trade and cooperation agreement with the EC in December 1989 which granted it most-favored-nation status and gradually abolished the quantitative restrictions on EC imports from the Soviet Union by 1995, Soviet membership in the EC was not on the agenda and was unlikely to be in the near future because of both the size of its economy and the slower pace of its economic reform. After outlining the Chairman of the Commission of the EC's vision of "a future Europe consisting of three concentric rings: the European Economic Community at the center, then the European Free Trade Association states, and then the East European States," one Soviet commentator lamented, "Won't we find ourselves, however, outside even the third ring, at the very fringes of Europe?"[36] Continued economic cooperation with Eastern Europe offered a way to avoid this fate.

The attractiveness of continued economic cooperation with Eastern Europe also increased when the Soviet Union found that it was more affected by a drop in regional trade than had been anticipated. The Soviets, along with many Western economists, had believed that they would benefit the most from the switch to hard currency because "while Soviet raw materials can be successfully sold on any market, finished goods from the East European countries are not very competitive outside the CMEA economic space and certainly won't sell for freely convertible currency in all cases."[37] However, the switch to hard currency led to a serious drop in regional trade because of a shortage of hard currency, and the Soviets discovered that the benefits of mutual trade were indeed mutual. For example, a *Pravda* editorial stated that the Soviet Union receives from Eastern Europe "products without which a number of economic branches could not function normally and public demand for medicines, clothing, footwear, etc. could not be met."[38] Also, due to a drop in world market prices for oil, the East Europeans were paying above world market prices for Soviet oil so regional trade was not as disadvantageous as it had been previously.[39] Thus, although the Soviet Union was vitally interested in rejoining the world and especially Europe, the realities of the situation insured that the Soviet Union had both economic and security interests in continued cooperation with Eastern Europe.

East European Interests

Like the Soviet Union, many of the East European states

continued to be dissatisfied with the performance of CMEA. The more reformist states, in particular, feared that continued membership in CMEA would hinder their ability to reform their economies. The East Europeans were also interested in expanding trade and economic cooperation with the West, and concrete steps had been taken to achieve these goals. However, it had become clear that some goals, such as membership in the EC, might not be achieved for at least several years. Also, the short-term costs of the transition to a market economy were going to be high. The East European economies were small and very dependent on foreign trade so the transition was likely to be accompanied by high social costs in the form of inflation and unemployment as inefficient industries were forced out of business by foreign competition and the subsidized imports of Soviet oil came to an end. Therefore, the East Europeans were interested in continued economic cooperation with the Soviet Union as a means of easing the social costs of the transition to a market economy by providing a secure market for output that might otherwise be difficult to export. They also believed that it was in their security interest to ensure that the Soviet Union was not isolated from Europe.

Many of the East European states continued to be dissatisfied with their economic performance. The attempts at regional specialization had largely failed to increased economic efficiency. Therefore, the East European states had turned to imports of Western technology in the 1970s as a possible solution. However, their economies were unable to absorb the technology effectively so the major result, as shown in Table 5.1, was that their foreign debt rose, often to staggering levels.[40]

Table 5.1: External Debts of the CMEA Members, 1960

	Net debt (billions of dollars)	**Debt per capita (dollars)**
Bulgaria	9.8	1,090
Czechoslovakia	6.3	400
Hungary	20.3	1,910
Poland	41.8	1,100
Romania	1.3	60
Soviet Union	43.4	150

Source: John Williamson, *The Economic Opening of Eastern Europe* (Washington, DC: The Institute for International Economics, 1991), p. 12.

As Table 5.2 illustrates, growth rates then stagnated further in the 1980s, partially as a result of attempts to repay these debts.[41] Czechoslovakia, Poland, and Hungary even experienced negative economic growth during this period.

Table 5.2: Annual Growth Rates of CMEA Members, 1976-1985

	1976-1980	**1981-1985**
Bulgaria	6.1	3.7
Czechoslovakia	3.7	1.8
Hungary	2.8	1.4
GDR	4.1	4.5
Poland	1.2	-0.8
Romania	7.2	4.4
Soviet Union	4.3	3.5

Source: Ondrej Ler and Ludek Urban, "European CMEA Countries in 1985-1986," *Czechoslovak Economic Digest* 1986, No. 7, p. 5.

It became apparent, especially in Poland, that the population would not tolerate the social costs of the economic reforms necessary to redress the decline in growth rates without political reforms. When the Soviet Union signalled that it would no longer prevent political reforms, a whole new range of possibilities opened up.

Like the Soviets, the East Europeans were vitally interested in rejoining the world economy. After the revolutions in 1989, there was an expansion in trade with the West and in Western aid for economic reconstruction. As mentioned earlier, the CoCom controls over exports to the region were relaxed, and the U.S. began to gradually remove barriers to East European exports. The East European states that had not already done so also began to join international economic organizations as a means to gain access to Western markets and capital.[42] Progress was finally made on Bulgaria's application to accede to the GATT, and Czechoslovakia and Bulgaria joined the IMF and the World Bank in September 1990.[43] The East European states also joined the EBRD.

The ultimate goal of the East Europeans though was membership in the EC. The Bulgarian Foreign Minister Boyko Dimitrov even went so far as to say that joining the EC was Bulgaria's "only salvation."[44] The first step toward this goal, which had been taken by all the East European states, was the signing of trade and cooperation agreements.[45] These agreements provided for "unilateral access to the markets of Europe, followed by a transitional period during which duties on goods from the EC are also eliminated" in the East European state.[46] This was to allow the East Europeans time to adapt their economies to market conditions. The trade and cooperation agreements were of great significance for the East European economies. Hungary, for example, estimated that the lifting of EC quotas on Hungarian industrial products in January 1990 "yielded a surplus income of 120 million dollars for Hungarian exporters," and the "extension of preferential tariffs to manufactured goods and some farm produce may yield another 80 million dollars a year."[47]

The second step to membership in the EC was the signing of association agreements. These agreements offered free trade into the EC, joint projects, loans, and political cooperation. Hungary, Czechoslovakia, and Poland were negotiating association agreements in the first half of 1991, and the other East European states had expressed interest in signing similar agreements.

The East Europeans were also taking other steps in their attempt to return to Europe. One of these was membership in the Council of Europe. Hungary's application for full membership was approved in

November 1990 and Czechoslovakia's in February 1991. The other East European states had all been granted special guest status and hoped to achieve full membership before long.[48] They hoped to use membership as a staging ground for eventual membership in the EC as Spain, Portugal, and Greece had.[49] As the Hungarian Foreign Minister Geza Jeszenszky stated, "'Our CE membership goes hand in hand with the acceptance of a European legal order and a system of conventions which Hungarian laws have to adapt to, and this will help us attain our highest aim, namely our accession to the EEC.'"[50] Membership in the European Free Trade Association (EFTA) was also being considered as a temporary alternative and possible avenue to EC membership.[51]

Another step which some East Europeans had also taken on the path to eventual EC membership was the formation of regional associations which transcended the old blocs. One of these was the Pentagonal Initiative which had begun as a quadrilateral association of Italy, Hungary, Austria, and Yugoslavia in November 1989 and had expanded to include Czechoslovakia in May 1990.[52] One of the announced goals of the Pentagonal Initiative was "to facilitate the entry of its members into the European Community."[53] The Balkan states (Albania, Bulgaria, Greece, Romania, Turkey, and Yugoslavia) and the Black Sea states (Romania, Bulgaria, Turkey, and the Soviet Union) were also pursuing closer regional cooperation.[54] Finally, proposals for increased Baltic cooperation had been made by Sweden and Poland.[55]

The Central European states (Poland, Hungary, and Czechoslovakia) were confident that they would be ready for membership in the EC by the end of the century. Romania and Bulgaria were aware that their lower levels of development and slower reforms would probably delay their entry longer than that, but they too were confident of their eventual success. They believed that continued membership in CMEA might impede their attempts to reform their economies and to join the EC.[56] In particular, the East European states wanted to divest themselves of the "unwanted baggage of diverse and formal complications" represented by the membership of Cuba, Vietnam, and Mongolia. As a Polish commentary observed, "the integration of these three economies into the world economy may prove to be beyond the powers of, for example, Poland, which is now more preoccupied with securing its own position on the world market."[57] However, there were also factors that increased their interest in regional cooperation.

Despite all the diplomatic activity and the East Europeans' hopes, the official policy of the EC was that the association agreements would not automatically lead to full membership, that it would not begin talks on membership until 1995, and that even then there were several states in line ahead of the East Europeans -- Austria, Turkey, Cyprus, and Malta.[58] The experience of Turkey which had signed an association agreement in 1964 which was intended to lead to full membership and still was not a member almost 30 years later demonstrated how slow the process could be.

The East Europeans also felt somewhat vulnerable when the CSCE failed to create a pan-European security structure, and it became apparent that the Warsaw Pact would collapse. For the first time in decades there was no one to guarantee their security. This led them to try to strengthen their ties to "the only functioning security organization" in Europe, NATO.[59] Although NATO was unwilling to admit the East Europeans as members, it did declare that "any 'coercion or intimidation' aimed at the countries of Central and Eastern Europe would be treated as a matter of 'direct and material concern'" to the members of the alliance.[60] The East Europeans were also having some success in negotiating bilateral security arrangements within the region. However, they realized that it was not in their security interest for the Soviet Union to be isolated from Europe. As the Czechoslovak Foreign Minister Jiri Dienstbier observed, "If the USSR were isolated and pushed back beyond the Asian border, then a Greater Russian nationalism might emerge."[61] In the past, that had proved detrimental to East European interests.

However, the major reason that the East Europeans continued to be interested in regional economic cooperation was that otherwise they faced the loss of a major export market and a major source of their raw material imports. Since the establishment of CMEA in 1949, the Soviet Union had traditionally been the largest trading partner of the East European states, and the East European industrial structure had been developed or adapted to fit the needs of the Soviet market. Thus, many East European enterprises produced solely for the Soviet market. For example, Poland compiled a list of about 100 plants that produced exclusively for the Soviet market.[62] Moreover, a portion of these products could not be sold elsewhere because of their low technical level and quality. A Hungarian study of the exports of 22 firms in the machine building industry found that in the first nine months of 1990 their ruble-based exports shrank by 32 percent leading to a total decrease of 32 percent.[63] As the industries producing for the Soviet market were quick to point out, a significant reduction in trade with the Soviet Union over a short period of time, such as occurred in 1991, could lead to massive unemployment and social unrest in these fragile new democracies.[64] Moreover, they stressed that trade with the Soviet Union could be an important component of future economic success because the Soviet market was large and offered many export opportunities. This was also a market in which the East European states had some competitive advantages over Western suppliers. As a Hungarian observed, "'We know the market, we can speak the language and we know how to move about in the country.'"[65] Thus, maintaining economic cooperation with the Soviet Union was a way for the East Europeans to reduce the social costs of the transformation to a market economy and to preserve the advantages that they had in trade with that huge country.

The East Europeans were also interested in maintaining trade relations with the Soviet Union because it had been their major supplier of raw materials, and they believed that it would be difficult for them to switch to alternate suppliers quickly. Their hard currency exports were still insufficient to finance massive imports of oil and other raw materials from hard currency areas.[66] The transportation problems involved in a switch to Western suppliers were also enormous. The East Europeans were connected to supplies of Soviet raw materials by natural gas pipelines, oil pipelines, and a joint electricity grid which are the cheapest and most efficient means of transporting these commodities. Some other oil pipelines, such as the Adria pipeline which connects Hungary to the Adriatic Sea, did exist, but establishing connections with West European natural gas pipelines and electricity grids would take time and would require a considerable investment.[67] Finally, importing oil from other sources would probably mean converting their refineries at great expense to process different types of oil.[68]

The East European states had a vested interest in raw material trade with the Soviet Union because of joint investments made in Soviet extraction and fuel industries as a result of the CMEA Multilateral Plan and Comprehensive Program. The East Europeans had contributed labor and material supplies to the construction of facilities, which remained the property of the Soviet Union, in return for guaranteed deliveries of the commodity produced. Their investments were substantial. For example, Czechoslovakia estimated that it had outstanding investments in joint projects of 2.3 to 2.4 billion rubles.[69] These projects were in various stages of the repayment cycle. In some cases, the original investment had been repaid by deliveries of the commodity, but the East Europeans were still eligible to receive deliveries for another period of time. In other cases, the original investment was still being repaid. Finally, some projects were not yet finished so deliveries had not even begun.

However, these joint investment projects also posed problems for future economic cooperation because the conversion to trade in convertible currencies raised the question of how to revalue them.[70] The original investments were valued in transferable rubles "on the basis of the norms, rates and charges, etc., of the country where the project is located."[71] Therefore, the original contribution, which was the basis for repayment, had to be revalued in convertible currency, a process which was fraught with complications. The East Europeans also took this opportunity to raise the question of how their contributions were originally valued because they asserted that the "methodology of fixing prices on construction-assembly services within the frames of the CMEA countries . . . was profitable only for the USSR."[72] For example,

Hungary wanted to renegotiate the agreement on its participation in the construction of the Yamburg natural gas pipeline which was two-thirds completed. It claimed that over 170 forints had to be 'invested' to produce one transferable ruble "owing to prices on the Soviet domestic market."[73] Czechoslovakia also expressed concerns about the effectiveness of its continued participation in the construction of an ore dressing plant near Krivoj Roj.[74] Another major problem was that "the prices of the products . . . are generally determined at the time of shipping, in accordance with the pricing practices and methods prevailing in the CMEA countries."[75] Thus, the change to convertible currencies could make investments which looked profitable initially very unprofitable because the goods delivered by the Soviet Union would be valued much higher than the East European inputs were valued.

Changes in the interests of the Soviet Union and of the East European states had led to an increase in the centrifugal forces within CMEA. However, there was still interest in some form of regional cooperation. For example, various proposals for the creation of "cooperation circles" among the East European states were being mooted.[76] The idea of a Czechoslovak-Polish federation was revived,[77] and Czechoslovak President Vaclav Havel organized a summit meeting of Czechoslovak, Polish, and Hungarian leaders in Bratislava on April 9, 1990 to discuss a coordinated return to Europe. Another, better organized, meeting of these states was held in Visegrad in February 1991. Romania and Bulgaria both expressed interest in participating in future meetings, but the participants decided that "it would not be expedient to increase the number of states taking part in the co-operation beyond the present three countries, which are at present at a similar level of development."[78] Romania was also pressing for the establishment of "a Central and Eastern European union."[79] The East Europeans realized that "it is important to be able to solve our regional problems on our own. That would be the best possible illustration of our readiness to take part in European integration."[80] To explain why the members were unable to create a successor organization despite these interests, it is necessary to look at the power of the states, the institutional structure of

CMEA, and cognitive factors.

Soviet and East European Power Capabilities

Although the Soviet Union was still far more powerful than Eastern Europe, its absolute power capabilities were declining. Its population and territory remained approximately the same, but its economic capability was dropping. The United Nations estimated that the Soviet Union's net material product had declined four percent in 1990. Industrialized nations last experienced declines of this magnitude in the Great Depression of the 1930s, and the Soviet decline was continuing and even accelerating in 1991.[81]

The Soviet Union's conventional military capability had also diminished as a result of conscious decisions by the government to cut the military budget and as a result of social unrest. Under the terms of the Treaty on Conventional Armed Forces in Europe which was signed in November 1990, the Soviet Union had agreed to dramatically reduce its conventional weaponry in Europe. Soviet military capability was also threatened by widespread draft refusals. More than 30,000 men had failed to report for the Spring 1990 draft, and three times as many may have ignored the fall callup.[82]

Although it still possessed enormous reserves, the Soviet Union was having difficulty with its production of raw materials, in particular oil. Production of oil had plummeted by almost a million barrels a day since 1988, an eight percent decline. The decline for 1990 alone was 18 million tons.[83] The oil industry was suffering from a deteriorating infrastructure; labor unrest; uncertainty about who controlled the resource, the republics or the center; and ethnic unrest in Azerbaijan which was the main service and supply center for the oil fields.

Less quantifiable indicators of power capability such as political stability and competence also seemed to be declining. The fate of the union itself was in question due to increasing separatist tendencies. Four of the fifteen union republics (Armenia, Estonia, Latvia, and Lithuania) had declared independence, and most of the remaining republics had declared sovereignty. Actual fighting among rival ethnic groups had broken out in the Nagorno-Karabakh region of Azerbaijan and in the Abkhazia region of Georgia, and Soviet troops had forcibly seized several public buildings in the Baltic republics.[84] Gorbachev was attempting to reform the structure of the union to restrain these separatist tendencies, but he had only received the approval of nine republics for a new union treaty scheduled to be signed in August 1991.[85] Gorbachev's government had been shaken by the dramatic resignation of his Foreign Minister Eduard Shevardnadze in December 1990.[86] He was also under attack by conservatives who had tried to unseat him as the party leader in April and who were proposing a transfer of presidential power to the chairman of the Supreme Soviet, Anatoly Lukyanov.

However, the East European states faced their own serious economic and political problems. They were also suffering from declining production. It is estimated that in 1990 net material product declined from a high of 13.6 percent in Bulgaria to a low of three percent in Czechoslovakia.[87] As part of their economic recovery programs, the East Europeans were reducing the size of their militaries. Hungary, for example, decided to reduce army personnel by 30 percent.[88] The political stability of ethnically divided states embarking on such dramatic transformations and the competence of the new leaderships which often had little or no political experience were also questionable.

As the debate over declining American hegemony demonstrates, it is difficult to establish whether the changes in relative power capabilities amounted to a loss of Soviet hegemony over Eastern Europe or not.[89] The Soviet Union was willing to compromise on some of its demands in order to achieve mutual benefit. For example, an agreement signed between the Soviet Union and Czechoslovakia in September 1990 provided that "as of Jan. 1, 1991, trade accounts between the two countries will be settled at current world market prices, and payments will be made in freely convertible currency."[90] Thus, only the balances would be payable in hard currency, and barter trade would continue. According to another agreement signed in November 1990,

Czechoslovakia would pay for its oil imports from the Soviet Union in three ways: "partly in hard currency, partly in equipment to modernize the USSR's oil production industry, and partly in consumer goods for oil workers."[91] The Soviet Union also allowed Czechoslovakia "to pay for the raw materials it receives using its positive trade balance with the Soviet Union."[92]

However, the Soviet Union did not provide the leadership to create a new regional economic infrastructure. After the transfer to trade in convertible currencies in January 1991, it became obvious that some sort of clearing arrangement was necessary if the desired levels of mutual trade were to be maintained, but the East Europeans had to turn to West European organizations to provide these crucial arrangements. The EBRD guaranteed a bilateral clearing system for Hungary and the Soviet Union.[93] Other East European states expressed an interest in EC financing for Soviet imports of their products.[94] The Soviet Union's failure to provide hegemonic leadership as it had in the past made it more difficult to create a successor organization because there was no one willing or able to provide side payments to encourage states to cooperate.[95] However, there were other changes that also intensified the pressures for reform and at the same time made it more difficult to achieve.

The Institutional Structure of CMEA

Changes in the organizational structure of CMEA, which had become bloated, were firmly put on the agenda by Gorbachev at the October 1985 Warsaw Pact session. Gorbachev wanted "CMEA to have less administrative regimentation, fewer committees and commissions, and to pay greater attention to economic incentives, initiative, the socialist spirit of enterprise, and to an increase in the involvement of work collectives in the process."[96] At the 43rd Council Session in October 1987, it was agreed to streamline CMEA. According to Jozef van Brabant's calculations, "of the 36 official organs in place in October

1987, 19 were abolished, merged, or replaced; and 6 new ones were set up, so that by early 1988 only 24 official organs survived."[97] The Executive Committee also reported that "the number of tenured positions for employees of the CMEA Secretariat was reduced by almost one-third."[98] Further simplification of CMEA's structure was called for at the 44th Council Session in July 1988.

Despite these organizational changes, CMEA had not been granted any additional authority, and the egalitarian features of the organization were not changed. Indeed under Gorbachev's leadership, the Soviet Union began to gradually revise its definition of national sovereignty until it matched the Romanian definition. Rather than emphasizing the class base of national sovereignty, the Soviet Union began to stress the importance of national interests. In a speech on the 70th Anniversary of the October Socialist Revolution, Gorbachev stated that relations among socialist countries should be built on generally recognized principles including "the responsibility of the ruling party for affairs in its state, and patriotic service to its people."[99] However, until 1989 his pronouncements continued to contain statements about the common interests of the socialist community. Then in Helsinki in October 1989, Gorbachev proclaimed that the Brezhnev doctrine was dead, that the Soviet Union had "no right, moral or political right, to interfere in events" in Eastern Europe. His spokesman Gennadi Gerasimov referred to this as the Sinatra doctrine, a reference to the famous Sinatra song "I Did It My Way."[100] The Soviet Union demonstrated its commitment to this interpretation of national sovereignty when it did not intervene in Eastern Europe despite the overthrow of communist party rule in all the states but Romania and Bulgaria.

Perhaps most important of all, there was no change in the decision rule of CMEA. Although the interested party principle provided a way around the unanimity rule in some circumstances, it appears that there was still resistance to it. For example, the Soviet Deputy Permanent Representative noted that the principle of decision-making used by the Council is that of acceptance on the part of the countries concerned. It's another matter that the actual approach to this principle may vary and even that attempt may be made to question the possibility of working in the CMEA in a given sphere of cooperation by agreement between some member countries even when not all members are prepared for it.[101]

The combination of all these factors made it difficult for CMEA to respond to the rapidly changing events in Eastern Europe in any meaningful way. As Vaclav Klaus lamented, "When one CEMA member cut contractual deliveries, for instance crude oil from the USSR, there was no CEMA to intervene. When one CEMA country (the German Democratic Republic) disappeared from the scene, there was no CEMA to negotiate, in the interest of the other member countries, on compliance with its obligations toward the other countries." He concluded that CMEA had become "an inoperative and dead organization" long before its official demise.[102] Thus, it was clear to the members that the existing institutional structure could not meet their needs. A new organization was necessary.

If a legal successor to CMEA was to be created, the negotiations would have to occur within the existing framework. Under any conditions, but especially given the continuing resistance to the interested party principle, it was necessary to achieve unanimity on an institutional structure for the successor organization and on the principles underlying future cooperation.

Cognitive Factors

If the cracks in the monolithic unity of doctrine had widened in the late 1960s, by 1990 that unity had shattered. Gorbachev had disavowed the leading role of the Soviet Communist party stating that "no one has the right to claim a special position in the socialist world,"[103] He had also rejected a single model of socialism. In his book *Perestroika,* he stated,

Marx, Engels and Lenin, who theoretically substantiated the principles on which the concept

> of socialism is founded, did not seek to give a detailed picture of the future society. And this is in general impossible to do. This picture acquired its outlines and is still in the making as a result of the revolutionary creative work of all the socialist states.[104]

This change in doctrine made possible the complete abandonment of the Stalinist or neo-Stalinist model of economic development in Eastern Europe and further erosion of that model in the Soviet Union. For example, the Soviet economist Oleg Bogomolov observed that "real socialism of the Stalinist or neo-Stalinist type is thoroughly discredited and that faith in its 'advantages' has been lost."[105] Thus, the 1991 attempt to reform CMEA differed from previous attempts because a consensus had finally been reached on the necessity to abandon the autarkic model of economic development.

It also differed from previous attempts in that the doctrinal changes were being accompanied by major shifts in domestic economic structure. Some states were finally "creating the legal, organization and economic conditions necessary for enterprises to become directly involved in foreign economic activity and to be equal participants in it along with various central agencies and ministries."[106] Poland had liberalized domestic prices and made its currency convertible in January 1990, and Czechoslovakia and Hungary were beginning to follow suit. The same three states were also making the transition to private property by selling off state-owned industries, and central planning was being abandoned. These changes in the domestic economic structure of at least some members meant that it would no longer be possible for CMEA to function as it had in the past. As Nikolae Ryzhkov concluded, "a profound incompatibility has arisen between the very system of international economic ties and the economic reforms being carried out in most of the CMEA countries, an incompatibility that is having an increasingly marked negative impact on reciprocal economic ties."[107] In combination, these two changes meant that a reform of CMEA would no longer be sufficient.

However, agreement needed to be reached on the principles on which future economic cooperation would be based. Prior to 1989, the emphasis had been on refining the concept of the international socialist division of labor (ISDL). A program entitled *Collective Concept of the ISDL for the Years 1991-2005* was to have been presented at the June 1988 Council Session. The core of the new concept of the ISDL was the creation of a unified CMEA market, and although a draft was debated, the new program was never published. After 1989, there was widespread agreement that it was necessary to create an open market economy based on commodity-money relations, but there was disagreement, both within the individual states and in the region as a whole, on the appropriate speed for such a transformation. Poland had opted for "shock therapy" while Czechoslovakia and Hungary were moving more slowly. The Soviets also favored opening their economy "to the world gradually, by establishing an open sector encompassing all the regions and industries that are more prepared than others for foreign economic activity."[108] Romania and Bulgaria had made virtually no progress. This lack of agreement on the appropriate role of the state in regulating the economy was a significant impediment to the creation of a successor organization to CMEA.

The members also began to question the role of regional economic cooperation in stimulating the restructuring of their economies and generating growth. Some Western economists, such as Jozef van Brabant, argued that maintaining intraregional trade was an important factor in the transition to a market economy because in addition to the short-term dependence on regional trade due to the existing transportation infrastructure, demand for spare parts, etc., there were comparative advantages to be exploited. Others, such as Jeffrey Sachs, argued that efforts to maintain intraregional trade were counterproductive because significant comparative advantages did not exist. Instead effort should be concentrated on expanding trade with Western Europe. In the absence of significant marketization, reliable information on real costs of production and demand which was necessary to compute the costs and benefits of these possible trading patterns did not exit. One economist attempted "to infer the true comparative advantage of East European countries from their trade with the rest of the world since this trade was conducted, for the most part, on the basis of market principles." Nonetheless, he still had to make adjustments for cheap petroleum inputs.[109]

As Ernst Haas reminds us, the choice between these alternatives is "not 'pure' because it is constrained by what the choosers have already experienced."[110] For the most developed states, in particular, membership in CMEA was associated with relative economic decline. Czechoslovakia, for example, is estimated to have had approximately the same standard of living as Austria before World War II whereas forty years later its standard of living was about half that of Austria.[111] Therefore, their past experiences made some members skeptical about the benefits to be derived from future intraregional cooperation especially when membership in the EC, which was widely regarded as successfully promoting growth, had become a possibility, no matter how remote. Finally, a Hungarian economist observed that in Eastern Europe "there is a desire to make use of newly won opportunities as soon as possible. The changes are considered to be fleeting; as past experience has been that opportunities for modernization in the region open up and then suddenly close again."[112]

Conclusion

Although both the Soviet Union and Eastern Europe were dissatisfied with CMEA and interested in rejoining Europe and the world economy, their economic and security interests did provide support for the continuation of some form of economic cooperation. It would not be easy for any of these countries to rejoin the world economy after the forty year existence of CMEA. Their economies were structured around a particular pattern of trade which was fostered by the rules and procedures of CMEA, and restructuring would be difficult and would carry high social costs. Property rights had also been created. Finally, it was in no one's interest for the Soviet Union to be isolated from Europe.

Despite these interests, this attempt to reform CMEA failed for many of the same reasons as the previous attempts. However, what distinguished this attempt to reform CMEA was the failure of the Soviet Union to provide the leadership necessary to create a new economic infrastructure. This was necessary because of the changes in doctrine and the domestic economic structures of many members as well as the demonstrated inability of CMEA to respond effectively to the problems resulting from the changes. There was widespread agreement that the creation of an open market economy based on commodity-money relations was necessary. Differences in the pace of domestic reform and the resulting differences in domestic economic institutions made it impossible though to reach unanimous agreement upon principles for future economic cooperation. Therefore, the members disbanded CMEA without creating a successor organization.

Notes

1. "CMEA -- On the Threshold," p. 12.

2. "Visit with Hungarian Workers," p. 6.

3. The Socialist Republic of Vietnam became a member of CMEA in 1978, and Cuba became a member in 1972.

Discussions of the events of this period can be found in Zwass, *The Council for Mutual Economic Assistance* and Stone, *Satellites and Commissars.*

4. "Today is not 1968," p. 1.

5. "CSSR's Calfa Interviewed," p. 6.

6. Quoted in Zhmyrev, "Good Foundation Laid," p. 18.

7. "CMEA at a Sharp Turning Point," p. 14.

8. "Nemeth Comments," p. 5.

9. "CSFR Minister Comments," p. 1.

The GDR had terminated its membership in CMEA before unification in October 1990 so Germany did not participate in the negotiations on the restructuring of the organization.

10. "Official on Postponement of CEMA Session," p. 18.

11. "Organization Disbands," p. 6.

12. See Ruggie, "International Regimes, Transactions, and Change." On the difference between a change in regime and a change of regime, see Krasner, "Structural Causes," pp. 3-4.

13. Bunce, "Decline of a Regional Hegemon," p. 241.

14. Marrese and Vanous estimate that Soviet subsidies to Eastern Europe grew from less than a quarter of a billion dollars a year in the early 1960s to over $10 billion per year in the late 1970s and early 1980s. *Soviet Subsidization of Trade*. Again critics assert that these estimates are inflated due to methodological problems. See, for example, Dietz, "Advantages and Disadvantages" and Poznanski, "Opportunity Cost in Soviet Trade."

In another recalculation of Soviet subsidies, Poznanski argues that as the producer of the lowest quality machinery in the bloc, the Soviet Union received subsidies through the CMEA price structure. On this basis he concludes that the flow of subsidies was not consistently from the Soviet Union to the East European states. Poznanski, "Pricing Practices in the CMEA Trade Regime." These studies demonstrate that because it was so difficult to determine who was benefitting from trade, it was possible for everyone to believe that they were being exploited.

15. Reisinger, *Energy and the Soviet Bloc*, Chapter 6.

16. According to Bunce, the deficits had reached 13 billion rubles by 1985. "Decline of a Regional Hegemon," p. 252.

17. Bunce, "Decline of a Regional Hegemon," p. 242.

18. Lavrovsky, "Should We Sell Our Oil Abroad," p. 22.

19. For another statement to this effect, see Marrese and Wittenberg, "Implicit Trade Subsidies within the CMEA," p. 11.

20. Karavayev, "Eastern Europe is Opening Itself," p. 35.

21. Apple, "Bush Vows to Put Soviets in Group Favored in Trade," pp. A1, A4. For a discussion of Soviet concerns about this process, see Kovalenko, "What Will the New COCOM Be Like?" p. 15.

22. Kovalenko, "What Should the New Bank Be Like?" pp. 18-19.

23. Quoted in Norman, "The BERD Gets Ready to Fly," p. 25.

24. Kovalenko, "Bank for Eastern Europe is Being Set Up," p. 23. For a further discussion, see M. Berger, "The European Bank," p. 5.

25. Norman, "The BERD Gets Ready to Fly," p. 25.

26. Ivanov, "We Answer the Reader," p. 14.

27. Haus, *Globalizing the GATT*, p. 96. Chapter 6 details the Soviet attempt to gain observer status. See also, Kosinsky, "Step Toward a World Market," p. 22.

28. Zhagel, "We're Being Studied," p. 22.

29. "Bush's Remarks on Aid to Kremlin," p. A6.

30. Farnsworth, "Soviet Economic Output," p. 6.

31. Weitz, "The Expanding Role of the Council of Europe," p. 50.

32. Deryabin, "Milestones of the 'Year of Europe,'" p. 64.

33. The Warsaw Pact was dissolved on July 1, 1991, and the last Soviet troops left Hungary and Czechoslovakia in June 1991. Soviet troops were scheduled to leave Germany by 1994, and talks were continuing on Soviet troop withdrawals from Poland.

An overview of the debate in the Soviet Union over policy in Eastern Europe and its implications for Soviet security can be found in Crow, "'Who Lost Eastern Europe?'"

34. Even Bulgaria which had been a very loyal ally objected to this clause. "Difficulties on Draft Bulgarian-Soviet Treaty," p. 15.

35. Linden, "The New Eastern Europe," p. 30.

36. Pushkov, "In Proud Solitude?" p. 13.

37. Guseinov, "The Moment of Truth is Coming," p. 25.

38. "Let's Wait Another Month," p. 15. For more detailed figures on the importance of East European trade to the Soviet economy, see Rybakov, "The Economic Platform of Interaction," p. 68.

39. According to Rybakov, "in the current year we will sell oil to the European countries of the CMEA at about 95 rubles per ton, while the world price on the free market at the end of January was between 86 and 87 rubles, and the domestic retail price is 30 rubles." "The Economic Platform of Interaction," p. 68.

40. Czechoslovakia, which dramatically reduced its imports of Western technology in the 1970s, did not have high levels of debt, but as a result, "the average age of machinery and equipment in Czechoslovakia is about a third higher than in other developed countries." Altmann, "Czechoslovakia," p. 117.

Romania had also accumulated a high foreign debt which Ceausescu had managed to pay by severely lowering domestic consumption.

41. Compare these with the growth rates given in Table 3.1.

42. Hungary, Poland, and Romania were already members of the IMF, the World Bank, and GATT. For an overview of the involvement of the East European states in these international economic organizations, see Brabant and Marer, "Reform and Membership."

43. See Haus, *Globalizing the GATT*, Chapter 5 for a discussion of Bulgaria's accession negotiations with the GATT.

Czechoslovakia had helped found the IMF, but it was stripped of its membership in 1954 because it "refused to provide detailed information about its economic development, foreign trade and especially the state of its balance of payments and foreign exchange reserves." "CTK Views IMF Application," p. 41.

44. "Dimitrov Says Joining EC 'Only Salvation,'" p. 8.

45. Hungary signed such an agreement in September 1988, Poland in August 1989, and Czechoslovakia and Bulgaria in May 1990. A similar agreement for Romania was initialled in June 1990, but it was not ratified until October of that year because of the brutal dispersion of anti-government protestors in Bucharest in June. "EC Economic Agreement Suspended," p. 49.

46. Gornenski, "Only the Opposition," p. 8.

47. "Deputy Minister Urges Links With EC, EFTA," p. 57. For a statement about the benefits to the Polish economy, see "EEC Preferences Apply to Country 1 Jan," p. 60.

48. Poland needed to hold free parliamentary elections before it could become a full member. The Romanian request for special guest status was not granted until February 1991 because of concerns about continuing violations of human and political rights. "Government Spokesman Comments," p. 41.

49. Weitz, "The Expanding Role of the Council of Europe," p. 54.

50. Quoted in Arato, "The Advantage of Our Council of Europe Membership," p. 24.

51. See, for example, Dezseri, "Hungarian Orientation Toward Western Europe."

52. Moore, "New Dimensions for the Alpine-Adria Project." Polish membership which became official in August 1991 was also on the agenda. Morawski, "From Pentagon to Hexagon."

53. Kusin, "The Initiative from Venice," p. 26.

54. Zanga, "The Balkan Foreign Ministers' Conference." "Black Sea Countries Discuss Economic Cooperation," p. 2.

55. Grzybowski, "Report on progress of Ronneby conference," pp. 43-4.

56. Hungary had been complaining about this since the introduction of the New Economic Mechanism in 1968. See, for example, Apatini, "Characteristics and Problems of the Comecon Market," p. 13. For a detailed account of Hungary's failing economy, see Kadar, "What We Inherited," pp. 3-7.

57. Wroblewska, "Is There A Need for CMEA," pp. 22, 21.

58. See, for example, "EC Commission Spokesman on Trade Ties," p. 40.

59. Tucek, "Our View of European Security," p. 13. This phrase was repeatedly used in statements by the leaders of other East European states.

60. Friedman, "NATO Tries to Ease Military Concerns," p. A1.

61. "Dienstbier: CSFR Wants to Remain in Pact," p. 13. For a Hungarian statement to this effect, see "Katona on Warsaw Pact Resolution," p. 33.

62. Weydenthal, "Prospects for Soviet-Polish Trade," p. 23.

63. Vanyai and Viszt, "Foreign-Trade Reorientation," pp. 90-91.

64. The Hungarian International Economic Relations Minister estimated a halt in trade with the Soviet Union "could result in the closure of 30-40 big plants and 200,000 unemployed." "Minister Interviewed on USSR Trade Problems," p. 24.

65. Quoted in Bohlen, "As the Soviet Rut Deepens," p. 6.

66. See, for example, Paral, "Are Oil Supplies to Czechoslovakia Guaranteed?" p. 8.

67. Salay, "Restructuring the Energy System," p. 20.

The Czechoslovak Finance Minister Vaclav Klaus phrased it rather bluntly: "Simply from the technical point of view, [speeding up oil imports from the rest of the world] cannot solve a drop of oil importation problems from the Soviet Union." "Klaus on Fuel Shortage, Price Increase," p. 17. One reason for Czechoslovakia's interest in the Pentagonal Commission was the creation of links to oil pipelines in the other member states. "Pentagonal Countries View Energy, Pipeline Link," pp. 17-18.

68. Gavrilov, "Energy Crisis Looming," p. 4.

69. "Trade Relationship with USSR Assessed," p. 16.

70. For a discussion of the East European concerns about the joint investments, see Csaba, "Joint Investments and Mutual Advantages."

71. Valek, "Selected Questions Concerning the Effectiveness of Joint Investment Activity by CMEA Members," p. 51.

72. "Planning Chief on Polish-Soviet Trade, Debt," p. 51. See also Sielanko, "A Break in the Deadlock," p. 41. According to the Hungarian economist Laszlo Csaba, 1929 Soviet construction norms were used in costing, norms which even Soviet enterprises were unable to meet. Csaba, "Joint Investments and Mutual Advantages," p. 239.

73. "Soviet Gas Supply Situation, Prospects Reported," p. 59.

74. "Should Construction be Suspended or Continued," p. 21.

75. Poller and Tesner, "Socialist Economic Integration," p. 14.

76. "Mazowiecki: The Changes," p. 46.

77. "Federation with CSSR Suggested," p. 58.

78. "Visegrad Talks Detailed," p. 9.

79. See, for example, "Further on Chebeleu Statements," p. 32. The other East European states were not very enthusiastic about this proposal. "Hungary Critical of Romanian Proposal," p. 4.

80. Quoted in Kolodziejczyk, "A Question of Perception," p. 44. See also "More Active Attitude," p. 21 and "Neagu Attends Black Sea Region Countries' Meeting," p. 53.

81. Farnsworth, "Soviet Economic Output," p. 6. Apple, "In Washington, Moscow's Moment Has Arrived," p. 1.

82. Rutherford, "Draft Dodgers," p. A18. Kamm, "Estonia Gives the Draftable Civilian Work," p. A11.

83. Yergin, "The Next Oil Surprise," p. 8. Mikheyev, "Europe Without the CMEA," p. 17.

84. For coverage, see Clines, "Blood Feud Feeding Soviet Violence;" Keller, "Soviet Army Raids Lithuania Offices;" and Schmemann, "Soviet Commandos Stage Latvia Raid."

85. For a draft of the proposed union treaty, see Smith, *Soviet Politics*, Appendix B.

86. Keller, "Shevardnadze Stuns Kremlin.'"

87. Silk, "Trickle Down." For estimates of declines in GDP, see Michael Bruno, "Stabilization and Reform in Eastern Europe," pp. 754-55.

88. Desi, "What Do We Need the Army for?" p. 38.
See also "Proposal of Minister of National Defense," p. 15 and "Slimak on 26 Feb Pullout, Army Troop Cuts," p. 11.

89. See, for example, Strange, "The Myth of Lost Hegemony;" Russett, "The Mysterious Case of Vanishing Hegemony;" Kennedy, *The Rise and Fall of the Great Powers*; and Nye, *Bound to Lead.*

90. Kornilov, "At World Market Prices," p. 26.

91. "Is it Good to be Neighbors?" p. 22. For further of evidence of the continuation of barter trade, see "USSR to Trade Oil for Industrial Products, Food," pp. 33-4.

92. Kornilov, "At World Market Prices," p. 26.

93. "Outline of Soviet-EBRD Clearing Account," pp. 14-15.

94. "Skubiszewski Hopes Aid Will Restore Soviet Trade," p. 17.

95. The East Europeans themselves seemed to lean toward the explanation that the Soviet Union was unwilling rather than unable. When asked if the Soviet Union did not pay for East European imports because it could not pay, the Hungarian Finance Minister replied, "I am aware of the problems there, but I also know that the Soviet Union has very good trade relations with South-east Asia. In other words, the Soviet Union is selecting the areas where it wants to pay." Kocsi, "Too Many Compromises," p. 18.

96. Gorbachev, *Perestroika*, p. 168.
For a detailed description of CMEA's organizational structure, see Nicolae, "CMEA in Theory and Practice."

97. Brabant, "Toward a Renewal of Socialist Economic Integration" p. 42. For a complete accounting of the fate of the various organs, see Ikonnikov, "Sovershenstvovanie struktury SEV."

98. "Rohlicek Speech," p. 3.

99. Gorbachev, "October and Restructuring," p. 16. This point was also stressed in his book. See Gorbachev, *Perestroika*, p. 165.

100. Gwertzman and Kaufman, eds, *The Collapse of Communism*, p. 163.

101. "The Socialist Community," p. 127. This article discusses the Council Session in July 1988. Several decisions were reached at this meeting, and it is unclear from the context which one he is referring to.

102. "CEMA: Born 1949, Deceased 1991," p. 12 as corrected in FBIS-EEU-91-018, January 28, 1991, pp. 23-24.

103. "Czechoslovak-Soviet Friendship Rally," p. 9.

104. Gorbachev, *Perestroika*, p. 163.

105. Bogomolov, "The Changing Nature of Socialism," p. 16.

106. "What is Slowing Us Down," p. 8.

107. "CMEA -- On the Threshold," p. 12.

108. Karavayev, "Eastern Europe is Opening Itself," p. 39.

109. Salvatore, "Privatization, Economic Restructuring, and Foreign Trade," p. 33. As an example of the problems with piecemeal reforms, Jeffrey Sachs told how Poland, due to absurdly low fuel prices before the price liberalization in January 1990, became an exporter of semitropical flowers. Williamson, *The Economic Opening of Eastern Europe*, p. 9.

110. E. Haas, *When Knowledge is Power*, p. 14.

111. Williamson, *The Economic Opening of Eastern Europe*, p. 12. The least developed members, Bulgaria and Romania, did not experience relative declines so its is not surprising that they demonstrated more support for the continuance of regional economic cooperation.

112. Inotai, "Transforming the East," p. 42.

Chapter Six

Post CMEA: Disintegration or Reintegration?

> "We ended CEMA. However, I feel that we might have also thrown out the baby with the bathwater in the heat of emotions. In other words, we also eliminated those areas of cooperation that we could have continued after renegotiating them and adjusting them to the new conditions." -- Lech Walesa[1]

In some ways the situation in Eastern Europe in the 1990s is similar to the situation after World War II. The previous pattern of trade has been seriously disrupted, and the states in the region are experimenting with new economic and political models. In 1949 the Soviet Union had the capability and the willingness to create a new international economic infrastructure for the region. The East Europeans clearly hoped that the European Union (EU) would provide that infrastructure. However, the EU was unwilling to expand its membership rapidly. Instead it encouraged the former socialist states to organize economic cooperation among themselves first. Theories of international economic cooperation suggest that this will be difficult though.

As discussed earlier, structural theories of international economic cooperation suggest that cooperation is most likely to emerge when there is either a hegemonic state, one willing and able to provide leadership, or a group of small, developed states.[2] Cognitive theories, on the other hand, stress the importance of "convergent expectations and patterns of behavior or practice."[3] Neither approach would predict the rapid reemergence of regional economic cooperation. Russia, although by far the most powerful state in the former CMEA, is unable to provide leadership due to its failing economy and domestic political problems. There are also large variations in the size and level of development of the states within the region. Finally, as discussed in the previous chapter, there are differences in the speed of economic reform which impede economic cooperation.

Rather than region wide economic cooperation, states outside the region have provided the leadership to create foci for cooperation or groups of states within the region at similar levels of development have provided that infrastructure themselves. However, one of the legacies of the past forty years is a deep distrust of highly institutionalized regional cooperation, and this has hindered the development of cooperation.

The following sections of this chapter examine the collapse of the regional market, the response of the EU, and the emergence of new foci of cooperation. The conclusion discusses the impediments to further economic cooperation.

Collapse of the Regional Market

As discussed in the previous chapter, the switch to trade in convertible currencies at the beginning of 1991 led to a precipitous drop in regional trade. After the collapse of CMEA, the Soviets and the East Europeans hoped that they would quickly be reintegrated into world markets. However, the Western states feared that this reintegration would not occur quickly enough to counter the disintegration of the existing regional market and that the economic and political results would be disastrous. For example, a World Bank study concluded that "if the volume of East European trade were to remain fixed, then the collapse of the CMEA and the decline in income in Eastern Europe and the USSR would require that nearly 70% of East European exports be directed toward the West."[4] This fear was only been strengthened by the continuing disintegration of the regional market as the result of the collapse of the Soviet Union in the fall of 1991, the war in the former Yugoslavia, and the division of Czechoslovakia at the end of 1992.

Two months after the final meeting of CMEA, conservatives in the Soviet Union staged a coup which ultimately led to the breakup of that state and the emergence of fifteen newly independent states. Although the East Europeans remain vitally interested in this huge market, the breakup of the union has made it even more difficult for them to trade with one of their largest trading partners. One of their main advantages in this market was their knowledge of the personnel and business practices. However, this advantage was largely lost after the coup. As the Polish minister of foreign economic relations complained, "we do not even know what the people in those factories with which we used to cooperate are doing today." He also observed that the continuing political uncertainty impeded trade; "negotiations are difficult in view of the fact that the decision-making powers of individual departments are not clear."[5]

The problems with payments which had plagued East European trade with the former Soviet Union since the switch to hard currency were only exacerbated by its breakup. The Bulgarian Trade Minister complained, "Our companies' storage premises are full of goods sought after in the republics of the former USSR. The problem is that they cannot pay."[6] Since the East Europeans are not in a financial position to be able to extend credit to buyers, their only option is barter, and it is difficult to maintain the previous level of trade because of the limitations of barter when it is not managed centrally.

These problems led to a further decline in regional trade. For example, in 1992 Czechoslovakia's exports to the countries of the former Soviet Union decreased by about 45 percent following a decrease of 38 percent the previous year.[7] Given the level of political turmoil throughout the former Soviet Union, trade is unlikely to rebound soon.

Regional trade was also disrupted by the war in the former Yugoslavia. The war itself led to the slowing of traffic on the Danube, diminished transit trade in the region, and the closure of the Adria pipeline. The UN embargo on trade with Yugoslavia, which these states honored for the most part, led to further disruptions in trade. Hungary estimates that its loss of income from railroad, public road, and pipeline transit fees could total "a few tens of millions of dollars."[8] Romania estimated that its losses from the embargo totalled more than $7 billion by February 1993, and Bulgaria \$1.2 billion by the end of 1992.[9] Shortly before sanctions were lifted at the end of 1995, Greece, Bulgaria, Romania, Moldova, and Ukraine issued a joint statement which declared that "the burden of sanctions is surpassing economic and social tolerance."[10]

The division of Czechoslovakia into the Czech Republic and Slovakia at the end of 1992 also led to a further decrease in regional trade. Trade between the two countries dropped more than 30 percent despite a customs union agreement which includes a clearing system. The agreement provides that goods up to 130 million ECU per month are paid in local currencies while any additional amounts must be paid in hard currency. "The Czechs have exceeded the limit every month since mid-1994, blaming a 10% import surcharge imposed by Slovakia and a 5% overvaluation of the Slovak koruna."[11] This imbalance and the Czech plans to make its currency convertible led the Czech Republic to unilaterally cancel the clearing system in May 1995.

As the Western states feared, the disintegration of the regional market has had a negative impact on the economies of these states. One result has been a decline in GDP and industrial production, in particular. While it is difficult to measure the effect precisely because many other economic changes were occurring simultaneously, Table 6.1 presents an estimate of the fall of GDP owing to the fall of exports.

Table 6.1: Percent Change of GDP, 1991

	Total	**Due to fall in exports**
Bulgaria	-23	-16
Czechoslovakia	-16	-9
Hungary	-8	-8
Poland	-8	-4
Romania	-12	-10

Source: Michael Bruno, "Stabilization and Reform in Eastern Europe: A Preliminary Evaluation," *IMF Staff Papers* 39 (December 1992), pp. 754-55.

The fall in production may be economically justifiable since many of the industries affected were not profitable, but it creates other problems. For example, it has led to increases in unemployment which can cause political instability and a slowing of the economic reform process as voters take out their frustrations on the governing parties. The successes of the former communists in parliamentary elections in Poland in October 1993 and Hungary in May 1994 are cases in point.

Given these consequences, it is not surprising that there has been concern about the collapse of regional trade. The Bulgarian Trade Minister noted, "I am convinced that Bulgaria should restore its markets in the former socialist countries. The best market for us is the most likely market. Considering the present quality of our goods, it would be a delusion to strive for a hasty breakthrough in Western markets."[12]

The European Union

Nonetheless, the East Europeans have continued to place their greatest hope for reintegration into world markets in the EU. As the Hungarian Foreign Minister Geza Jeszenszky observed, "undoubtedly, there is a kind of expectation of a miracle, some kind of need to belong to an empire, that comes from the misconception that a more real messiah will come in place of the eastern messianism."[13] The progress in increasing the level of cooperation with the EU varies across the region. Poland, the Czech Republic, Slovakia, Hungary, Bulgaria, Romania, and the Baltic states have made the most progress and the other republics of the former Soviet Union the least.

In December 1991 Poland, Hungary, and Czechoslovakia signed association agreements with the EU. These were referred to as Europe Agreements which indicates that they cover "a wider range of problems than simply those of a commercial character."[14] The agreements provide for an asymmetrical lifting of trade barriers with barriers to trade with the EU being lifted before the barriers to trade with the Central European states. Trade barriers for sensitive industrial products will be kept longer than for others, and trade liberalization for industrial products will be more comprehensive than for agricultural products. The negotiations were difficult. They were based on a draft in English prepared by the EU which gave it an advantage in the bargaining over terms. Since analogous drafts were given to these three states, they "came to the conclusion that cooperation and exchange of information improved the bargaining position of each candidate for association, even though the negotiations were held separately."[15] Similar association agreements with Bulgaria and Romania were signed in December 1992 and February 1993, respectively.[16] Europe Agreements with the three Baltic states were initialed in April 1995, and there are plans to sign a similar agreement with Slovenia.[17]

The significance of these agreements was widely hailed. For example, Polish Premier Leszek Balcerowicz referred to Poland's association with the EU as "one of the turning points of postwar history."[18] The financial benefits were also touted. The Czechoslovak government estimated that the direct financial gain from the trade part of the agreement would total $183 million per year.[19]

However, there were several problems with the association agreements. First, while the agreements recognized that membership was a goal for the Central European states, the EU did not specifically commit itself to this nor did it set a timetable or list of conditions for membership. This was a problem because the barriers to entry were increasing. The Maastricht treaty establishing the European Union was signed on February 7, 1992. This declared the intention to tighten cooperation in foreign, economic, and monetary policies as well as in culture, security, and law. One consequence is the growing quantity of EU rules and legislation, the so called *acquis communautaire*, which are obligatory for members. Balcerowicz observed that "the condition of Poland's integration into the EC remains bringing Polish regulations into line with community norms and passing around 8,000 laws which are obligatory on the twelve member nations."[20] A Hungarian government official complained that "those East and South European countries interested in EC membership cannot be forced to accept stiffer conditions just because--for historic and political reasons--they knocked on the door of European integration only later."[21] Requiring full implementation of the *acquis* in environmental and social legislation could in fact delay access indefinitely.[22]

There is also increased competition for membership in the EU. Austria, Sweden, and Finland became members in January 1995, pressure for Turkey, Cyprus, and Malta to join is increasing, and the breakup of the Soviet Union has increased the number of potential applicants. Within the EU, there are concerns about the impact of widening (expanding membership) on deepening (intensifying cooperation) and a sense that there is some natural limit to the size of the EU if it is to be effective.[23] This leads to a heightened sense of fear by the East Europeans that they might be left out. One EU analyst noted that "any enlargement which goes beyond the three to five industrialized EFTA states could trigger a dynamic process in the rest of eastern Europe; no country would want to be the last to have the door slammed in its face because the EC is overcrowded."[24]

Finally, there is a problem with the pattern of trade envisioned. Barriers are highest on those goods that the East Europeans traditionally produce and can export most competitively: agricultural products, textiles, and steel. These sensitive goods account for about 50 percent of Poland and Hungary's exports to the EU and about 35 percent of the former Czechoslovakia's.[25] No free trade in agriculture is planned, even in the longer term. Exports under preferential terms can only increase ten percent a year. A Hungarian economist observed that since

> Hungarian agricultural exports to the EC increased by 17 percent in 1990 and by 25 percent in 1991, the 10 percent export increment possibility does not seem a generous offer. This observation is reinforced by the fact that the quantities exportable under preferential terms were based on 1989 export performance, which was not a peak year for Hungarian agricultural exports.[26]

Also, the asymmetrical nature of the concessions does not automatically benefit the Central European states. For example, Hungary had lower nominal tariff rates for agricultural products than the EU so this "would not result in an equal degree of protection and/or opening up."[27] Finally, some provisions of the new trade agreements actually make it easier to erect extra barriers to Central European exports by, for example, initiating anti-dumping actions. In August 1992 the EU Commission fixed quotas on Czechoslovak steel exports, which had not initially been subject to quantitative limits, because Czechoslovak exports of some steel products had increased by as much as 620 percent over the previous year, and Czechoslovak products were 20 to 30 percent less expensive than the current market price in the EU states. Czechoslovak officials vehemently denied charges of dumping, and they pointed out that Czechoslovak steel accounted for only 0.6 percent of total EU consumption.[28] There were similar responses to Hungarian exports of steel tubes, plums, cherries, and sour cherries and Russian aluminum exports.[29] East European economists did not find the "modest depression" in the EU to be a compelling argument for renewed protectionism. "The argument that a 1-2 per cent economic decline justifies protectionism is hardly valid in Central (and Eastern) Europe where a double-digit shrinkage of GDP had been accompanied by (irrational) liberalization."[30] This is especially true given the disparity in trade dependence. For example, the Hungarian share of total EU trade is 0.27 percent while the EU share of total Hungarian trade is over 40 percent.[31]

The EU is trying to deal with the concerns about the Europe Agreements. At the Copenhagen summit in June 1993, it affirmed its commitment to the admission of the Central European states as members possibly by the end of the century and accelerated the transition to free access to EU markets.[32] At the Essen summit in December 1994, the EU reaffirmed its commitment to Central and Eastern European membership. The key issue is likely to be the interpretation of the phrase "when their economies are ripe for full membership."[33] In May 1995, the EU Commission issued a "white paper" on East European membership. Although it was stressed that the white paper "was neither legally binding nor a guarantee of EU membership," it outlines legislative changes that must be made before negotiations on membership can begin.[34] The Central European states are concerned though that "the recent reversion in the Community to a bloc mentality can be interpreted as a wish to delay Eastern attempts to join," especially since they are already "as developed as Greece was in 1981, or Portugal when negotiations on her accession started."[35]

Despite the problems with the association agreements, most of the former republics of the Soviet Union have not even made this much progress. In late 1992, the EU Commission started negotiations with Russia, Ukraine, Belarus, and Kazakstan on the conclusion of so-called Partnership and Cooperation Agreements. This new type of agreement adds provisions on measures of political and cultural cooperation to a normal trade and economic co-operation agreement. However, it does not include provisions for the establishment of a free trade area, nor does it provide for more far-reaching financial cooperation.[36] Russia has signed such an agreement, but the EU decided not to sign the interim trade agreement until a settlement was reached in Chechnya. As a result Russia "will be considered a country with a state-run economy that not only does not quality for most-favored-nation status but that, in general, can be unilaterally subjected to all kinds of sanctions and antidumping procedures."[37] Given the wide disparity in the size and level of development of the former republics, it is unlikely that the EU will attempt a uniform approach.

Other International Organizations

The lack of clear criteria or a timetable for EU membership led the East European states and the former republics of the Soviet Union to explore alternative avenues of economic cooperation. Some existing organizations have provided foci for cooperation, and some states have provided the leadership to create new organizations. The major impact of this has been to disperse trade across several regions.

The East European and Baltic states have primarily been looking West. Czechoslovakia, Poland, Hungary, Romania, Bulgaria, Latvia, Lithuania, and Estonia all signed trade agreements with the European

Free Trade Association (EFTA).[38] The Hexagonal expanded to include Poland and the former Yugoslav republics Bosnia-Herzegovina, Croatia, Macedonia, and Slovenia and was renamed the Central European Initiative (CEI). After an extensive debate over the boundaries of Central Europe, the CEI expanded again in 1996 to include Albania, Moldova, Belarus, Bulgaria, Romania, and Ukraine.[39] It maintains the goal of "supporting the efforts of other CEI members aimed at their association and integration with the European Community."[40] Rather than promoting free trade, the CEI is concentrating on infrastructure projects: railroads, highways, telecommunications, and energy as a way of facilitating both trade and "the spontaneous contacts connecting the Central European countries."[41] An international secretariat, funded by Italy and the EBRD, has also been created although there are still concerns that "the Initiative should remain a forum for discussion and that it should not launch into any activities merely to justify its existence."[42]

New organizations have been formed to facilitate economic cooperation with states to the south, the east, and the north. In June 1992 an agreement on Black Sea Economic Cooperation was signed by Albania, Armenia, Azerbaijan, Bulgaria, Georgia, Greece, Moldova, Romania, Russia, Turkey, and Ukraine. This includes commitments by the parties "to gradually lift restrictions on the movement of capital, goods and people. The agreement provides for the development of a transportation and communications infrastructure that will facilitate cooperation."[43] However, the East European members stress that it is "not intended to serve as an alternative to the EU, but rather as a means to speed up European integration."[44] Despite concerns about "excessive institutionalization,"[45] there are plans to establish a Black Sea Trade and Development Bank and a permanent Secretariat. However, the bank was still not operational in 1995 due to a lack of capital subscriptions.[46] In March 1992 the Council of Baltic Sea States was formed by Poland, Germany, Russia, Lithuania, Latvia, Estonia, Denmark, Sweden, Norway, and Finland for the "support of new democratic institutions, economic and technological cooperation, joint actions in the field of environmental protection, health, and energy."[47]

Some of the former republic of the Soviet Union, particularly the Central Asian republics, are looking to established economic organizations in the East. In November 1992, Azerbaijan, Kazakstan, Kyrgyzstan, Tajikistan, Turkmenistan, and Uzbekistan formally joined the Organization of Economic Cooperation (OEC) which was formed in 1964 by Iran, Pakistan, and Turkey. The OEC plans to lower tariffs, establish an investment bank and an airline, and develop satellite communications.[48] It was also decided to admit these states into the Asian Development Bank in May 1993.[49] Russia felt very threatened by this turn to the East,[50] but it is also exploring its own contacts with Asian states. For example, the Russian Foreign Minister participated in the July 1993 session of foreign ministers of the Association of South East Asian Nations (ASEAN) member countries. He proclaimed that "'Russia has found its place and its voice in this community.'"[51] In March 1995 Russia also applied to join the Asian Pacific Economic Cooperation (APEC) organization which includes Australia, Canada, China, the U.S., Japan, and the ASEAN members.[52]

Regional Cooperation

Visegrad Group

As the previous section indicates, the concepts of closer regional economic cooperation have tended to originate from outside the region, and it tends to be seen as a means to an end rather than an end in itself. However, cooperation within the region itself is developing. Perhaps the most successful regional organization has been the Visegrad group composed of Poland, Hungary, the Czech Republic, and Slovakia which has tried to model itself on the Benelux. This experience is attractive because the Benelux countries are also members of the EU. The Visegrad countries cooperated when negotiating the association agreements with the EU.[53]

Although there is resistance to further institutionalization of

Visegrad cooperation on the part of Hungary and the Czech Republic, pressure from the EU led to the signing of the Central European Free Trade Agreement (CEFTA) in December 1992. One of the major impetuses for this increased level of cooperation was the association agreements with the EU which "created a competition advantage for several products coming from the EC countries and has meant a disadvantage for the members of the Visegrad group."[54] Also, the rules of origin in the association agreements "include intraregional inputs, provided that the Visegrad countries commit themselves to dismantling barriers in their mutual trade." Finally, "the EU has been conveying the idea that success with higher forms of regional cooperation will be admitted as evidence of 'EU maturity.'"[55] CEFTA will affect about 25 percent of the goods traded in the initial stages "rising to 80-85 percent over the next four years. Trade involving textiles and foundry products is likely to be among the last to undergo liberalisation."[56]

High hopes were placed on the impact of this agreement because as Bela Kadar noted, it set "these countries free from the confinement of being small nations since a market of 65 million people is much more attractive for foreign investors."[57] However, there are problems. CEFTA is unlikely to have a major impact because, excluding the trade between the Czech Republic and Slovakia, mutual trade accounts for less than ten percent of these states' total foreign trade. Also, the trade liberalization under CEFTA initially lagged behind liberalization with the EU and EFTA which led the Czech Republic to request that liberalization be speeded up.[58] Finally, the division of Czechoslovakia created additional problems because it increased the differences in size, level of development, and pace of economic reform among the states. Poland is now much larger than the other states, and concerns about its "overwhelming political and economic potential" may increase.[59] The Czech Republic is the most developed state, and its interest in deeper regional cooperation has dropped. Also, economic reform in Slovakia is lagging, and this may slow down joint efforts to join the EU.

Although the growth in mutual trade has been slower than hoped, the CEFTA members continue to pursue trade liberalization. In July

1994 the members decided to accelerate the creation of a free trade zone, and in August 1995, they decided to accelerate the abolition of tariffs on agricultural commodities.[60] It was also decided that states which have signed association agreements with the EU and joined the GATT would be eligible to apply for membership. Slovenia became the fifth member in January 1996, and Romania, Bulgaria, and Lithuania have officially applied for membership.[61]

Commonwealth of Independent States

Progress in reconstructing economic cooperation within the former Soviet Union has been uneven despite fears about the impact of failure to cooperate on the already weak Soviet economy. On December 8, 1991 Russia, Ukraine, and Belarus formed the Commonwealth of Independent States (CIS) terminating the existence of the Soviet Union.[62] Later that month in Alma Ata eleven republics signed the documents on the creation of the Commonwealth.[63] Then in April 1992, nine republics signed an agreement on the creation of a uniform customs space.[64]

Over the years hundreds of agreements on cooperation have been signed by the CIS members, but few have been implemented. Russia has been unwilling to commit itself to forms of cooperation that it does not dominate for fear that it will end up subsidizing the other members' economies. Like Turkmenistan, most of the other members have resisted "attempts to revive the structures of central authority and to give the CIS the nature of a rigid structure that imposes collective obligations and collective responsibilities on its member states."[65] Instead of serving as an engine for reintegration, the CIS seems to be "a mechanism for a civilized divorce."[66] It has provided a forum for the former republics to discuss and resolve at least some of the many problems resulting from the disintegration of the Soviet Union. Deeper forms of cooperation are emerging around several regional cores.

The first of these cores is in the Baltic region. On September 13, 1993, the Baltic states signed a free trade agreement which came into effect on April 1, 1994. It abolished internal customs restrictions and

tariffs on industrial goods.[67] In June 1996 an agreement on agricultural free trade was also signed.[68] Although all three states are small and relatively developed, their levels of mutual trade are somewhat low, ranging from five percent to 12 percent, so the absolute economic benefits would be low. However, the signing of a free trade agreement is viewed "as the first step for an integration of the Baltic countries in the European Community."[69]

The second core is in Central Asia. Kazakstan, Uzbekistan, Turkmenistan, Kyrgyzstan, and Tajikistan announced the creation of a Central Asian Commonwealth in January 1993. They proposed the introduction of "common customs regulations, a common tax system, a common defense space and mutually agreed upon prices. In addition, priority in reciprocal deliveries of scarce raw materials and other goods is to be given to the countries' nearest neighbors."[70] Although agreement was reached on draft statues on an interstate council and an executive committee for this council in January 1994,[71] only Kazakstan, Uzbekistan and Kyrgyzstan actually participated in the formation of these bodies in February 1995.[72] These three states have continued to work out common positions on issues in the CIS and to pursue closer regional integration. However, interest in broader regional cooperation remains. For example, in 1994 they concluded an agreement on free trade (except for energy resources and non ferrous metals),[73] and they established the Central Asian Bank for Cooperation and Development in 1995.[74] However, interest in broader regional cooperation remains. At a meeting of the five states in April 1995, it was decided to create a permanent forum on sustained regional development,[75] and in May 1995 the Uzbek president called for the integration of all post-Soviet Central Asian states stating that "Turkestan must become a common home. . . If all five states in the region pool their efforts in this vast expanse, the threat from outside will disappear by itself, as will the 'elder brother' notion, which oppresses and alarms everybody."[76]

The third zone of cooperation centers around Russia. Russia responded forcefully to the emergence of economic cooperation in Central Asia.[77] In July 1993, Russia, Belarus, and Ukraine signed a joint

statement calling for the creation of their own economic union which provided for the creation of supranational organs where Russia was granted 70 percent of the votes, Ukraine 20 percent, and Belarus ten percent. Although the statement that others are free to participate if they are not members of other unions or associations was included, the other republics were not consulted, and it was generally accepted that "the 'Slavic alliance' is designed, among other things, to make it clear to the Central Asian republics and Kazakhstan that they must choose what path they are going to take."[78] The economic union was expanded in September 1993 to include most CIS members although Ukraine, Turkmenistan, and Georgia initially opted for associate rather than full membership.[79] Once the membership expanded, the Economic Union faltered as well. Russia again turned its attention to Belarus.

In November 1993 Belarus and Russia signed an agreement to unite their monetary systems. One analyst cited this as "evidence of the [Belorusian] Supreme Soviet's willingness to move as close to Russia as possible, even to the point of ignoring the concepts of 'sovereignty' and 'independence'" because under the terms of the agreement all credit and monetary policy would be set by the Central Bank of Russia.[80] Belarus was willing to surrender this in return for a one to one exchange of the Belarusian ruble for the Russian ruble and duty free access to Russian oil and gas. Many Russian reformers opposed the unification of monetary systems because it would add to Russia's budget deficit and fuel inflation.[81]

As Russia's economy began to recover, it shifted its emphasis from export controls to export promotion in order to further economic growth. In conjunction with this, Russia became more interested in the formation of a customs union, and in January 1995 Russia, Belarus, and Kazakstan formed a joint customs union.[82] In March 1996 Russia, Belarus, Kazakstan, and Kyrgyzstan signed the Quadripartite agreement which envisions the creation of "a single economic space with a common market of goods, services, capital and labor; unified transport, energy and information systems; coordinated price formation, industrial and agricultural policies; coordinated social security policies; and

support for a single cultural space." Several supranational organs are planned, and membership is open to other states.[83]

In April 1996 Belarus and Russia again forged ahead with a deeper form of cooperation. They signed a treaty "On Deepening Integration and Comprehensive Drawing Together" in which they agreed to form a union with a set of supranational institutions.[84] The Russian government became upset because the media were referring to this new body as the "Community of Sovereign Republics" which is abbreviated in Russian as SSR.[85] This is awkward because Yeltsin has insisted that it is not intended to be a recreation of the union.[86]

Although the reintegration of the former Soviet Union was one of the major issues in the 1996 Russian presidential election, the response of the former republics to the March 15 decision of the Duma to renounce the December 12, 1991 RSFSR Supreme Soviet decision to abrogate the 1922 treaty forming the USSR indicates that Russia will find this a difficult task. Only Belarus and Tajikistan responded positively, and even they recognized that "the USSR's full restoration is unrealistic and impossible."[87] Instead cooperation is likely to center around these three cores with some of the Central Asian states serving as a bridge between Central Asia and Russia.

Conclusion

The EU has been trying to promote regional economic cooperation as either a precondition for or a way station before membership in the EU. Region-wide cooperation is not emerging, but smaller forms of cooperation are developing more successfully where there is an outside party to provide leadership and inducements to cooperation or among smaller groups of states at similar levels of development. However, there are impediments to the further development of economic cooperation.

First, these states, especially the East European, have made a negative evaluation of past regional cooperation which they blame for

their economic backwardness, and they fear that continued economic cooperation will only lead to further backwardness. For example, Czech Prime Minister Vaclav Klaus asserts that "there is no way to restore former trade links without returning to central planning. The flow of trade in CEMA was not based on comparative advantages and cannot be renewed without direct coercion."[88] Even Bulgarian President Zhelyu Zhelev stated that his country was prepared to participate in regional cooperation, "but we fear that it might curb our move toward a modern state; we are counting on Europe to lead us toward progress. Otherwise, it will be like recreating CEMA, a grouping of backward countries."[89] Russian reformers have the same fears about continued cooperation with the less developed republics of the former Soviet Union.

Because of this concern that regional cooperation might impede progress toward joining Europe, there is a lack of interest in institutionalizing the various organizations in Eastern Europe. For example, the Czech Republic opposes institutionalization of both the CEI and the Visegrad. As Czechoslovak President Vaclav Havel observed of the Visegrad Group, "we did not agree on forming some sort of permanent bodies, or even less so, some sort of joint bureaucracy. Our three countries still have enough of their own bureaucracy."[90] In February 1993 the Bulgarian Parliament declined an invitation to participate in the meeting of the parliamentary leaders of the Black Sea Economic Cooperation because "Bulgaria believes that its institutionalization is not expedient at the present stage and attaches greater importance to bilateral economic contacts in the region and to economic cooperation under the aegis of the Council of Europe and the CSCE."[91]

Within the CIS there is a divergence of views on institutionalization. Based in part on its own experience with CMEA, Russia is insisting on institutions with supranational authority and weighted voting as a means to control the possible costs of economic cooperation. However, as some analysts point out, "one of the main reasons why most CIS bodies have been stillborn is Moscow's desire to play an openly dominant role in them. But the experience of the Council

for Mutual Economic Aid and the Warsaw Treaty Organization shows that such mechanisms only cause the weaker partners to break away."[92]

As the Czech Prime Minister Vaclav Klaus asserted, the collapse of communism represents "a challenge not only to the post-communist countries, but also to the countries of West Europe, and we are afraid that this was not--and has not yet been--understood."[93] If the EU continues to postpone the admission of the former socialist states, steps must be taken to encourage the development of other forms of economic cooperation for these states because cooperation is developing too slowly enough to prevent negative economic and political consequences. In addition to maintaining markets, international economic cooperation can assist in the restructuring process by allowing governments in the region to make a credible commitment to trade liberalization thus countering "enterprises' incentives to delay or indefinitely defer meeting the standards of foreign competitors."[94] International economic organizations can assist the development of economic cooperation among the former socialist states by creating financial incentives for states to cooperate. The EBRD is already proceeding in this direction as evidenced by its infrastructure loans to the CEI.[95]

However, regional cooperation is only part of the solution to the region's economic problems. As the East European states are quick to point out, "All the prospective focuses for modernization are located beyond the bounds of the Visegrad group, as is the anchor of political stability. Intraregional links can only play a complementary role, not become the engine for successful modernization."[96] Many states in the CIS feel the same way: "Russia today is unable to offer them middle-level, to say nothing of advanced, technologies. This circumstance prompts them to look for outside partners."[97]

Notes

1. Szalai, *et. al.*, "Twelve Questions," p. 6.

2. Krasner, "State Power," pp. 343-44.

3. Young, "Regime Dynamics," p. 94.

4. Brada, "The European Community," p. 29.

5. Kowlaczyk and Lipszycz, "Trade With Russia," pp. 19, 20. For a further account of the difficulties in trading with the Russians, see Gasiorowska, "The Retreat From Moscow."

6. Radeva, "One Does Not Expect Miracles in Trade," p. 14.

7. "CSFR 1992 Foreign Trade Figures Published," p. 11. Husak, "Into the 'G-7,'" p. 13.

Hungary's exports to the former Soviet Union grew by 14 percent in 1992. However, this followed an even more precipitous decline the previous year than that suffered by Czechoslovakia. "Minister Releases 1992 Foreign Trade Figures," p. 16.

8. Eszes, "Ban on Transportation of Goods," p. 19.

9. Iorgulescu, "We Will Choose Alternative Scenarios," p. 38 and "Economic Losses From Serbian Sanctions Reported," p. 7.

10. Tatic, "Stop the Embargo," p. 52.

11. OMRI Daily Digest II, 4 May 1995.

12. Videnova, "The Best Market," p. 3. For a similar statement by the Romanian President Ion Illiescu, see Vidal and Dupre, "As Far as People's Lives are Concerned," p. 17.

13. Erdelyi, "Instead of Expecting Miracles of Empire...," p. 12.

14. Stawarska, "Poland's Association with the EEC," p. 79.

15. Stawarska, "Poland's Association with the EEC," p. 81.

16. However, Bulgaria complained that these two states were being treated differently than the Central European states. For example, the EU "set a 0.4 percent quota for Bulgarian and Romanian farming exports against 4 percent for Czecho-Slovakia, Hungary, and Poland." "Fair Treatment in EC Association Talks Demanded," p. 3.

17. Omblus, "Free Trade Agreements."

18. "Balcerowicz: Accord 'Turning Point,'" p. 31. For other examples, see Kocsi, "Brussels Can Be Hungary's Historic Chance," p. 12 and Husak, "Into the 'G-7'," pp. 13-14. The Romanian response was a little more restrained. See Sirbu, "Things Must Evolve Well at Home," p. 31.

19. "Minister on Advantages of EC, EFTA Agreements," p. 10. Not all of the predictions of the impact of the agreements were so rosy. Polish economists estimated that in the short run, the opening of markets would be more favorable for the EU than for Poland. Stawarska, "Poland's Association with the EEC," p. 85. For a discussion of the varying points of view on Poland's association with the EU, see Walencik, "Hopes and Fears."

20. "Balcerowicz: Accord Turning Point," p. 31.

21. Balazs, "How Can the European Community be Expanded?" p. 54. For a similar lament by Vaclav Klaus, see Danes, "The Collapse of Communism," p. 10.

22. Preston, "Obstacles to EU Enlargement."

23. One analyst questions these concerns. He notes that "the 1981 and 1986 enlargements had no such restraining effects on deepening, despite widely expressed fears at that time that they would do so." Nugent, "The Deepening and Widening of the European Community," p. 317.

24. Kramer, "The European Community's Response," p. 239.

25. European Commission, "Trade and Aid," p. 2. For a deeper discussion of trade in these three areas, see Brada, "The European Community." As Brada reminds us, steel, textiles, and agriculture have been areas where it has been particularly difficult to liberalize world trade. Indeed agriculture was one of the major stumbling blocks in the Uruguay Round of the GATT talks.

26. Kiss, "Hungarian Agricultural Strategy," p. 80.

27. Kiss, "Hungarian Agricultural Strategy," p. 84.

28. "Limits Imposed on Czechoslovak Steel Exports," p. 6. For a discussion of EC anti-dumping policy, see Holmes, *et. al.*, "Comparative Advantage," pp. 87-94.

29. Inotai, "The Economic Impact of the Association Agreement," p. 62; Kiss, "Hungarian Agricultural Strategy," p. 86; and Portansky, "Restrictions on Russian Exports," p. 19. This last action may have been justified. For more on the Russian aluminum industry, see Imse, "Russia's Wild Capitalists," p. 4.

30. Inotai, "Transforming the East," p. 27.

31. Kiss, "Hungarian Agricultural Strategy," p. 84.

32. For details, see European Commission, "Trade and Aid," p. 7.

33. Csaba, "Ripeness is All," p. 4.

34. OMRI Daily Digest II, 4 May 1995.

35. Inotai, "Transforming the East," p. 35.

36. Kramer, "The European Community's Response," p. 233.

37. Bovt and Kalashnikova, "Sides Hold to Their Own Opinions," p. 19.

38. See "A Decade of Greater Advantages," pp. 14-15; "Negotiations Begin on EFTA Free Trade Agreement," p. 15; "European Free Trade Association Agreement Signed," p. 38; and "Delegation Returns From Europe Trade Talks," p. 10.

39. "CEI: Austrian President Greets Albania's Serrqi," p. 6.

40. "CEI Declaration," p. 5.

41. Decsi, "Spontaneous Contacts Instead of Conformity," p. 17.

42. Zahradnicek, "Poland Cannot Speak on Behalf of the Others," p. 11.

43. Guseinov, "Conflicts in Former Soviet Republics," p. 21.

44. "Melescanu Views Black Sea Cooperation Summit," p. 49.

45. "Zhelev Greets Black Sea Ministers Meeting," p. 2.

46. "Melescanu Views," p. 50.

47. "Polish Minister Comments on Baltic Conference," p. 4.

48. Mekhtiyev, "Teheran and Islamabad Casting Lot with ECO," p. 18. The major interest of the Central Asian states in joining this organization is apparently outlets to the sea. See the speeches in Kozlov, "The Second Meeting," p. 15.

49. The communique acknowledged that the simultaneous membership of these states in the EBRD violates the statutes of the bank and that "the problem of delimiting the powers and responsibilities in the Asian and European banks" has not been completely solved. Agafonov, "Asian Bank Admits New Members," p. 20.

50. Vasilyev, "Russian and the Moslem World."

51. Velekhov, "'Little Dragons' Make Big Impression," p. 22.

52. Kalashnikova, "APEC," p. 27.

53. See, for example, Wagrowska, "Membership Must Be Realistic," p. 23.

54. "Government Approves Visegrad Three Trade Agreement," p. 11.

55. Inotai and Sass, "Economic Integration," p. 8.

56. "Central Europe To Set Up Free Trade Zone," p. 25.

57. "Hungary's Kadar Details Agreement," p. 2.

58. Inotai and Sass, "Economic Integration," pp. 19, 17.

59. Inotai and Sass, "Economic Integration," p. 11.

60. "Changes in Customs Tariffs in CEFTA Countries," p. 1.

61. OMRI Daily Digest II, 16 September 1996.

62. "Agreement on the Creation of a Commonwealth of Independent States."

63. Dildyayev and Yesilbayev, "On New Contours," p. 2. Estonia, Latvia, Lithuania, and Georgia did not sign.

64. Yakov, "It Has Been Decided," p. 22. Ukraine and Moldova did not sign.

65. Zhukov, "Turkmenia is Cramped by the Limits of the Commonwealth," p. 27.

66. Lipsky, "The CIS a Year Later," p. 8.

67. "Baltic Free Trade Agreement Detailed," pp. 1-2.

68. OMRI Daily Digest II, 16 August 1996.

69. "Baltic Presidents' Statement on Trade Agreements," p. 3.

70. L. Levin and Niyazmatov, "Presidents Find it Warmer in Tashkent," p. 1. The motivation for this was apparently the perception that "in the area of financial policy Russia has been behaving--especially of late--like a monopolist that does not recognize others' interests."

At this meeting it was also decided to change the name of the region from Srednyaya Asia to Tsentralnaya Asia. "A New Turkestan." Although both words are translated into English as central, they have somewhat different connotations in Russian. This was both an attempt to move away from the Russian/Soviet colonial terminology and to include Kazakstan. Before, the "correct" term had been "Central Asia and Kazakstan." My thanks to Roger Kangas for his insights on this point.

71. "Leaders of Central Asian Republics Seek Greater Unity," p. 27.

72. Portnikov, "'Central Asian Troika,'" pp. 20-1.

73. Salimov and Lapin, "Prospects for Setting Up Eurasian Union," p. 1.

74. "Central Asian Bank Official Interviewed," LD0205125795 Almaty PANORAMA in Russian 29 Apr 95 in FBIS-SOV-95-085, May 3, 1995, pp. 2-3.

75. "Regional Conference Backs Plan for Permanent Forum," p. 39.

76. OMRI Daily Digest I, 8 May 1995.

77. Yartayev and Shestakov, "Asian Gas Will Flow West," pp. 16-17.

78. Demchenko, "Heads of Government of Three Slavic Republics," p. 13. This move harks back to the initial creation of the CIS when these same three republics decided without consultation to end the Union.

79. Kononenko, "CIS is Bolstered by Economic Union," p. 27.

80. Tsygankov, "Russia and Belarus Unite Monetary System," p. 33.

81. M. Berger, "Belorussia Exchanges Part of its Sovereignty," p. 1.

82. Rybak, "Customs Union Created," pp. 21-23. The benefits to Belarus and Kazakstan of this have not been large despite a certain loss of sovereignty. For example, Russia maintains a considerable customs barrier and limits Kazak access to its oil export pipelines (Jamestown Monitor, March 21, 1996). Also, in February 1996 Belarus had to draw up a new list of tariffs for imports to comply with a changed Russian list (OMRI Daily Digest II, 23 February 1996).

83. Jamestown Monitor, 1 April 1996. Yeltsin mentioned in particular the other members of the CIS, the Baltic states, and Bulgaria as potential members. This caused quite a furor in Bulgaria.

84. OMRI Daily Digest II, 29 March 1996.

85. OMRI Daily Digest I, 3 April 1996. The preferred terminology is Russo-Belarusian Community.

86. OMRI Daily Digest I, 28 February 1996.

87. Jamestown Monitor, 18 March 1996.

88. "Europe Today and Tomorrow," p. 8.

89. Shihab, "Interview with President Zhelyu Zhelev," p. 3.

90. "Leaders Hold News Conference," p. 5. On the CEI, see "Klaus, Meciar View CEI," p. 10.

91. "Parliament Declines To Attend Black Sea Meeting," p. 5.

92. Rogov, "Result is Distressing," p. 23.

93. Klaus, "One the Eve of the Copenhagen Summit," p. 8.

94. Hillman, "The Transition from the CMEA System of International Trade," p. 282.

95. For more discussion of the role of the EBRD in facilitating infrastructure projects and regional cooperation, see Weber, "The European Bank for Reconstruction and Development," pp. 26-27.

96. Inotai and Sass, "Economic Integration," p. 12.

97. Kirichenko, "The State of and Prospects for Economic Ties," p. 49.

Appendix:

Soviet and East European Power Capabilities, 1950-1990

Table 1: Soviet and East European Power Capabilities, 1950[1]

	Area (000 km²)	Population (000s)	GDP ($bil)	Military (000s)
Bulgaria	111	7,251	2.42	200
Czechoslovakia	128	12,389	9.11	300
GDR	108	18,389	7.99	42
Hungary	93	9,388	5.04	50
Poland	313	24,824	11.21	400
Romania	238	16,311	3.33	150
Total EE	991	88,501	39.10	1,142
USSR	22,402	193,200	68.38	2,874
%	4	46	57	40

Table 2: Production of Selected Raw Materials, 1950[2]

	Coal (000 long tons)	Iron Ore (000 short tons)	Crude Petroleum (000 barrels)
Bulgaria	5,712	80	0
Czechoslovakia	45,962	1,600	292
GDR	126,000	320	0
Hungary	13,250	368	3,700
Poland	82,838	790	1,205
Romania	3,100	395	32,000
Total EE	276,862	3.553	37,197
USSR	264,000	51,406	273,200
%	105	7	14

Table 3: Soviet and East European Power Capabilities, 1955[3]

	Area (000 km^2)	Population (000s)	GDP ($bil)	Military (000s)
Bulgaria	111	7,499	2.5	175
Czechoslovakia	128	13,093	8.9	245
GDR	108	17,832	13.9	100
Hungary	93	9,825	4.5	205
Poland	313	27,281	13.0	300
Romania	238	17,325	5.0	250
Total EE	991	92,855	46.9	1,275
USSR	22,402	193,200	92.7	5,763
%	4	48	51	22

Table 4: Production of Selected Raw Materials, 1955[4]

	Coal (000 long tons)	Iron Ore (000 short tons)	Crude Petroleum (000 barrels)
Bulgaria	11,211	111	1,103
Czechoslovakia	69,321	2,451	723
GDR	224,093	1,638	0
Hungary	24,599	347	24,599
Poland	110,805	1,672	1,334
Romania	6,730	627	78,670
Total EE	446,759	6,846	94,046
USSR	431,288	70,727	509,760
%	104	10	18

Table 5: Soviet and East European Power Capabilities, 1960[5]

	Area (000 km^2)	Population (000s)	GDP ($bil)	Military (000s)
Bulgaria	111	7,629	5.25	100
Czechoslovakia	128	13,581	18.59	150
GDR	108	17,280	21.03	65
Hungary	93	9,978	8.55	75
Poland	313	29,527	23.36	200
Romania	238	18,360	8.76	200
Total EE	991	96,350	85.54	790
USSR	22,402	215,000	179.95	3,623
%	4	45	48	22

Table 6: Production of Selected Raw Materials, 1960 (000 metric tons)[6]

	Coal	Iron Ore	Crude Petroleum
Bulgaria	15,986	412	200
Czechoslovakia	84,617	3,120	137
GDR	228,186	1,642	0
Hungary	26,524	516	1,127
Poland	113,765	2,182	194
Romania	8,163	1,460	11,500
Total EE	477,241	9,332	13,248
USSR	513,186	105,857	147,859
%	93	9	9

Table 7: Soviet and East European Power Capabilities, 1965[7]

	Area (000 km^2)	Population (000s)	GDP ($bil)	Military (000s)
Bulgaria	111	8,100	7.4	158
Czechoslovakia	128	14,000	19.6	235
GDR	108	17,000	25.9	112
Hungary	93	10,000	9.8	109
Poland	313	31,500	30.7	277
Romania	238	19,000	13.9	198
Total EE	991	99,600	107.3	1,089
USSR	22,402	228,000	251.3	3,150
%	4	44	43	35

Table 8: Production of Selected Raw Materials, 1965 (000 metric tons)[8]

	Coal	Iron Ore	Crude Petroleum
Bulgaria	25,042	1,804	229
Czechoslovakia	100,840	2,446	192
GDR	253,048	1,630	0
Hungary	31,437	762	1,802
Poland	141,457	2,862	339
Romania	12,095	2,479	12,571
Total EE	563,919	11,983	15,133
USSR	577,731	153,432	577,731
%	98	8	3

Table 9: Soviet and East European Power Capabilities, 1970[9]

	Area (000 km^2)	Population (000s)	GDP ($bil)	Military (000s)
Bulgaria	111	8,500	10.71	149
Czechoslovakia	128	14,475	27.70	168
GDR	108	17,150	31.13	129
Hungary	93	10,325	14.02	102
Poland	313	32,800	40.65	242
Romania	238	20,000	19.09	181
Total EE	991	103,250	143.30	971
USSR	22,402	244,000	347.30	3,305
%	4	42	41	29

Table 10: Production of Selected Raw Materials, 1970 (000 metric tons)[10]

	Coal	Iron Ore	Crude Petroleum
Bulgaria	29,251	2,409	334
Czechoslovakia	109,847	1,606	203
GDR	261,882	422	60
Hungary	27,060	629	1,937
Poland	172,867	2,554	424
Romania	22,835	3,206	13,377
Total EE	623,742	10,826	16,335
USSR	624,114	195,492	353,039
%	100	6	5

Table 15: Soviet and East European Power Capabilities, 1985[15]

	Area (000 km^2)	Population (000s)	GDP ($bil)	Military (000s)
Bulgaria	111	8,970	63.78	149
Czechoslovakia	128	15,600	151.32	203
GDR	108	16,800	197.10	174
Hungary	93	10,800	87.92	106
Poland	313	37,500	275.83	319
Romania	238	23,500	151.31	190
Total EE	991	113,170	927.26	1,141
USSR	22,402	276,500		5,300
%	4	41		22

Table 16: Production of Selected Raw Materials, 1985 (000 metric tons)[16]

	Coal	Iron Ore	Crude Petroleum
Bulgaria	30,880	1,985	1,300
Czechoslovakia	128,538	1,859	123
GDR	312,000	30	59
Hungary	24,042	311	2,012
Poland	249,442	11	194
Romania	49,819	2,287	10,718
Total EE	794,721	6,483	14,406
USSR	726,000	247,639	595,291
%	109	3	2

Table 17: Soviet and East European Power Capabilities, 1990[17]

	Area (000 km^2)	Population (000s)	GDP ($bil)	Military (000s)
Bulgaria	111	9,026	20.73	129
Czechoslovakia	128	15,692	45.63	198
GDR	108	16,664		138
Hungary	93	10,567	33.06	94
Poland	313	38,479	62.27	313
Romania	238	23,295	37.63	163
Total EE	991	113,759		1,035
USSR	22,402	288,561	1,535.14	3,988
%	4	39		26

Table 18: Production of Selected Raw Materials, 1990 (000 metric tons)[18]

	Coal	Iron Ore	Crude Petroleum
Bulgaria	31,700	1,079	900
Czechoslovakia	107,250	1,831	123
GDR	300,000	0	41
Hungary	17,578	0	1,974
Poland	215,208	2	163
Romania	40,874	2,002	7,928
Total EE	712,610	4,914	11,129
USSR	703,000	236,000	570,000
%	101	2	2

Notes

1.The data on area are from Sovet Ekonomicheskoi Vzaimopomoshchi *Statisticheski Ezhegodnik, 1988.*

The East European population data are from Meyers, "Population and Labor Force in Eastern Europe." The Soviet figure is an estimate for 1946 from *The Statesman's Yearbook 1949.*

The GDP data are in constant 1965 prices. Zeman, "Development in the Position of the Comecon Complex," p. 38. For a discussion of the problems with computing GNP or GDP for the socialist states, see Marer, "Economic Performance and Prospects in Eastern Europe."

The East European military data is from *The Statesman's Yearbook, 1949, 1951*, and *1952*, but it is not clear how comparable the figures are, i.e. whether they are all counting the same personnel. Some include the security police while others do not. Also, the figures are not all from the same year. The Soviet figure is Khrushchev's for 1948 which is cited in Evangelista, "Stalin's Postwar Army Reappraised."

2.Coal and crude petroleum were chosen because they were the major sources of industrial energy. Iron ore was chosen rather than steel because the East European states were developing significant steel industries based largely on imported iron ore. The figure for coal includes anthracite, bituminous, brown, and lignite coals. Bureau of Mines, *Minerals Yearbook, 1951.*

3.The East European population data are from Meyers, "Population and Labor Force in Eastern Europe." The Soviet figure is an estimate for 1946 from *The Statesman's Yearbook, 1949.* The GDP data are in 1955 US dollars. Since there are no readily available figures for total GDP of these countries in this year in a single currency, I multiplied the per capita figures from "Comparative GDP Levels" by the population figures from Meyers, "Population and Labor Force in Eastern Europe." The East European military data are from *The Statesman's Yearbook, 1956* and *1957.* Problems with the comparability and accuracy of the data still exist. The figures are not all for the same year, and it is unclear whether they are counting the same personnel. The Soviet figure is Khrushchev's for 1955 which is cited in The Institute for Strategic Studies, *The Military Balance, 1960.*

4.Bureau of Mines, *Minerals Yearbook, 1959,* Vol. 1 *Metals and Minerals (except fuels)* and Vol. 2 *Fuels.*

5.The population and military data are from Institute for Strategic Studies, *The Military Balance, 1960.* The GDP data is in constant 1965 prices. Zeman, "Development in the Position of the Comecon Complex," p. 38.

6.Bureau of Mines, *Minerals Yearbook, 1964*, Vol. 4 *Area Reports: International.*

7.The population and military data are from Institute for Strategic Studies, *The Military Balance, 1965-1966.* The GDP data are in 1965 US dollars. Once again I multiplied the per capita figures from "Comparative GDP Levels" by the population figures from Meyers, "Population and Labor Force in Eastern Europe."

8.Bureau of Mines, *Minerals Yearbook, 1968*, Vol. 4 *Area Reports: International.*

9.The population and military data are from Institute for Strategic Studies, *The Military Balance, 1970-1971.* The GDP data are in constant 1965 prices. Zeman, "Development in the Position of the Comecon Complex," p. 38.

10.Bureau of Mines, *Minerals Yearbook, 1972*, Vol. 3 *Area Reports: International.*

11.The population and military data are from Institute for Strategic Studies, *The Military Balance, 1975-1976*. The GDP data are in current US dollars. The per capita figures from the World Bank Atlas were multiplied by the total populations. A complete discussion of the methodology used and its failings can be found in Marer, *Dollar GNPs.*

12.Bureau of Mines, *Minerals Yearbook, 1977*, Vol. 3 *Area Reports: International.*

13.The population and military data are from Institute for Strategic Studies, *The Military Balance, 1980-1981*. The GDP data are in current US dollars. Marer, *Dollar GNPs*. Part of the increase in the figures is due to a change in the methodology used to calculate them.

14.Bureau of Mines, *Minerals Yearbook, 1984*, Vol 3 *Area Reports: International.*

15.The population and military data are from Institute for Strategic Studies, *The Military Balance, 1985-1986*. The GDP data are in constant 1988 US dollars. Alton, "East European GNP's."

16.Bureau of Mines, *Minerals Yearbook, 1987*, Vol. 3 *Area Reports: International.*

17.The population and military data are from Institute for Strategic Studies, *The Military Balance, 1990-1991*. The GDP data are in current US dollars at market exchange rates. United Nations, *Statistical Yearbook, 1992.*

18.Bureau of Mines, *Minerals Yearbook, 1991*, Vol. 3, Part 4 *Mineral Industries of Europe and Central Eurasia.*

Bibliography

Agafonov, Sergei. "Asian Bank Admits New Members." *Izvestia*, May 5, 1993. In *The Current Digest* 45 (June 2, 1993), p. 20.

Aggarwal, Vinod. *Liberal Protectionism: The International Politics of Organized Textile Trade*. Berkeley: University of California Press, 1985.

"Agreement on the Creation of a Commonwealth of Independent States." *Rossiiskaya gazeta*, December 10, 1991. In *CDSP* 43 (January 8, 1992), pp. 10-11.

Albinowski, Stanislaw. "There is Still no Conception . . . ." *Zycie Warszawy*, March 2, 1963. In *Polish Press Survey* No. 1497, Radio Free Europe Research, pp. 2-3.

______. "Fuel -- A Bottleneck." *Zycie Gospodarcze*, March 3, 1963. In *Polish Press Survey* No. 1497, Radio Free Europe Research, pp. 4-7.

______. *Commercial Policy of EEC*. Warsaw: Zachnodia Agencja Prasowa, 1965.

______. "Where to Get Petroleum." *Polityka*, September 24, 1966. In *Polish Press Survey* No. 2018, Radio Free Europe Research, pp. 1-6.

Altmann, Franz-Lothar. "Czechoslovakia: Internal Development and Foreign Economic Relations in the 1980s." In Joseph, Philip, ed. *The Economies of Eastern Europe and their Foreign Economic Relations*. Chichester, UK: NATO, 1986.

Alton, Thad P. "East European GNP's, Domestic Final Uses of Gross Product, Rates of Growth, and International Comparisons." In Joint Economic Committee, US Congress. *Pressures for Reform in the East European Economies*. Washington, DC: USGPO, 1989.

Amort, Jiri. "The Development and Structure of Czechoslovak Foreign Trade." *Czechoslovak Foreign Trade* 5 (March 1965), pp. 3-6.

Anderson, Sheldon. "A Dollar to Poland is a Dollar to Russia: United States Economic Diplomacy Toward Poland, 1945-1950." *East European Quarterly* 26 (March 1992), pp. 77-108.

Andreyev, D. and M. Makov. "The Common Market After Eleven Years." *International Affairs* [Moscow], January 1969, pp. 43-49.

Apatini, K. "Characteristics and Problems of the Comecon Market." *Penzugyi Szemle*, January 1971. In *Hungarian Press Survey* No. 2115, Radio Free Europe Research.

Apple, R. W., Jr. "In Washington, Moscow's Moment Has Arrived." *The New York Times*, June 9, 1991, Section 4, p. 1.

______. "Bush Vows to Put Soviets in Group Favored in Trade." *The New York Times*, July 31, 1991, pp. A1, A4.

Apro, Antal. "International Economic Cooperation and Our Development Over a Quarter of a Century." *Partelet*, March 1970. In *Hungarian Press Survey* No. 2074, Radio Free Europe Research.

Apro, Eva. "On the Economic Cooperation of the Socialist Countries." *Tarsadalmi Szemle*, February 1962. In *Hungarian Press Survey* No. 1126, Radio Free Europe Research, pp. 2-7.

Arato, Gabor. "The Advantage of Our Council of Europe Membership is Not Merely Symbolic." *Magyar Hirlap*, November 8, 1990. In FBIS-EEU-90-220, November 14, 1990, pp. 24-5.

Art, Robert and Robert Jervis, eds. *International Politics: Anarchy, Force, Political Economy, and Decision Making*. 2d ed. Boston: Little, Brown, and Company, 1985.

"At the International Conference of Communist and Workers' Parties." *Pravda*, June 7, 1969. In *CDSP* 21 (July 9, 1969), pp. 4-5.

"At the International Conference of Communist and Workers' Parties." *Pravda*, June 8, 1969. In *CDSP* 21 (July 9, 1969), pp. 5-8.

"At the International Conference of Communist and Workers' Parties." *Pravda*, June 10, 1969. In *CDSP* 21 (July 9, 1969), pp. 4-7.

"At the International Conference of Communist and Workers' Parties." *Pravda*, June 11, 1969. In *CDSP* 21 (July 23, 1969), pp. 3-6.

"At the International Conference of Communist and Workers' Parties." *Pravda*, June 18, 1969. In *CDSP* 21 (July 30, 1969), pp. 16-18, 48.

Ausch, Sandor. *Theory and Practice of CMEA Cooperation*. Budapest: Akademiai Kiado, 1972.

Avramov, Lachezar. "Our Foreign Trade and Its Role in the Socialist Construction of the People's Republic of Bulgaria." *Novo Vreme*, September 1962. In *Bulgarian Press Survey* No. 349, Radio Free Europe Research.

______. "On the Frontiers of Integration." *Pravda*, October 17, 1970. In *CDSP* 22 (November 17, 1970), pp. 14-15.

Balazs, Peter. "How Can the European Community be Expanded?" *New Hungarian Quarterly* 33 (Spring 1992), pp. 51-8.

"Balcerowicz: Accord Turning Point." LD1712014391 Warsaw PAP in English 001 GMT 17 Dec 91. In FBIS-EEU-91-242, December 17, 1991, p. 31.

"Baltic Free Trade Agreement Detailed." WS1602140794 Tallinn BNS in English 1038 GMT, 17 Feb 1994. In FBIS-SOV-94-033, February 17, 1994, pp. 1-2.

"Baltic Presidents' Statement on Trade Agreements." W53008142693 Riga LETA in English 1130 GMT 20 Aug 93. In FBIS-SOV-93-168, September 1, 1993, p. 3.

"Basic Principles of the International Socialist Division of Labor." *Pravda*, June 17, 1962. In *CDSP* 14 (July 11, 1962), pp. 3-8.

Bautina, N. "International Socialist Production Relations." *Mirovaia ekonomika i mezhdunarodnye otnosheniia*, 1968, no. 4. In *Soviet and Eastern European Foreign Trade* 4 (Fall 1968), pp. 87-104.

Belayev, Yu. "CMEA Cooperation Today." *International Affairs* [Moscow], December 1968, pp. 5-11.

Belli, Nicolae. "Equalizing the Economic Development Levels of the Socialist Countries." *Revista Economica*, September 1974. In *Rumanian Press Survey* No. 980, Radio Free Europe Research.

Belyaev, Y. "Economic Ties Between the Socialist Countries." *International Affairs* [Moscow], August 1966, pp. 16-22.

Benedek, I. G. "Relations Between Hungary and the Common Market." *Magyar Hirlap*, February 6, 1971. In *Hungarian Press Survey* No. 2112, Radio Free Europe Research.

Berend, I. T. "The Problem of Eastern European Economic Integration in a Historical Perspective." In Vajda, Imre and Mihaly Simai, eds. *Foreign Trade in a Planned Economy*. Cambridge: Cambridge University Press, 1971.

Berger, Mikhail. "The European Bank Does Not Want To Be a Gosplan." *Izvestiya*, June 18, 1991. In FBIS-SOV-91-120, June 21, 1991, p. 5.

______. "Belorussia Exchanges Part of its Sovereignty For Russian Rubles." *Izvestia*, April 14, 1994. In *The Current Digest* 46 (May 11, 1994), p. 1.

Berger, Wolfgang. "Socialist Economy and International Cooperation." *World Marxist Review* 7 (February 1964), pp. 30-5.

Binns, Christopher. "From USE to EEC: The Soviet Analysis of European Integration Under Capitalism." *Soviet Studies* 30 (April 1978), pp. 237-61.

Biro, Jozsef. "The Development of Hungarian-Soviet Economic Relationships." *Kozgazdasagi Szemle*, November 1967. In *Hungarian Press Survey* No. 1875, Radio Free Europe Research.

"Black Sea Countries Discuss Economic Cooperation." AU1203140191 Bucharest ROMPRES in English 1304 GMT 12 Mar 91. In FBIS-EEU-91-050, March 14, 1991, p. 2.

Bognar, Jozsef. "Principles of Foreign Trade in the New Economic Mechanism." *The New Hungarian Quarterly* 8 (Summer 1967), pp. 156-71.

Bogomolov, Oleg. "The International Socialist Division of Labor." *Voprosy Ekonomiki*, 1960, no. 1. In *Problems of Economics* 3 (June 1960), pp. 44-55.

______. "Strengthening of Cooperation is Path to New Successes." *Pravda*, August 4, 1964. In *CDSP* 16 (August 26, 1964), pp. 27-8.

______. "Problems in Production Specialization and Cooperation Among CMEA Countries." *Mirovaia ekonomika i mezhdunarodnye otnosheniia*, 1967, no. 5. In *Soviet and Eastern European Foreign Trade* 4 (Spring 1968), pp. 68-90.

______. "The Changing Nature of Socialism." *Kommunist*, 1989, No. 11. In *Problems of Economics* 32 (March, 1990), pp. 15-29.

Bohlen, Celestine. "As the Soviet Rut Deepens, Hungary Learns Some Tricks of New Trade." *The New York Times*, December 30, 1990, p. 6.

Bovt, Gregory and Natalya Kalashnikova. "Sides Hold to Their Own Opinions." *Kommersant-Daily*, March 10, 1995. In *The Current Digest* 47 (April 5, 1995), pp. 18-19.

Brabant, Jozef van. "On the Origins and Tasks of the Council for Mutual Economic Assistance." *Osteuropa Wirtschaft* 19 (September 1974), pp. 182-209.

______. *Socialist Economic Integration: Aspects of Contemporary Economic Problems in Eastern Europe*. Cambridge: Cambridge University Press, 1980.

______. *Adjustment, Structural Change and Economic Efficiency: Aspects of Monetary Cooperation in Eastern Europe*. Cambridge: Cambridge University Press, 1987.

______. "Toward a Renewal of Socialist Economic Integration (SEI)?" In Joint Economic Committee, US Congress. *Pressures for Reform in the East European Economies*. Washington, DC: USGPO, 1989.

______ and Paul Marer. "Reform and Membership of the Planned Economies in the GATT, the IMF, and the World Bank." In Joint Economic Committee, US Congress. *Pressures for Reform in the East European Economies*. Washington, DC: USGPO, 1989.

Brada, Josef. "The European Community and Czechoslovakia, Hungary, and Poland." *Report on Eastern Europe* 2 (December 6, 1991), pp. 27-32.

Breslauer, George. "Soviet Economic Reforms Since Stalin: Ideology, Politics, and Learning." *Soviet Economy* 6, no. 3, pp. 252-80.

Brown, J. F. "Rumania Steps out of Line." *Survey* No. 49 (October 1963), pp. 19-34.

Brozik, M. "The Truth About Czechoslovak-Soviet Trade in Raw Materials." *Rude Pravo*, October 17, 23, and November 11, 1969. In *Czechoslovak Press Survey* No. 2277, Radio Free Europe Research.

Bruno, Michael. "Stabilization and Reform in Eastern Europe: A Preliminary Evaluation." *IMF Staff Papers* 39 (December 1992), pp. 741-77.

Brzezinski, Zbigniew. *The Soviet Bloc: Unity and Conflict*. Rev. ed. Cambridge: Cambridge University Press, 1967.

Bunce, Valerie. "Decline of a Regional Hegemon: The Gorbachev Regime and Reform in Eastern Europe." *East European Politics and Society* 3 (Spring 1989), pp. 235-67.

Bureau of Mines. *Minerals Yearbook*. Washington, DC: USGPO, annually.

Burks, R. V. "The Decline of Communism in Czechoslovakia." *Studies in Comparative Communism* 2 (January 1969), pp. 21-49.

"Bush's Remarks on Aid to Kremlin and Plans for Summit." *The New York Times*, December 13, 1990, p. A6.

Butler, William E., ed. *A Source Book on Socialist International Organizations*. Alphen aan den Rijn, The Netherlands: Sijthoff & Noordhoff, 1978.

Bykov, A. "CMEA: International Importance of Its Experience." *International Affairs* [Moscow], February 1965, pp. 16-22.

Campbell, John. *The United States in World Affairs, 1947-1948*. New York: Harper & Brothers, 1948.

"CEI: Austrian President Greets Albania's Serrqi." AU0306085296 Tirana ATA in English, 1914 GMT, 31 May 96. In FBIS-EEU-96-107, June 3, 1996, p. 6.

"CEI Declaration." LD1807120993 Budapest MTI in English 1525 GMT 17 Jul 93. In FBIS-EEU-93-136, July 19, 1993, pp. 4-6.

"Central Asian Bank Official Interviewed." LD0205125795 Almaty PANORAMA in Russian 29 Apr 95. In FBIS-SOV-95-085, May 3, 1995, pp. 2-3.

"Central Europe To Set Up Free Trade Zone." LD3011210792 Warsaw PAP in English 2023 GMT 30 Nov 92. In FBIS-EEU-92-231, December 1, 1992, p. 25.

"CEMA: Born 1949, Deceased 1991." *Verejnost*, January 16, 1991. In FBIS-EEU-91-015, January 23, 1991, pp. 12-13.

"Changes in Customs Tariffs in CEFTA Countries." AU2208132795 Bratislava SME in Slovak 19 Aug 95. In FBIS-EEU-95-163, August 23, 1995, p. 1.

"Charter of the Council on Mutual Economic Aid." *Vedmosti Verkhonovo Soveta SSSR*, No. 15 [999] (April 21, 1960). In *CDSP* 12 (July 6, 1960), pp. 9-12.

Chistyakov, A. "Growth in Economic Cooperation Among Countries of the Socialist Camp." *Kommunist*, October 1954. In *CDSP* 6 (January 19, 1955), pp. 3-8.

Ciulea, Octavian and Marina Rudareanu. "The Development of Rumanian Foreign Trade." *Lupta de Clasa*, December 1968. In *Rumanian Press Survey* No. 784, Radio Free Europe Research.

Cizkovsky, M. *Mezinarodni Planovani - Zkusenost a Moznosti RVHP* [International Planning - The Experience and Possibilities of CMEA]. Prague: Academia, 1971.

Clines, Francis X. "Blood Feud Feeding Soviet Violence." *New York Times*, May 13, 1991, p. A6

"CMEA at a Sharp Turning Point." *Pravda*, January 11, 1990. In *CDSP* 42 (February 14, 1990), p. 14.

"CMEA -- On the Threshold of Major Changes. -- At the 45th Session of the Council for Mutual Economic Aid." *Pravda*, January 10, 1990. In *CDSP* 42 (February 14, 1990), pp. 12-14.

Comanici, G. "Interchim -- A Form of Collaboration Among Comecon Member Countries in the Field of Small-Scale Chemical Production." *Viata Economica*, January 8, 1971. In *Rumanian Press Survey* No. 870, Radio Free Europe Research.

"Combine National and International Interests." *Izvestia*, June 4, 1964. In *CDSP* 16 (July 1, 1964), pp. 4-5.

"Communique on Conference of First Secretaries of Central Committees of Communist and Workers' Parties and Heads of Government of Member Countries of Council for Mutual Economic Aid." *Pravda*, July 28, 1963. In *CDSP* 15 (August 21, 1963), pp. 24-6.

"Communique on Conference of Representatives of Communist and Workers' Parties." *Pravda*, December 2, 1960. In *CDSP* 12 (December 28, 1960 and January 4, 1961).

"Communique on 23rd Special Session of Council for Mutual Economic Aid," *Pravda*, April 27, 1969. In *CDSP* 21 (May 14, 1969), pp. 18-20.

"Communique on the 24th Session of the Council for Mutual Economic Aid." *Pravda*, May 17, 1970. In *CDSP* 22 (June 16, 1970), pp. 16-17.

"Comparative GDP Levels." *Economic Bulletin for Europe* 31, no. 2.

"Concerning Imperialist 'Integration' in Western Europe." *Pravda*, August 26, 1962. In *CDSP* 14 (September 19, 1962), pp. 9-16.

Constantinescu, Gh. "The Historical Function of the Relations Between the Socialist Countries." *Viata Economica*, 1968, No. 48. In *Rumanian Press Survey* No. 777, Radio Free Europe Research, pp. 5-7.

Constantinescu, Radu. "The Development and Improvement of Collaboration Within Comecon." *Probleme Economice*, 1969, No. 5. In *Rumanian Press Survey* No. 804, Radio Free Europe Research.

______. "Collaboration and Cooperation in Material Production Among the Socialist Countries." *Viata Economica*, February 23, 1973. In *Rumanian Press Survey* No. 945, Radio Free Europe Research, pp. 4-10.

______. "Economic Collaboration and Cooperation in Material Production Among the Socialist Countries." *Viata Economica*, March 9, 1973. In *Rumanian Press Survey* No. 946, Radio Free Europe Research.

"Cooperation in the Development of Crude Oil Extraction." *Rude Pravo,* September 24, 1966. In *Czechoslovak Press Survey* No. 1850, Radio Free Europe Research, pp. 7-9.

Crow, Suzanne. "'Who Lost Eastern Europe?'" *Report on the USSR* 3 (April 12, 1991), pp. 1-5.

Csaba, Laszlo. "Joint Investments and Mutual Advantages in the CMEA -- Retrospection and Prognosis." *Soviet Studies* 37 (April 1985), pp. 227-47.

______. "Ripeness is All: From Comecon to the European Union." *The Hungarian Quarterly* 36 (Spring 1995), pp. 3-18.

"CSFR Minister Comments." LD0501145791 Prague CTK in English 1419 GMT 5 Jan 91. In FBIS-EEU-91-005, January 8, 1991, pp. 1-2.

"CSFR 1992 Foreign Trade Figures Published." AU1902184493 Prague CTK in English 1948 GMT 17 Feb 93. In FBIS-EEU-93-033, February 22, 1993, pp. 11-12.

"CSSR's Calfa Interviewed." Prague Television Service in Czech 1830 GMT 8 Jan 90. In FBIS-EEU-90-006, January 9, 1990, p. 6.

"CTK Views IMF Application." LD2301140990 Prague CTK in English 1305 GMT 23 Jan 90. In FBIS-EEU-90-019, January 29, 1990, pp. 41-2.

"Czechoslovak-Soviet Friendship Rally." *Pravda,* April 11, 1987. In *CDSP* 39 (May 13, 1987), pp. 8-11.

Danes, Martin. "The Collapse of Communism Also Represents a Challenge for the European Community." *Cesky Denik,* June 9, 1993. In FBIS-EEU-93-113, June 15, 1993, p. 10.

"A Decade of Greater Advantages." *Hospodarske Noviny,* May 26, 1992. In FBIS-EEU-92-107, June 3, 1993, pp. 14-15.

"Declaration of Conference of Representative of Communist and Workers' Parties of Socialist Countries, Held in Moscow Nov. 14-16, 1957." *Pravda,* November 22, 1957. In *CDSP* 9 (January 1, 1958), pp. 3-7.

Decsi, Katalin. "Spontaneous Contacts Instead of Conformity." *Nepszava,* December 5, 1992. In FBIS-EEU-92-239, December 11, 1992, pp. 16-17.

"Delegation Returns From Europe Trade Talks." AU2901184693 Sofia BTA in English 1621 GMT 29 Jan 93. In FBIS-EEU-93-019, February 1, 1993, p. 10.

Demchenko, Irina. "Heads of Government of Three Slavic Republics Agree on International Integration Once Again." *Izvestia,* July 13, 1993. In *The Current Digest* 45 (August 11, 1993), pp. 12-13.

Department of State. *Treaties and Other International Agreements of the United States of America, 1931-1945.* Vol. 3 *Multilateral.* Washington, DC: USGPO, 1969.

______. *Treaties and Other International Agreements of the United States of America, 1946-1949.* Vol. 4 *Multilateral.* Washington, DC: USGPO, 1970.

______. *Foreign Relations of the United States, 1947.* Vol. 3 *The British Commonwealth; Europe.* Washington, DC: USGPO, 1972.

______. Decimal files. National Archives, Washington, DC.

"Deputy Minister Urges Links With EC, EFTA." LD1602155490 Budapest MTI in English 1316 GMT 16 Feb 90. In FBIS-EEU-90-037, February 23, 1990, p. 57.

Deryabin, Yuri. "Milestones of the 'Year of Europe,'" *International Affairs* [Moscow], February 1990, pp. 56-67.

Desi, Janos. "What Do We Need the Army for? -- Lajos Fur on Relations With the Warsaw Pact, Army Reserve Ranks, and the Generals' Power." *Magyar Nemzet,* May 30, 1990. In FBIS-EEU-90-107, June 4, 1990, p. 38.

Dezseri, Kalman. "Hungarian Orientation Toward Western Europe: Will it Be to the EC and/or to the EFTA?" *Kulgazdasag* 24, no. 6. In *Soviet and Eastern European Foreign Trade* 26 (Winter 1990-91), pp. 50-64.

D'iachenko, V. "Main Trends in Improving Prices in Trade Among Comecon Members." *Voprosy ekonomiki* 1967, no. 12. In *Problems of Economics* 11 (June 1968), pp. 40-9.

"Dialectics of National and International in Socialist World System." *World Marxist Review* 15 (July 1972), pp. 17-59.

"Dienstbier: CSFR Wants to Remain in Pact." LD0506180990 Hamburg DPA in German 1720 GMT 5 Jun 90. In FBIS-EEU-90-109, June 6, 1990, p. 13.

Dietz, Raimund. "Advantages and Disadvantages in Soviet Trade with Eastern Europe." In Joint Economic Committee, U.S. Congress. *East European Economies: Slow Growth in the 1980s*. Washington, DC: USGPO, 1985.

"Difficulties on Draft Bulgarian-Soviet Treaty." AU1005165091 Sofia BTA in English 1455 GMT 10 May 91. In FBIS-EEU-91-092, May 13, 1991, pp. 14-15.

Dildyayev, Gregory and Tleuzhan Yesilbayev. "On New Contours." *Pravda*, December 23, 1991. In *CDSP* 43 (January 22, 1992), p. 2.

"Dimitrov Says Joining EC 'Only Salvation.'" AU2205210090 Sofia BTA in English 2002 GMT 22 May 90. In FBIS-EEU-90-100, May 23, 1990, p. 8.

"The Directives of the 23rd C.P.S.U. Congress for the Five-Year Plan for the Development of the U.S.S.R. National Economy in 1966-1970." *Pravda*, April 6, 1966. In *CDSP* 18 (April 27, 1966), pp. 3-21, 28.

Djilas, Milovan. *Conversations with Stalin*. Transl. Michael B. Petrovich. New York: Harcourt, Brace, & World, Inc., 1962.

Dobozy, Istvan. "Raw Materials Supply in the Comecon Area." *Nepszagadsag*, January 23, 1974. In *Hungarian Press Survey* No. 2338, Radio Free Europe Research.

Drewnowski, Jerzy. "The Problem with Problems." *Zycie Gospodarcze*, March 19, 1967. In *Polish Press Survey* No. 2061, Radio Free Europe Research, pp. 1-6.

Duculescu, V. "The Sovereign State in International Relations." *Era Socialista*, 1973, No. 13. In *Rumanian Press Survey* No. 955, Radio Free Europe Research.

Dudinskii, I. "The Problem of Fuels and Raw Materials in the Comecon Countries, And the Ways to Solve It." *Voprosy ekonomiki*, 1966, No. 4. In *Soviet and Eastern European Foreign Trade* 3 (September-October 1966), pp. 19-39.

______. "Economic Integration -- Law of Development of the Socialist Community." *International Affairs* [Moscow], December 1970, pp. 3-10.

"EC Commission Spokesman on Trade Ties." LD1607120890 Budapest MTI in English 1059 GMT 16 Jul 90. In FBIS-EEU-90-137, July 17, 1990, pp. 40-1.

"EC Economic Agreement Suspended." AU1506094490 Paris AFP in English 0943 GMT 15 Jun 90. In FBIS-EEU-90-116, June 15, 1990, p. 49.

Eckstein, Harry. "Case Study and Theory in Political Science." In Greenstein, Fred and Nelson Polsby, eds. *Handbook of Political Science*. Vol. VII. Reading, Mass.: Addison-Wesley, 1975.

"Economic Losses From Serbian Sanctions Reported." AU1012151092 Sofia BTA in English 1449 GMT 10 Dec 92. In FBIS-EEU-92-239, December 11, 1992, p. 7.

Economic Research Institute, Academy of Social and Political Science of Socialist Republic of Rumania. "New Stage in International Economic Interdependence." *World Marxist Review* 16 (December 1973), pp. 35-9.

"EEC Preferences Apply to Country 1 Jan." LD0301193990 Warsaw PAP in English 1841 GMT 3 Jan 90. In FBIS-EEU-90-006, January 9, 1990, p. 60.

Erdelyi, Andras. "Instead of Expecting Miracles of Empire...." *Uj Magyarorszag*, April 18, 1992. In FBIS-EEU-92-082, April 28, 1992, pp. 12-13.

Eremia, N. "The International Investment Bank." *Viata Ekonomica*, January 22, 1971. In *Rumanian Press Survey* No. 872, Radio Free Europe Research.

"Establishment of the Council for Mutual Economic Aid." *Pravda*, January 25, 1949. In *CDSP* 1 (February 22, 1949), p. 11.

Eszes, Tibor. "Ban on Transportation of Goods, With Days of Grace." *Nepszabadsag*, June 4, 1992.

In FBIS-EEU-92-111, June 9, 1992, pp. 19-20.
"Europe Today and Tomorrow From the Central European Perspective." *Telegraf,* May 13, 1993. In FBIS-EEU-93-093, May 17, 1993, pp. 7-9.
European Commission. "Trade and Aid in Relations Between the European Union, the Countries of Central and Eastern Europe, and the Countries of the Commonwealth of Independent States." December 1993.
"European Free Trade Association Agreement Signed." LD1112041592 Warsaw PAP in English 2358 GMT 10 Dec 92. In FBIS-EEU-92-240, December 14, 1992, pp. 38-9.
Evangelista, Matthew. "Stalin's Postwar Army Reappraised." *International Security* 7 (Winter 1982/1983), pp. 110-38.
"Facts About the Economic Links Between the CSSR and USSR." *Nove Slovo*, November 7, 1968. In *Czechoslovak Press Survey* No. 2143, Radio Free Europe Research.
Faddeev, Nikolai V. *Sovet Ekonomicheskoi Vzaimopomoshchi* [The Council for Mutual Economic Assistance]. Moscow: Ekonomika, 1974.
______. "CMEA: Cooperation of Equal Nations." *International Affairs* [Moscow], April 1967, pp. 7-12.
Fainsod, Merle. *How Russia is Ruled.* Rev. ed. Cambridge: Harvard University Press, 1963.
"Fair Treatment in EC Association Talks Demanded." AU1011124792 Sofia BTA in English 1052 GMT 10 Nov 92. In FBIS-EEU-92-219, November 12, 1992, p. 3.
Farnsworth, Clyde. "Soviet Economic Output Off Sharply." *The New York Times*, December 22, 1990, p. 6.
Fazekas, Laslo. "Traditions in Fetters." *Nepujsag,* June 6, 1963. In *Hungarian Press Survey* No. 1346, Radio Free Europe Research, pp. 2-4.
______. "Socialist Economic Integration -- Independence Turned Upside Down." *Nograd*, February 24, 1972. In *Hungarian Press Survey* No. 2188, Radio Free Europe Research.
"Federation with CSSR Suggested." LD0401135190 Warsaw PAP in English 1210 GMT 4 Jan 90. In FBIS-EEU-90-008, January 11, 1990, p. 58.
Fierlinger, Zdenek. "The Truth About Czechoslovakia's Attitude to the Marshall Plan." *Novaya i Noveishaya Istoria*, 1963, no. 1. In *CDSP* 15 (April 24, 1963), pp. 17-19, 40.
Fikus, Dariusz. "The Change." *Polityka,* August 2, 1969. In *Polish Press Survey* No. 2219, Radio Free Europe Research.
Filipov, Grisha. "The Main Economic Task and Bulgaria's Problems of Economic Cooperation with the Socialist Countries." *Trud,* July 23, 1963. In *Bulgarian Press Survey* No. 468, Radio Free Europe Research, pp. 2-7.
Fischer-Galati, Stephen. *The New Rumania: From People's Democracy to Socialist Republic.* Cambridge: The M.I.T. Press, 1967.
Foldes, Istvan. "Economic Cooperation and Internationalism." *Nepszabadsag*, November 7, 1962. In *Hungarian Press Survey* No. 1252, Radio Free Europe Research, pp. 2-4.
______. "On Cooperation and Nationalism." *Nok Lapia*, July 6, 1963. In *Hungarian Press Survey* No. 1349, Radio Free Europe Research, pp. 8-10.
"For Strengthening the Solidarity of Communists, For a New Upswing in the Anti-Imperialist Struggle." *Pravda*, June 8, 1969. In *CDSP* 21 (July 2, 1969), pp. 3-17.
Forte, David. "The Response of Soviet Foreign Policy to the Common Market, 1957-63." *Soviet Studies* 19 (January 1968), pp. 373-86.
Friedman, Thomas. "NATO Tries to Ease Military Concerns in Eastern Europe." *The New York Times*, June 7, 1991, pp. A1, A6.
Friesen, Connie M. *The Political Economy of East-West Trade.* New York: Praeger, 1976.
"Further on Chebeleu Statements." AU0205190791 Bucharest ROMPRES in English 1839 GMT 2 May 91. In FBIS-EEU-91-086, May 3, 1991, pp. 31-2.
Gamarnikow, Michael. "The Future of Comecon." *East Europe* 11 (June 1962), pp. 3-10.

Gasiorowska, Anna. "The Retreat From Moscow." *Gazeta Wyborcza*, May 26, 1993. In FBIS-EEU-93-104, June 2, 1993, pp. 20-21.

Gavrilov, Vera. "Energy Crisis Looming." *Report on Eastern Europe* 1 (August 24, 1990), pp. 3-5.

Gelman, Harry. *The Brezhnev Politburo and the Decline of Detente*. Ithaca: Cornell University Press, 1984.

George, Alexander. "Case Studies and Theory Development." Paper presented at the Second Annual Symposium on Information Processing in Organizations, Carnegie-Mellon University, October 15-16, 1982.

Georgiyev, Yu. "Yugoslavia: 'New Variant of Socialism'?" *Kommunist*, October 1968. In *CDSP* 20 (January 15, 1969), pp. 3-8, 24.

Gertzovitch, G. "The Economic Development of the Socialist World System." *Voprosy Ekonomiki*, April 1959. In *Problems of Economics* 2 (August 1959), pp. 75-84.

Gilpin, Robert. "Economic Interdependence and National Security in Historical Perspective." In Knorr, Klaus and Frank N. Trager, eds. *Economic Issues and National Security*. Kansas City: Regents Press of Kansas, 1977.

Goldstein, Judith. "Ideas, Institutions, and American Trade Policy." *International Organization* 42 (Winter 1988), pp. 179-217.

Gorbachev, Mikhail. *Perestroika: New Thinking for Our Country and the World*. New York: Harper and Row, 1987.

______. "October and Restructuring: The Revolution Continues." *Pravda*, November 3, 1987. In *CDSP* 39 (December 9, 1987), pp. 12-16.

Gornenski, Petur. "Only the Opposition Disputes This Agreement." *Duma*, May 22, 1990. In FBIS-EEU-90-103, May 29, 1990, pp. 8-9.

"Government Approves Visegrad Three Trade Agreement." LD1712181092 Budapest Kossuth Radio Network in Hungarian 1225 GMT 17 Dec 92. In FBIS-EEU-92-244, December 18, 1992, p. 11.

"Government Spokesman Comments." AU0102170091 Bucharest ROMPRES in English 1530 GMT 1 Feb 91. In FBIS-EEU-91-023, February 4, 1991, p. 41.

Greenstein, Fred and Nelson Polsby, eds. *Handbook of Political Science*. Reading, Mass.: Addison-Wesley, 1975.

Griffith, William E. *The Sino-Soviet Rift*. Cambridge: The M.I.T. Press, 1964.

Grigorov, M. "New Problems and Accelerated Socialist Advance in Bulgaria." *World Marxist Review* 2 (October 1959), pp. 26-31.

Gross, George. "Rumania: The Fruits of Autonomy." *Problems of Communism* 15 (January-February 1966), pp. 16-27.

Grzybowski, Adam. "Report on progress of Ronneby conference on protection of environment in Baltic zone." *Dziennik Baltycki*, September 4, 1990. In FBIS-EEU-90-188, September 27, 1990, pp. 43-4.

Guseinov, Elmar. "The Moment of Truth is Coming in Relations Among CMEA Partners." *Izvestia*, January 15, 1991. In *CDSP* 43 (February 13, 1991), p. 25.

______. "Conflicts in Former Soviet Republics are Major Topic at Istanbul Meeting." Izvestia, June 25, 1992. In *The Current Digest* 44 (July 22, 1992), p. 21.

Gvishiani, D. "Soviet Scientific and Technical Cooperation with Other Countries." *International Affairs* [Moscow], February-March 1970, pp. 46-52.

Gwertzman, Michael and Michael T. Kaufman, eds. *The Collapse of Communism*. New York: Random House, 1990.

Gyulai, Istvan. "The Socialist Program for Economic Integration." In *Hungarian Press Survey* No. 2151, Radio Free Europe Research.

Haas, Ernst. "Why Collaborate? Issue Linkage and International Regimes." *World Politics* 32 (April 1980), pp. 347-405.

______. *When Knowledge is Power: Three Models of Change in International Organizations.* Berkeley: University of California Press, 1990.

Haas, Peter. "Introduction: Epistemic Communities and International Policy Coordination." *International Organization* 46 (Winter 1992), pp. 1-35.

Haggard, Stephan and Beth A. Simmons. "Theories of International Regimes." *International Organization* 41 (Summer 1987), pp. 491-517.

Hansenclever, Andreas, Peter Mayer, and Volker Rittberger. "Interests, Power, Knowledge: The Study of International Regimes." *Mershon International Studies Review* 40 (October 1996), pp. 177-228.

Haus, Leah. *Globalizing the GATT: The Soviet Union's Successor States, Eastern Europe, and the International Trading System.* Washington, DC: Brookings Institution, 1992.

Hedri, Gabriella. "Changes in the West European Closed Economic Groups." *Kulkereskedelem*, September 1962. In *Hungarian Press Survey* No. 1227, Radio Free Europe Research, pp. 8-9.

Herman, Leon. "The Promise of Economic Self Sufficiency Under Soviet Socialism." *Studies on the Soviet Union* 7, no. 1, pp. 67-102.

______. "The New Soviet Posture in World Trade." *Problems of Communism* 3 (November-December 1954), pp. 9-16.

Hewett, Edward A. *Foreign Trade Prices in the Council for Mutual Economic Assistance.* London: Cambridge University Press, 1974.

Hillman, Arye L. "The Transition from the CMEA System of International Trade." In Keren, Michael and Gur Ofer, eds. *Trials of Transition: Economic Reform in the Former Communist Bloc.* Boulder, CO: Westview Press, 1992.

Holloway, David and Jane Sharp, eds. *The Warsaw Pact: Alliance in Transition?* Ithaca: Cornell University Press, 1984.

Holmes, Peter, *et. al.* "Comparative Advantage, Changes in Poland's Trade, and the EC Response." *Russian and East European Finance and Trade* 29 (Fall 1993), pp. 73-97.

Holsti, Ole, *et al*, eds. *Change in the International System.* Boulder, CO: Westview Press, 1980.

Holzman, Franklyn D. *Foreign Trade Under Central Planning.* Cambridge: Harvard University Press, 1974.

"How the CMEA Countries Tackle Their Energy Problems." *World Marxist Review* 28 (March 1985), pp. 116-23.

"Hungarian Anxieties About European Economic Integration." *Background Report* (Hungarian Unit), Radio Free Europe Research, July 10, 1962.

"Hungary Critical of Romanian Proposal." LD2504220291 Budapest MTI in English 2044 GMT 25 Apr 91. In FBIS-EEU-91-082, April 29, 1991, pp. 4-5.

"Hungary's Kadar Details Agreement." LD2112182392 Budapest MTI in English 1742 GMT 21 Dec 92. In FBIS-EEU-92-246, December 22, 1992, p. 2.

Husak, Petr. "Into the 'G-7' With a Great Deal of Effort?" *Lidove Noviny*, January 21, 1992. In FBIS-EEU-92-016, January 24, 1992, pp. 12-14.

Ikonnikov, I. "The CMEA Countries in 1966-1970." *International Affairs* [Moscow], October 1967, pp. 27-32.

______. "CMEA's Role in Cooperation Between the Socialist Countries." *International Affairs* [Moscow], April 1969, pp. 65-70.

______. "Sovershenstvovanie Struktury SEV." [The Having Been Improved Structures of CMEA] *Ekonomicheskoe sotrudnichestvo stran-chlenov SEV* 1988, no. 2, pp. 21-2.

Imse, Ann. "Russia's Wild Capitalists Take Aluminum for a Ride." *New York Times*, February 13, 1994, p. 4.

Inotai, Andras. "Transforming the East: Western Illusions and Strategies." *The Hungarian Quarterly* 35 (Spring 1994), pp. 24-43.

______. "The Economic Impact of the Association Agreement: The Case of Hungary." *Russian and East European Finance and Trade* 31 (January-February 1995), pp. 48-73.
______ and Magdolna Sass. "Economic Integration of the Visegrad Countries." *Eastern European Economics* (November-December 1994), pp. 6-28.
Institute for Strategic Studies. *The Military Balance*. London: The Institute for Strategic Studies, annually.
Iorgulescu, Iulia. "We Will Choose Alternative Scenarios." *Libertatea*, January 30, 1993. In FBIS-EEU-93-024, February 8, 1993, pp. 38-9.
"Is it Good to be Neighbors?" *Pravda*, November 3, 1990. In *CDSP* 42 (December 5, 1990), p. 22.
Iskra, Wieslaw. "Economic Integration of the Socialist Countries." *Zagagnienia I Materialy*, January 15-18, 1969. In *Polish Press Survey* No. 2192, Radio Free Europe Research, pp. 7-14.
______. "The Mechanisms of Integration." *Kulkereskedelem* 1971, no. 1. In *Soviet and Eastern European Foreign Trade* 7 (Spring 1971), pp. 119-28.
Ivanov, I. "We Answer the Reader: For Constructive Cooperation." *Pravda*, September 1, 1986. In *CDSP* 38 (October 1, 1986), p. 14.
Jakubowicz, Syzmon. "After the 20th Comecon Session." *Zycie Warszawy*, December 18-19, 1966. In *Polish Press Survey* No. 2041, Radio Free Europe Research, pp. 1-4.
Jamestown Monitor, various issues.
John, Ieuan, ed. *EEC Policy Towards Eastern Europe*. Westmead: Saxon House, 1975.
______. "The Soviet Response to Western European Integration." In John, Ieuan, ed. *EEC Policy Towards Eastern Europe*. Westmead: Saxon House, 1975.
Joint Economic Committee, US Congress. *Reorientation and Commercial Relations of the Economies of Eastern Europe: A Compendium of Papers*. Washington, DC: USGPO, 1970.
______. *East European Economic Assessment: A Compendium of Papers*. Washington, DC: USGPO, 1981.
______. *East European Economies: Slow Growth in the 1980s*. Washington, DC: USGPO, 1985.
______. *Pressures for Reform in the East European Economies*. Washington, DC: USGPO, 1989.
Jones, Christopher. *Soviet Influence in Eastern Europe: Political Autonomy and the Warsaw Pact*. New York: Praeger, 1981.
Joseph, Philip, ed. *The Economies of Eastern Europe and their Foreign Economic Relations*. Chichester, UK: NATO, 1986.
Jowitt, Ken. "Moscow 'Centre,'" *East European Politics and Societies* 1 (Fall 1987), pp. 296-348.
Kadar, Bela. "Small-Sized Developing Countries in the Regional Arrangements." *Acta Oeconomica*, 1973, no. 2, pp. 217-31.
______. "What We Inherited." *Kulgazdasag* 34, no. 6. In *Soviet and Eastern European Foreign Trade* 26 (Winter 1990-91), pp. 1-24.
Kalashnikova, Natalya. "APEC: If Things Don't Work Out in the West, Try Your Luck in the East." *Kommersant-Daily*, March 18, 1995 in *The Current Digest* 47 (April 12, 1995), p. 27.
Kamm, Henry. "Estonia Gives the Draftable Civilian Work." *The New York Times*, December 18, 1990, p. A11.
Kanet, Roger. "Integration Theory and the Study of Eastern Europe." *International Studies Quarterly* 18 (September 1974), pp. 368-92.
Kaplan, Karel. "The Council for Mutual Economic Aid, 1949 - 1951: Excerpts of documents with commentary." Research Project "The Experience of the Prague Spring." Working Study No. 4, June 1979.
Karaivanov, Ivan. "Unequal Relations Between USSR and Bulgaria." *Review of International Affairs* [Belgrade], June 7, 1950, pp. 17-19.
Karavayev, Valeri. "Eastern Europe is Opening Itself to the World." *International Affairs* [Moscow], April 1990, pp. 35-49.
Karpich, V. "CMEA Countries' Plan to Develop Integration." *International Affairs* [Moscow],

August 1970, pp. 8-13.
Kaser, Michael. *Comecon: Integration Problems of the Planned Economies.* 2d ed. London: Oxford University Press, 1967.
"Katona on Warsaw Pact Resolution." LD2606141990 Budapest Domestic Service in Hungarian 0908 GMT 26 Jun 90. In FBIS-EEU-90-124, June 27, 1990, pp. 33-4.
Keh, Zygmunt. "The International Specialization of Production." *Zycie Gospodarcze*, April 28, 1963. In *Polish Press Survey* No. 1532, Radio Free Europe Research, pp. 3-4.
Keller, Bill. "Shevardnadze Stuns Kremlin by Quitting Foreign Ministry and Warning of 'Dictatorship,'" *The New York Times*, December 21, 1990, pp. A1, A6.
______. "Soviet Army Raids Lithuania Offices." *New York Times*, January 12, 1991, pp. 1, 4
Kennedy, Paul. *The Rise and Fall of the Great Powers: Economic Change and Military Conflict from 1500 to 2000.* New York: Random House, 1987.
Keohane, Robert. "The Theory of Hegemonic Stability and Changes in International Economic Regimes, 1967-1977." In Holsti, Ole, *et al*, eds. *Change in the International System.* Boulder, CO: Westview Press, 1980.
______. "International Institutions: Two Approaches." *International Studies Quarterly* 32 (December 1988), pp. 379-96.
______ and Joseph Nye. *Power and Interdependence: World Politics in Transition.* Boston: Little, Brown, and Company, 1977.
Keren, Michael and Gur Ofer, eds. *Trials of Transition: Economic Reform in the Former Communist Bloc.* Boulder, CO: Westview Press, 1992.
Khrushchev, Nikita S. "On Control Figures for Development of the U.S.S.R. National Economy in 1959-1965." *Pravda*, January 28, 1959. In *CDSP* 11 (February 18 and 25 and March 4 and 11, 1959).
______. "On Peaceful Coexistence." *Foreign Affairs* 38 (October 1959), pp. 1-18.
______. "On the Program of the Communist Party of the Soviet Union." *Pravda*, October 19, 1961. In *CDSP* 13 (November 29 and December 6, 1961).
______. "Vital Questions of the Development of the World Socialist System." *Kommunist*, 12 (August 1962). In *CDSP* 14 (September 26 and October 3, 1962).
Khrushchev Remembers. Trans. and ed. Strobe Talbott. Boston: Little, Brown & Company, 1970.
Khrushchev Remembers: The Last Testament. Trans. and ed. Strobe Talbott. Bantam Book edition. New York: Bantam Books, 1974.
Kiraly, Bela. "Hungary's Army Under the Soviets." *East Europe* 7 (March 1958), pp. 3-14.
Kirichenko, Vadim. "The State of and Prospects for Economic Ties in the CIS." *Svobodnaia mysl'*, 1993, no. 3. In *Problems of Economic Transition* 36 (January 1994), pp. 39-56.
Kiss, Judit. "Hungarian Agricultural Strategy Toward the EC and the CAP." *Russian and East European Finance and Trade* 31 (January-February 1995), pp. 74-93.
Kiss, T. "Integration of CMEA Countries' National Markets." *Acta Oeconomica* 1970, no. 3, pp. 207-24.
"Klaus, Meciar View CEI." LD1707194193 Prague CTK in English 1742 GMT 17 Jul 93. In FBIS-EEU-93-136, July 19, 1993, p. 10.
"Klaus on Fuel Shortage, Price Increase." LD1707191890 Prague Domestic Service in Czech 1630 GMT 16 Jul 90. In FBIS-EEU-90-137, July 17, 1990, p. 17.
Klaus, Vaclav. "One the Eve of the Copenhagen Summit." *Cesky Denik*, June 18, 1993. In FBIS-EEU-93-118, June 22, 1993, pp. 7-8.
Knorr, Klaus and Frank N. Trager, eds. *Economic Issues and National Security.* Kansas City: Regents Press of Kansas, 1977.
Kocsi, Ilona. "Brussels Can Be Hungary's Historic Chance." *Magyar Hirlap*, December 16, 1991. In FBIS-EEU-91-243, December 18, 1991, pp. 12-13.
______. "Too Many Compromises, Too Few Decisions." *Magyar Hirlap*, May 13, 1991. In FBIS-

EEU-91-094, May 15, 1991, pp. 17-19.
Kohlmey, G. "World Economic Structures and International Socialist Division of Labor." *World Marxist Review* 9 (May 1966), pp. 43-50.
Kolodziejczyk, Kataryzna. "A Question of Perception." *Rzeczpospolita*, November 7, 1990. In FBIS-EEU-90-223, November 19, 1990, p. 44.
Kononenko, Vasily. "CIS is Bolstered by Economic Union, and will Perhaps Gain New Members." *Izvestia*, September 25, 1993. In *The Current Digest* 45 (October 27, 1993), p. 27.
Korbonski, Andrzej. "Comecon." *International Conciliation* No. 549 (September 1964).
Kormnov, Iu. "Economic Stimulation of the Development of International Production Specialization." *Voprosy ekonomiki* 1968, no. 6. In *Problems of Economics* 11 (January 1969), pp. 45-54.
______ and M. Cheburakov. "Improving the Management of Branch Integration of Comecon Member Nations." *Voprosy ekonomiki* 1973, no. 7. In *Problems of Economics* 16 (January 1974), pp. 69-90.
Kornilov, L. "At World Market Prices." *Izvestia*, September 4, 1990. In *CDSP* 42 (October 10, 1990), p. 26.
Kosinsky, Yu. "Step Toward a World Market -- USSR Becomes Observer in GATT." *Izvestia*, May 17, 1990. In *CDSP* 42 (June 20, 1990), p. 22.
Kosnar, Josef. "Does the Economic Cooperation Among the Comecon Countries Actually Pay?" *Pravda* [Prague], May 20, 1963. In *Czechoslovak Press Survey* No. 1260, Radio Free Europe Research, pp. 2-6.
______. "Prices and International Socialist Division of Work in Comecon." *Pravda* [Prague], May 27, 1963. In *Czechoslovak Press Survey* No. 1266, Radio Free Europe Research, pp. 2-6.
Kotyk, V. "Some Aspects of the History of Relations Among Socialist Countries." *Ceskoslovensky Casopis Historicky* 1967, no. 4. In *Czechoslovak Press Survey* No. 1973, Radio Free Europe Research.
Kouril, Frantisek. "Division of Work." *Rude Pravo*, April 10, 1963. In *Czechoslovak Press Survey* No. 1236, Radio Free Europe Research, pp. 4-6.
Kovalenko, Yu. "What Should the New Bank Be Like?" *Izvestia*, January 19, 1990. In *CDSP* 42 (February 21, 1990), pp. 18-19.
______. "Bank for Eastern Europe is Being Set Up." *Izvestia*, April 10, 1990. In *CDSP* 42 (May 16, 1990), pp. 23-4.
______. "What Will the New COCOM Be Like?" *Izvestia*, June 9, 1990. In *CDSP* 42 (July 11, 1990), p. 15.
Kovalev, S. "Sovereignty and the Internationalist Obligations of Socialist Countries." *Pravda*, September 26, 1968. In *CDSP* 20 (October 16, 1968), pp. 10-12.
Koves, Andras. *The CMEA Countries in the World Economy: Turning Inwards or Turning Outwards*. Budapest: Akademiai Kiado, 1985.
Kowlaczyk, Krzysztof and Jan Bazyl Lipszycz. "Trade With Russia." *Gazeta Wyborcza*, September 10, 1991. In FBIS-EEU-91-185, September 24, 1991, pp. 19-21.
Kozlov, Sergei. "The Second Meeting of the Leaders of the OEC's Member Countries." *Nezavisimaya gazeta*, July 14, 1993. In *The Current Digest* 45 (August 11, 1993), pp. 15-16.
Kozma, Ferenc. "The Effects of the International Division of Labour on National Economies." *Acta Oeconomica*, 1972, nos. 3-4, pp. 343-57.
______. "Dialectics of Equalizing Development Levels and Socialist Integration." *World Marxist Review* 16 (August 1973), pp. 39-48.
Kramer, Heinz. "The European Community's Response to the 'New Eastern Europe,'" *Journal of Common Market Studies* 31 (June 1993), pp. 211-44.
Krasner, Stephen, ed. *International Regimes*. Ithaca: Cornell University Press, 1983.
______. "Structural Causes and Regime Consequences: Regimes as Intervening Variables." In Krasner, Stephen, ed. *International Regimes*. Ithaca: Cornell University Press, 1983.

______. "Regimes and the Limits of Realism: Regimes as Autonomous Variables." In Krasner, Stephen, ed. *International Regimes*. Ithaca: Cornell University Press, 1983.

______. "State Power and the Structure of International Trade." Reprinted in Art, Robert and Robert Jervis, eds. *International Politics: Anarchy, Force, Political Economy and Decision Making*. 2d ed. Boston: Little, Brown, and Company, 1985.

Kresta, Jaromir. "Problems of Exchange in Consumer Goods with the Comecon Countries." *Planovane Hospodarstvi* 1968, no. 3. In *Soviet and Eastern European Foreign Trade* 4 (Fall 1968), pp. 44-57.

Kruczkowski, Andrzej. "The Whys and Wherefores of Integration." *Zycie Warszawy*, January 7, 1969. In *Polish Press Survey* No. 2172, Radio Free Europe Research, pp. 7-11.

Krylova, J. and R. Rohan. "The Development of the Socialist System." *Nova Mysl*, September 1963. In *Czechoslovak Press Survey* No. 1327, Radio Free Europe Research, pp. 4-8.

Kusin, Vladimir. "The Initiative from Venice." *Report on Eastern Europe* 1 (August 17, 1990), pp. 26-29.

Kuzinski, Stanislaw. "About the International Socialist Division of Work." *Nowe Drogi*, September 1963. In *Polish Press Survey* No. 1590, Radio Free Europe Research, pp. 2-5.

______. "Integrating Eastern Europe." *Polish Perspectives* 13 (November 1970), pp. 11-18.

Kuzminov, I. "Lenin and Problems of the Economic Theory of Socialism." *Pravda*, April 16, 1969. In *CDSP* 21 (May 7, 1969), pp. 13-14, 16.

Larrabee, Stephen. "Soviet Crisis Management in Eastern Europe." In Holloway, David and Jane Sharp, eds. *The Warsaw Pact: Alliance in Transition?* Ithaca: Cornell University Press, 1984.

Lavrovsky, I. "Should We Sell Our Oil Abroad." *Izvestia*, November 20, 1989. In *CDSP* 41 (December 20, 1989), p. 22.

"Laws Governing the Development of World Socialist System." *World Marxist Review* 14 (October 1971), pp. 3-43.

"Leaders Hold News Conference." LD0610212591 Warsaw Radio Warszawa Network in Polish 1818 GMT 6 Oct 91. In FBIS-EEU-91-195, October 8, 1991, pp. 5-7.

"Leaders of Central Asian Republics Seek Greater Unity." *Sevodnya*, January 12, 1995. In *The Current Digest* 46 (February 9, 1995), p. 27.

Ler, Ondrej and Ludek Urban. "European CMEA Countries in 1985-1986." *Czechoslovak Economic Digest* 1986, no. 7, pp. 3-20

Leonhard, Wolfgang. *Child of the Revolution*. Trans. C. M. Woodhouse. Chicago: Henry Ragnery Company, 1967.

"Let's Wait Another Month." *Pravda*, March 18, 1991. In *CDSP* 43 (April 17, 1991), p. 15.

Levin, I. D. "On the Essence and Significance of the Principle of Sovereignty." *Sovetskoya Gosudarstvo i Pravo*, 1949, no. 6. In *CDSP* 1 (October 25, 1949), pp. 3-7.

Levin, Lev and Vilor Niyazmatov. "Presidents Find it Warmer in Tashkent." *Pravda*, January 5, 1993. In *The Current Digest* 45 (February 3, 1993), pp. 1-2.

Levy, Robert. "The 'Right Deviation' of Ana Pauker." *Communist and Post-Communist Studies* 28, no. 2, pp. 239-54

Liberman, Evsei. "Plan, Pribyl', Premiia" [Plan, Profit, and Bonus] *Pravda*, September 9, 1962, p. 3.

Lijphart, Arend. "The Comparable-Case Strategy in Comparative Research." *Comparative Political Studies* 8 (July 1975), pp. 158-77.

"Limits Imposed on Czechoslovak Steel Exports." *Hospodarske Noviny*, August 19, 1992. In FBIS-EEU-92-163, August 21, 1992, p. 6.

Linden, Ronald. "The New Eastern Europe and East-West Relations." *Report on Eastern Europe* 1 (November 16, 1990), pp. 26-31.

Lipsky, Andrei. "The CIS a Year Later: Results and Prospects." *Nezavisimaya gazeta*, December 22, 1992. In *The Current Digest* 45 (February 3, 1993), pp. 8-9.

Liu Shao-Chi. "Internationalism and Nationalism." *Pravda*, June 7, 8, and 9, 1949. In *Soviet Press Translations* 4 (July 15, 1949), pp. 423-39.

Loshchakov, A. I. "35 Let SEV: Istoki i Sovremennost'" [35 Years of CMEA: The Sources and the Present], *Ekonomicheskoe sotrudnichestvo stran-chlenov SEV* 1984, no. 5, pp. 34-6.

Lukaszewski, Jerzy, ed. *The People's Democracies After Prague: Soviet Hegemony, Nationalism, Regional Integration?* Bruges: De Temple, 1970.

Lukin, L. I. "Pervoe Desiatiletie Soveta Ekonomicheskoi Vzaimopomoshchi" [The First Decade of the Council for Mutual Economic Assistance], *Voprosy Istorii* 1974, no. 4, pp. 39-57.

Mackintosh, Malcolm. "The Warsaw Treaty Organization: A History." In Holloway, David and Jane Sharp, eds. *The Warsaw Pact: Alliance in Transition?* Ithaca: Cornell University Press, 1984.

March, James G. and Johan P. Olsen. "The New Institutionalism: Organizational Factors in Political Life." *American Political Science Review* 78 (September 1984), pp. 734-49.

______. *Rediscovering Institutions*. New York: Macmillian, 1989.

Marer, Paul. *Soviet and East European Foreign Trade, 1946-69: Statistical Compendium and Guide*. Bloomington: Indiana University Press, 1972.

______. "Economic Performance and Prospects in Eastern Europe: Analytical Summary and Interpretation of Findings." In Joint Economic Committee, US Congress. *East European Economic Assessment: A Compendium of Papers*. Washington, DC: USGPO, 1981.

______. "The Political Economy of Soviet Relations with Eastern Europe." In Terry, Sarah M., ed. *Soviet Policy in Eastern Europe*. New Haven: Yale University Press, 1984.

______. *Dollar GNPs of the U.S.S.R. and Eastern Europe*. Baltimore: Johns Hopkins University Press, 1985.

Marrese, Michael and Jan Vanous. *Soviet Subsidization of Trade with Eastern Europe: A Soviet Perspective*. Berkeley: Institute of International Studies, University of California, Berkeley, 1983.

______ and Lauren Wittenberg. "Implicit Trade Subsidies within the CMEA: A Historical Perspective." *Economic Systems* 16 (April 1992), pp. 1-32.

Maryska, Egon. "For the Closest Cooperation Between the Comecon Countries." *Rude Pravo*, October 11, 1962. In *Czechoslovak Press Survey* No. 1132, Radio Free Europe Research, pp. 2-6.

Mastanduno, Michael. *Economic Containment: CoCom and the Politics of East-West Trade*. Ithaca: Cornell University Press, 1992.

"Mazowiecki: The Changes Should Not Lead to a Balkanization of Europe." *Nepszabadsag*, January 12, 1990. In FBIS-EEU-90-022, February 1, 1990, pp. 46-7.

Medvedev, E. "Soviet Trade Agreements with Socialist Countries." *Vneshniaia torgovlia* 1960, no. 3. In *Problems of Economics* 3 (August 1960), pp. 55-7, 64.

Medvedkov, Iu. "The Scientific-Technical Revolution and Economic Collaboration Among Socialist Countries." *Mirovaia ekonomika i mezhdunarodnye otnosheniia* 1969, no. 12. In *Problems of Economics* 13 (July 1970), pp. 34-52.

Mekhtiyev, Aidyn. "Teheran and Islamabad Casting Lot with ECO." *Nezavisimaya gazeta*, December 2, 1992. In *The Current Digest* 44 (December 30, 1992), pp. 18-19.

"Melescanu Views Black Sea Cooperation Summit." AU1107080095 Bucharest AZI in Romanian 6 Jul 95. In FBIS-EEU-95-132, July 11, 1995, pp. 49-50.

Melnikov, D. "Western Europe and the Marshall Plan." *Izvestia*, July 21, 1948. In *Soviet Press Translations* 3 (September 1, 1948), pp. 451-53.

Meyers, Paul F. "Population and Labor Force in Eastern Europe: 1950 to 1996." In Joint Economic Committee, US Congress. *Reorientation and Commercial Relations of the Economies of Eastern Europe: A Compendium of Papers*. Washington, DC: USGPO, 1970.

Mikheyev, O. "Europe Without the CMEA." *Pravda*, August 10, 1990. In *CDSP* 42 (September 12,

1990), p. 17.

Mikulsky, K. "Economic Efficiency in the CMEA Countries." *International Affairs* [Moscow], March 1969, pp. 59-64.

______. "New Scientific and Technological Horizons in the CMEA Countries." *International Affairs* [Moscow], June 1970, pp. 38-43.

Miller, Dorothy. "East Germany -- Trade Loophole in the Common Market." *Background and Situation Reports*, Radio Free Europe Research, October 27, 1965.

"Minister Interviewed on USSR Trade Problems." LD2502142191 Budapest Domestic Service in Hungarian 0545 GMT 25 Feb 91. In FBIS-EEU-91-038, February 26, 1991, pp. 24-5.

"Minister on Advantages of EC, EFTA Agreements." LD0903213192 Prague CSTK in English 1739 GMT 9 Mar 92. In FBIS-EEU-92-049, March 12, 1992, p. 10.

"Minister Releases 1992 Foreign Trade Figures." LD1002144893 Budapest MTI in English 1404 GMT 10 Feb 93. In FBIS-EEU-93-027, February 11, 1993, p. 16.

Moisiuc, Constantin. "National vs. World Economy." *Viata Economica*, June 25, 1971. In *Rumanian Press Survey* No. 898, Radio Free Europe Research, pp. 1-4.

Moldovan, Roman. The Socialist International Division of Labor." *World Marxist Review* 3 (August 1960), pp. 73-4.

______. "Equalizing the Levels of Economic Development -- A Law on Co-operation Among the Socialist Countries." *Scanteia*, May 19, 1974. In *Rumanian Press Survey* No. 974, Radio Free Europe Research, pp. 16-20.

Montias, John Michael. *Economic Development in Communist Rumania*. Cambridge: The M.I.T. Press, 1967.

Moore, Patrick. "New Dimensions for the Alpine-Adria Project." *Report on Eastern Europe* 1 (March 2, 1990), pp. 53-6.

Morawski, Zdzislaw. "From Pentagon to Hexagon." *Contemporary Poland* 1991, no. 6, pp. 1-3.

"More Active Attitude Toward the World." *Lidove Noviny*, December 27, 1990. In FBIS-EEU-90-249, pp. 21-2.

Moreton, Edwina. "Foreign Policy Goals." In David Holloway and Jane Sharp, eds. *The Warsaw Pact: Alliance in Transition?* Ithaca: Cornell University Press, 1984.

Murgescu, Costin. "Rumania's Industrialization and Experience." *Contemporanul*, September 23, 1962. In *Rumanian Press Survey* No. 325, Radio Free Europe Research.

Murgu, Gh. and Gh. Barbu. "Rumania's Economic Cooperation with West European Countries." *Probleme Economice* 1968, no. 8. In *Rumanian Press Survey* No. 768, Radio Free Europe Research, pp. 5-8.

"The Nation in the Contemporary World, a Round Table Discussion." *Lupta de Clasa*, October 1967. In *Rumanian Press Survey* No. 729, Radio Free Europe Research, pp. 2-11.

"Neagu Attends Black Sea Region Countries' Meeting." AU2112155890 Bucharest ROMPRES in English 2249 GMT 20 Dec 90. In FBIS-EEU-90-247, December 24, 1990, pp. 53-4.

"Negotiations Begin on EFTA Free Trade Agreement." AU2309125392 Bucharest ROMPRES in English 0942 GMT 23 Sep 92. In FBIS-EEU-92-187, September 25, 1992, p. 15.

Negru, Radu. "Development of Rumania's Economic Relations with the Socialist Countries." *Viata Economica* 1968, no. 34. In *Rumanian Press Survey* No. 768, Radio Free Europe Research, pp. 1-3.

Nelson, Sonia. "Czechoslovak Political Economy and US Foreign Economic Policy, 1943-1948." Paper presented at the American Association for the Advancement of Slavic Studies National Convention, Phoenix, AZ, November 1992.

"Nemeth Comments." LD1401214190 Budapest Television Service in Hungarian 1800 GMT 14 Jan 90. In FBIS-EEU-90-010, January 16, 1990, p. 5.

Nettl, J. P. *The Eastern Zone and Soviet Policy in Germany 1945-50*. London: Oxford University Press, 1951.

"New Machinery -- New Problems." *Rolnicke Noviny*, July 18, 1963. In *Czechoslovak Press Survey* No. 1302, Radio Free Europe Research, pp. 11-12.

"A New Turkestan." *Nezavisimaya gazeta*, January 6, 1993. In *The Current Digest* 45 (February 3, 1993), pp. 3-4.

Nicolae, Petre. "CMEA in Theory and Practice." Monograph Series on Soviet Union, Delphic Associates, 1984.

Norman, Peter. "The BERD Gets Ready To Fly." *Financial Times*, May 29, 1990, p. 25.

North, Douglass. *Institutions, Institutional Change, and Economic Performance*. New York: Cambridge University Press, 1990.

"Notes." *Nova Svoboda*, November 28, 1967. In *Czechoslovak Press Survey* No. 2000, Radio Free Europe Research, pp. 4-5.

Nove, Alec. *An Economic History of the USSR 1917-1991*. 3d ed. London: Penguin Books, 1992.

Novozamsky, Jiri. "A United Economy -- The Aim of the Socialist System." *Nova Mysl*, October 1962. In *Czechoslovak Press Survey* No. 1143, Radio Free Europe Research.

Nugent, Neill. *The Government and Politics of the European Community*. Basingstoke: Macmillan Education, 1989.

______. "The Deepening and Widening of the European Community: Recent Evolution, Maastricht, and Beyond." *Journal of Common Market Studies* 30 (September 1992), pp. 311-28.

Nye, Joseph S. "Soft Power." *Foreign Policy*, Fall 1990, pp. 153-71.

______. *Bound to Lead: The Changing Nature of American Power*. New York: Basic Books, 1990.

Nyerges, Janos. "Hungary and GATT." *Magyar Hirlap*, March 2, 1970. In *Hungarian Press Survey* No. 2070, Radio Free Europe Research, pp. 1-4.

"Nyers, Bogomolov Discuss Socialist Economics." LDO305013489 Budapest Television Service in Hungarian, 1745 GMT, 2 May 1989. In FBIS-EEU-89-084, May 3, 1989, pp. 16-18.

"Official on Postponement of CEMA Session." LD2702162891 Budapest MTI in English 1451 GMT 27 Feb 91. In FBIS-EEU-91-040, February 28, 1991, p. 18.

Oleinik, I. P. "A Law of Development of Socialist Countries." *Ekonomicheskaia Gazeta*, October 19, 1960. In *Problems of Economics* 3 (February 1961), pp. 62-4.

______. "Forms of International Division of Labor in the Socialist Camp." *Voprosy Ekonomiki* 1961, no. 5. In *Problems of Economics* 4 (October 1961), pp. 56-63.

______. "The Equalization of the Economic Development Level of the Socialist Countries." *Probleme Economice*, April 1962. In *Rumanian Press Survey* No. 322, Radio Free Europe Research.

______. "Leninism and the International Significance of the Experience Gained in Socialist Construction." *International Affairs* [Moscow], February-March 1970, pp. 27-34.

Omblus, Jaan. "Free Trade Agreements in the Transition of the Estonian Economy." *Russian and East European Finance and Trade* 32 (September-October 1996), pp. 5-15.

OMRI Daily Digest, various issues.

"On the Eve of the Consultative Meeting." *Pravda*, February 22, 1968. In *CDSP* 20 (March 13, 1968), pp. 8-11.

"On the Nature of Relations Between Socialist Countries." *Izvestia*, May 31, 1964. In *CDSP* 16 (July 1, 1964), pp. 3-7.

"On the Principles of Development and Further Strengthening of Friendship and Cooperation Between the Soviet Union and Other Socialist States." *Pravda*, October 31, 1956. In *CDSP* 8 (November 14, 1956), pp. 10-11.

"Organization Disbands." LD3006092291 Moscow Central Television First Program Network in Russian 1800 GMT 28 Jun 91. In FBIS-SOV-91-127, July 2, 1991, p. 6.

Orlov, N. "The Foreign Trade of the Soviet Union Under Present Conditions." *Voprosy ekonomiki*, May 1959. In *Problems of Economics* 2 (September 1959), pp. 26-33, 56.

"Outline of Soviet-EBRD Clearing Account." LD0406144791 Budapest MTI in English 1342 GMT

4 Jun 91. In FBIS-EEU-91-109, June 6, 1991, pp. 14-15.

Palairet, Michael. "'Lenin' and 'Brezhnev': Steel Making and the Bulgarian Economy, 1956-90." *Europe-Asia Studies* 46, no. 3, pp. 493-505.

Paral, Pavel. "Are Oil Supplies to Czechoslovakia Guaranteed?" *Rude Pravo*, February 15, 1990. In FBIS-EEU-90-035, February 21, 1990, p. 8.

Paraluta, Mihai. "Setting International Economic Relations on New Bases." *Viata Economica*, October 12, 1973. In *Rumanian Press Survey* No. 963, Radio Free Europe Research, pp. 5-6.

"Parliament Declines To Attend Black Sea Meeting." AU2502222593 Sofia BTA in English 1739 GMT 25 Feb 93. In FBIS-EEU-93-037, February 26, 1993, p. 5.

Patolichev, N. "The Present Day and Problems of European Security: May Economic Ties Grow Stronger." *Izvestia*, December 11, 1969. In *CDSP* 21 (January 13, 1970), pp. 5, 7.

Pawlicki, M. B. "The Starting Point -- Price." *Glos Pracy*, April 19, 1967. In *Polish Press Survey* No. 2067, Radio Free Europe Research, pp. 4-6.

Penev, Dimiter. "Trade Between the People's Republic of Bulgaria and the German Federal Republic Under the Conditions of the Common Market." *Vanshna Targovila*, January 1963. In *Bulgarian Press Survey* No. 402, Radio Free Europe Research, pp. 2-6.

"Pentagonal Countries View Energy, Pipeline Link." AU0910135090 Prague CTK in English 1820 GMT 5 Oct 90. In FBIS-EEU-90-196, October 10, 1990, pp. 17-18.

Petrov, K. "Political Integration in Western Europe." *International Affairs* [Moscow], November 1969, pp. 15-21.

"Planning Chief on Polish-Soviet Trade, Debt." LD0904212490 Warsaw PAP in English 2022 GMT 9 Apr 90. In FBIS-EEU-90-073, April 16, 1990, pp. 51-2.

Plechac, Valstimil. "Iranian Oil in Addition to Soviet Oil." *Svoboda*, November 24, 1969. In *Czechoslovak Press Survey* No. 2287, Radio Free Europe Research, pp. 11-12.

Podklyuchnikov, M. "Mezhdunarodnoe Obozrenie" [International Survey], *Pravda*, June 11, 1962, p. 4.

"Polish Comments on Comecon Meetings." *Polish Situation Report*, Radio Free Europe Research, October 13, 1966.

"Polish Minister Comments on Baltic Conference." LD0603220492 Warsaw Radio Warszawa Network in Polish 1800 GMT 6 Mar 92. In FBIS-EEU-92-046, March 9, 1992, p. 4.

Poller, Roland and Istvan Tesner. "Socialist Economic Integration and the Investment Cooperation of the CMEA Countries." *Kozgazdasagi Szemle*, September 9, 1982. In *Soviet and Eastern European Trade* 20 (Spring 1984), pp. 6-26.

Pomelov, I. "Common Principles and National Characteristics in the Development of Socialism." *Pravda*, August 14, 1968. In *CDSP* 20 (September 4, 1968), pp. 3-5.

Popisakov, Grigor. "Successes and the Future of Economic Cooperation: New Horizons." *Pravda*, August 4, 1969. In *CDSP* 21 (August 27, 1969), pp. 11-12.

Portansky, Aleksei. "Restrictions on Russian Exports Contradict West's Statements of Support for Our Reforms." *Izvestia*, August 13, 1993. In *The Current Digest* 45 (September 8, 1993), p. 19.

Portnikov, Vitaly. "'Central Asian Troika' is Creating its own Structures." *Nezavisimaya gazeta*, February 14, 1995. In *The Current Digest* 47 (March 15, 1995), pp. 20-1.

Poznanki, Kazimierz. "Opportunity Cost in Soviet Trade with Eastern Europe: Discussion of Methodology and New Evidence." *Soviet Studies* 15 (April 1988), pp. 290-307.

______. "Pricing Practices in the CMEA Trade Regime: A Reappraisal." *Europe-Asia Studies* 45, no. 5, pp. 923-30.

Preston, Christopher. "Obstacles to EU Enlargement: The Classical Community Method and the Prospects for a Wider Europe." *Journal of Common Market Studies* 33 (September 1995), pp. 451-63.

"Progress and Difficulties in Comecon." *Zycie Warszawy*, August 6, 1966. In *Polish Press Survey* No. 2011, Radio Free Europe Research, pp. 2-4.

"Proposal of Minister of National Defense to Reduce Length of Military Service." *Duma*, April 21, 1990. In FBIS-EEU-90-080, April 25, 1990, p. 15.

Pryor, Frederic. *The Communist Foreign Trade System*. Cambridge: The M.I.T. Press, 1963.

Puiu, Al. "The Federal Republic of Germany -- Rumania's Trade Partner." *Viata Economica*, May 14, 1971. In *Rumanian Press Survey* No. 891, Radio Free Europe Research, pp. 1-4.

______ and C. Cuilea. "The Development of Trade Exchanges Between Socialist and Advanced Capitalist Countries." *Probleme Economice*, 1968, No. 5. In *Rumanian Press Survey* No. 767, Radio Free Europe Research.

Pushkov, Aleksei. "In Proud Solitude?" *Izvestia*, April 25, 1990. In *CDSP* 42 (May 30, 1990), pp. 12-13.

Rachmuth, I. "The Importance of Establishing a Rate of Development Which Will Level Off the Economic Progress of All Socialist Countries." *Probleme Economice*, July 1963. In *Rumanian Press Survey* No. 377, Radio Free Europe Research.

Radeva, Mira. "One Does Not Expect Miracles in Trade." *Trud*, June 3, 1993. In FBIS-EEU-92-114, June 12, 1992, pp. 14-15.

"Regional Conference Backs Plan for Permanent Forum." LD0706201795 Moscow INTERFAX in English 1827 GMT, 7 June 1995. In FBIS-SOV-95-110, June 8, 1995, p. 39.

Reisinger, William. *Energy and the Soviet Bloc: Alliance Politics After Stalin*. Ithaca: Cornell University Press, 1992.

Remington, Robin Alison, ed. *Winter in Prague: Documents on Czechoslovak Communism in Crisis*. Cambridge: The MIT Press, 1969.

"Report of the C.P.S.U. Central Committee to the 23rd Congress of the Communist Party of the Soviet Union." *Pravda*, March 30, 1966. In *CDSP* 18 (April 13, 1966), pp. 5-24.

"A Report on Antal Apro's Lecture on Cooperation with the Comecon Countries." *Nepszabadsag*, July 16, 1966. In *Hungarian Press Survey* No. 1731, Radio Free Europe Research.

"Report on 1st Session of PZPR Plenum." In FBIS, *Daily Report*, January 21, 1960, pp. GG 1 - GG 13.

"The Reserves Have Been Exhausted." *Zycie Warszawy*, November 7, 1969. In *Polish Press Survey* No. 2222, Radio Free Europe Research, pp. 1-2.

Reutt, Boguslaw Wladyslaw. "Comecon -- Specialization Ties." *Zycie Gospodarcze*, January 5, 1969. In *Polish Press Survey* No. 2171, Radio Free Europe Research.

Rice, Condoleezza. *The Soviet Union and the Czechoslovak Army, 1948-1983: Uncertain Allegiance*. Princeton: Princeton University Press, 1984.

Ripka, Hubert. *Czechoslovakia Enslaved*. London: Victor Gollancz, Ltd., 1950.

Rogov, Sergei. "Result is Distressing, But There is a Way Out of the Impasse." *Nezavisimaya gazeta*, December 31, 1994. In *The Current Digest* (February 1, 1995), pp. 22-4.

"Rohlicek Speech." *Rude Pravo*, July 6, 1988. In FBIS-EEU-88-136, July 15, 1988, pp. 2-4.

Rostow, W. W. *The Dynamics of Soviet Society*. A Mentor Book. New York: The New American Library, 1954.

Rothschild, Joseph. *Return to Diversity: A Political History of East Central Europe Since World War II*. 2d ed. New York: Oxford University Press, 1993.

Ruggie, John. "International Regimes, Transactions, and Change: Embedded Liberalism in the Postwar Economic Order." In Krasner, Stephen, ed. *International Regimes*. Ithaca: Cornell University Press, 1983.

"A Rumanian Manifesto." *East Europe* 13 (June 1964), pp. 25-8.

Russett, Bruce. "The Mysterious Case of Vanishing Hegemony; Or is Mark Twain Really Dead." *International Organization* 39 (Spring 1985), pp. 207-31.

Rutherford, Andrea. "Draft Dodgers May Cause a Shake-up of Soviet Army." *Wall Street Journal*, November 1, 1990, p. A18.

Rybak, Sergei. "Customs Union Created." *Nezavisimaya gazeta*, January 31, 1995. In *The Current*

Digest 47 (March 1, 1995), pp. 21-3.
Rybakov, O. "The Economic Platform of Interaction." *Kommunist* 1990, no. 6. In *Soviet and Eastern European Foreign Trade* 26 (Winter 1990-91), pp. 65-80.
Salay, Juergen. "Restructuring the Energy System." *Report on Eastern Europe* 1 (August 31, 1990), pp. 16-21.
Salimov, Marat and Yevgeniy Lapin. "Prospects for Setting Up Eurasian Union." *Kommersant-Daily*, September 16, 1994. In FBIS-SOV-94-181, September 19, 1994, p. 1.
Salvatore, Dominick. "Privatization, Economic Restructuring, and Foreign Trade in Eastern Europe." *Russian and East European Finance and Trade* 28 (Spring 1992), pp. 29-40.
Sanakoyev, Sh. "Proletarian Internationalism: Theory and Practice." *International Affairs* [Moscow], April 1969, pp. 9-15.
______ and N. Kapchenko. "Triumph of the Principles of Proletarian Internationalism." *International Affairs* [Moscow], August 1969, pp. 32-9.
Schaefer, Henry Wilcox. *Comecon and the Politics of Integration*. New York: Praeger Publishers, 1972.
Schapiro, Leonard. *The Communist Party of the Soviet Union*. New York: Vintage Books, 1960.
Schmemann, Serge. "Soviet Commandos Stage Latvia Raid: 4 Civilians Killed." *New York Times*, January 21, 1991, pp. A1, A11.
Sebesta, Josef. "USSR's Second Largest Trading Partner." *Czechoslovak Life*, November 1967, pp. 8-9.
Sekera, Jiri. "In the Spirit of the Progressive Tradition." *Nova Mysl*, May 1963. In *Czechoslovak Press Survey* No. 1263, Radio Free Europe Research.
Selucky, Radoslav. "The Dynamic Force of Socialist Advance from the Economic Viewpoint." *Kulturny Zivot*, August 10, 1963. In *Czechoslovak Press Survey* No. 1311, Radio Free Europe Research, pp. 2-6.
______. "The Impact of the Economic Reforms on the Foreign Economic Relations of the Socialist Countries." *Mezinarodni Vztahy* 1968, no. 1. In *Soviet and Eastern European Foreign Trade* 4 (Fall 1968), pp. 72-86.
Shaffer, Harry G. "An Economic Model in Eclipse." *Problems of Communism* 17 (November-December 1968), pp. 50-6.
Shihab, Sophie. "Interview with President Zhelyu Zhelev." *Le Monde*, December 6, 1991. In FBIS-EEU-91-238, December 11, 1991, pp. 3-4.
Shiryayev, N. "USSR Trade with CMEA Countries in the Ninth Five-Year Period." *International Affairs* [Moscow], October 1971, pp. 113-14.
"Should Construction be Suspended or Continued." *Hospodarske Noviny*, June 28, 1990. In FBIS-EEU-90-128, July 3, 1990, p. 21.
Sielanko, Anna. "A Break in the Deadlock." *Rzeczpospolita*, March 20, 1990. In FBIS-EEU-90-059, March 27, 1990, pp. 40-1.
Sik, Ota. "Prague's Spring: Roots and Reasons." *Problems of Communism* 20 (May-June 1971), pp. 1-10.
Silk, Leonard. "Trickle Down: At the Summit a Chance to Set the Stage for Growth." *New York Times*, July 14, 1991, Section 4, p. 3.
Siluyanov, N. "Brotherly Collaboration and Mutual Assistance on the Part of the Socialist Countries." *Voprosy Ekonomiki*, March 1959. In *Problems of Economics* 2 (July 1959), pp. 14-24.
Sirbu, Crina. "Things Must Evolve Well at Home in Order To Be Able To 'Sell' a Positive Image Abroad." *Romania Libera*, January 25, 1993. In FBIS-EEU-93-020, February 2, 1993, pp. 30-1.
"Skubiszewski Hopes Aid Will Restore Soviet Trade." LD0706054791 Warsaw PAP in English 2154 GMT 6 Jun 91. In FBIS-EEU-91-110, June 7, 1991, p. 17.
"Slimak on 26 Feb Pullout, Army Troop Cuts." LD2202205490 Prague CTK in English 1658 GMT

22 Feb 90. In FBIS-EEU-90-037, February 23, 1990, p. 11.
Smilek, Jaroslav. "Coordination of the Economic Development of Comecon Member States." *Hospodarske Noviny*, July 22, 1966. In *Czechoslovak Press Survey* No. 1832, Radio Free Europe Research, pp. 1-7.
Smith, Gordon. *Soviet Politics: Struggling with Change*. 2d ed. New York: St. Martin's Press, 1992.
Sobell, Vlad. *The CMEA in Crisis: Toward a New European Order*. New York: Praeger, 1990.
"The Socialist Community: Democratisation and Renewal." *International Affairs* [Moscow], January 1989, pp. 123-32, 95.
Sojak, Z. and L. Riha. "Cooperation with the Socialist Countries." *Zivot Strany*, January 1968. In *Czechoslovak Press Survey* No. 2000, Radio Free Europe Research, pp. 1-5.
Sokolov, A. "Socialist Countries: Highroad of Economic Development." *International Affairs* [Moscow], June 1971, pp. 16-23.
______ and Y. Shirayev. "Important Trend in Socialist Countries' Co-operation." *International Affairs* [Moscow], January 1966, pp. 39-45.
Soldaczuk, Josef. "Regional Integration and East-West Trade." *Polish Perspectives* 9 (January 1966), pp. 110-17.
______ and Jan Giezgala. "Economic Integration of Comecon Countries and the Means and Methods of Hastening It." *Gospodarka Planowa*, November 1968. In *Polish Press Survey* No. 2170, Radio Free Europe Research.
Solska, A. "A Joint Bank." *Trybuna Luda*, June 2, 1970. In *Polish Press Survey* No. 2236, Radio Free Europe Research.
Sovet Ekonomicheskoi Vzaimopomoshchi. Sekretariat. *Statisticheski Ezhegodnik Stran-Chlenov Soveta Ekonomicheskoi Vzaimopomoshchi, 1988* [Statistical Yearbook of the Member Countries of the Council for Mutual Economic Assistance]. Moscow: Financi i Statistika, 1988.
"Soviet Crude Oil and Czechoslovak Credits." *Prace*, May 17, 1968. In *Czechoslovak Press Survey* No. 2084, Radio Free Europe Research, pp. 11-12.
"Soviet Gas Supply Situation, Prospects Reported." LD0806180490 Budapest MTI in English 1540 GMT 8 Jun 90. In FBIS-EEU-90-112, June 11, 1990, p. 59.
"Soviet-Rumanian Communique on Transfer to Rumanian People's Republic of Soviet Share in Joint Soviet-Rumanian Companies." *Pravda*, September 25, 1954. In *CDSP* 6 (November 10, 1954), pp. 16-17.
"Speech by Comrade L. I. Brezhnev." *Pravda*, May 8, 1970. In *CDSP* 22 (June 2, 1970), pp. 10-12.
Spulber, Nicolas. *The Economics of Communist East Europe*. New York: The M.I.T. Press, 1957.
"Stagnation in Comecon." *Czechoslovak Situation Report*, Radio Free Europe Research, November 7, 1966.
Stalin, Joseph V. *Ekonomicheskie Problemy Sotsializma v SSSR* [Economic Problems of Socialism in the USSR]. Moscow, 1952.
Stanescu, N. S. "Common Market Autarky: A Barrier to International Trade." *Scanteia*, June 14, 1968. In *Rumanian Press Survey* No. 760, Radio Free Europe Research, pp. 3-5.
The Statesman's Yearbook: Statistical and Historical Annual of the States of the World. New York: The MacMillian Company, annually.
Stawarska, Renata. "Poland's Association with the EEC." *Polish Western Affairs* 33 (January 1992), pp. 77-92.
Stein, Arthur A. "Coordination and Collaboration: Regimes in an Anarchic World." In Krasner, Stephen, ed. *International Regimes*. Ithaca: Cornell University Press, 1983.
Stone, Randall W. *Satellites and Commissars: Strategy and Conflict in the Politics of Soviet-Bloc Trade*. Princeton: Princeton University Press, 1996.
Strange, Susan. "The Myth of Lost Hegemony." *International Organization* 41 (Autumn 1987), pp. 551-74.

Stransky, F. "Toward Further Progress in the Economic Cooperation of the Socialist Countries." *Rude Pravo*, July 20, 1962. In *Czechoslovak Press Survey* No. 1089, Radio Free Europe Research.

Suslov, Mikhail. "Po povodu statei P. Fedoseeva" [In connection with the articles of P. Fedoseev], *Pravda*, December 24, 1952, p. 2.

______. "Leninism and the Revolutionary Transformation of the World." *Kommunist*, October 1969. In *CDSP* 21 (November 19, 1969), pp. 3-7.

Szabo, Melinda. "Hungarian Foreign Trade and the Growth of the Economy, *The New Hungarian Quarterly* 14 (Autumn 1973), pp. 215-20.

Szalai, Attila, *et. al.* "Twelve Questions for the Visegrad Three." *Uj Magyarorszag*, March 14, 1992. In FBIS-EEU-92-058, March 25, 1992, pp. 2-11.

Szawlowski, Richard. *The System of International Organizations of the Communist Countries*. Leyden: A. W. Sijthoff, 1976.

Szilagyi, Mihaly. "The Policy of Europe's Division." *Nepzabadsag*, August 2, 1961. In *Hungarian Press Survey* No. 1026, Radio Free Europe Research, pp. 2-5.

Szita, Janos. "On Intra-European Economic Cooperation and East-West Trade." *Acta Oeconomica* 1974, nos. 3-4, pp. 275-93.

Tait, Jack. "Pole in London Derides Paris Parley as 'Fake,'" *New York Herald Tribune*, July 15, 1947, p. 11.

Takhnenko, Galina. "Anatomy of a Political Decision: Notes on the Marshall Plan." *International Affairs* [Moscow], July 1992, pp. 111-15.

Tarnovskii, O. "Price Formation on the World Socialist Market." *Den'gi i kredit* 1969, no. 4. In *Problems of Economics* 12 (October 1969), pp. 42-57.

Tatic, S. "Stop the Embargo." *Vecernje Novosti*, April 15, 1995. In FBIS-EEU-95-110, June 8, 1995, pp. 52-3.

Terry, Sarah M., ed. *Soviet Policy in Eastern Europe*. New Haven: Yale University Press, 1984.

Toczek, Stanislaw. "Most-Favoured-Nation Treatment." *Polish Perspectives* 12 (August 1969), pp. 39-47.

"Today is not 1968." *Rzeczpospolita* [Warsaw], January 4, 1990. In FBIS-EEU-90-005, January 8, 1990, pp. 1-2.

"Trade Relationship with USSR Assessed." LD1007202190, Prague Domestic Service in Czech 1000 GMT 10 Jul 90. In FBIS-EEU-90-133, July 11, 1990, pp. 15-16.

"Treaty Between the Union of Soviet Socialist Republics and the Federal Republic of Germany." *Pravda*, August 13, 1970. In *CDSP* 22 (September 15, 1970), pp. 2-3.

Trend, Harry. "Comecon Confronted by Hard Economic Facts." *Background and Situation Reports*, Radio Free Europe Research, December 14, 1966.

______. "Romania Favors Even More Limited Comecon Council." *Background and Situation Reports*, Radio Free Europe Research, February 9, 1967.

Tucek, Josef. "Our View of European Security." *Mlada Fronta Dnes*, March 7, 1991. In FBIS-EEU-91-050, March 14, 1991, pp. 13-14.

Tsygankov, Vitaly. "Russia and Belarus Unite Monetary System." *Nezavisimaya gazeta*, November 20, 1993. In *The Current Digest* 45 (December 22, 1993), p. 33.

Tyszko, Celina. "The Development and the Prospects of Trade Exchange Between the GFR and the Socialist Countries." *Rynki Zagraniczne*, September 19, 1970. In *Polish Press Survey* No. 2256, Radio Free Europe Research, pp. 1-8.

"US Poses Czech Trade Obstacles." *Prague News Letter*, September 16, 1967, pp. 1, 4.

United Nations. *Statistical Yearbook 1992*. New York: United Nations, 1994.

"Unity Essential to Socialist Economies." Moscow in Rumanian to Rumania 0700 GMT 30 May 1964. In FBIS, *Daily Report*, June 3, 1964, p. BB7.

"USSR to Trade Oil for Industrial Products, Food." LD0606213990 Budapest MTI in English 1928

GMT 6 Jun 90. In FBIS-EEU-90-111, June 8, 1990, pp. 33-4.
Vajda, Imre and Mihaly Simai, eds. *Foreign Trade in a Planned Economy*. Cambridge: Cambridge University Press, 1971.
Valek, Vratislav. "Selected Questions Concerning the Effectiveness of Joint Investment Activity by CMEA Members." *Finance a uver* 1982, no. 3. In *Soviet and Eastern European Foreign Trade* 19 (Winter 1983-84), pp. 45-61.
Valenta, Jiri. *Soviet Intervention in Czechoslovakia, 1968*. Baltimore: Johns Hopkins University Press, 1979.
Valyi, Peter. "Hungary and International Integrations." *The New Hungarian Quarterly* 13 (Winter 1972), pp. 22-32.
Vanyai, Judit and Erzsebet Viszt. "Foreign-Trade Reorientation and the Freeze on Ruble-Based Exports: The Lessons of a Machine-Industry Survey." *Kulgazdasag* 35, no. 8. In *Russian and East European Finance and Trade* 28 (Fall 1992), pp. 76-92.
Vasilyev, Aleksei. "Russian and the Moslem World--Partners or Adversaries." *Izvestia*, March 10, 1992. In *The Current Digest* 44 (April 8, 1992), pp. 1-3.
Velekhov, Leonid. "'Little Dragons' Make Big Impression." *Sevodnya*, July 30, 1993. In *The Current Digest* 45 (August 25, 1993), p. 22.
Verona, Sergiu. *Military Occupation and Diplomacy: Soviet Troops in Romania, 1944-1958*. Durham: Duke University Press, 1992.
Vetrov, A. "Economic Ties Between Socialist and Capitalist States." *International Affairs* [Moscow], September 1970, pp. 7-11.
Vidal, Dider and Jean Dupre, "As Far as People's Lives are Concerned, ..." *Dimineata*, April 3-4, 1993. In FBIS-EEU-93-066, April 8, 1993, p. 17.
Videnova, Lyudmila. "The Best Market is the Most Likely Market." *Kontinent*, July 1, 1992. In FBIS-EEU-92-135, July 14, 1992, pp. 3-4.
Vinogradov, K. "Collaboration of Socialist Countries in the Development of Machine Building." *Voprosy Ekonomiki* 1960, no. 2. In *Problems of Economics* 3 (June 1960), pp. 51-5.
Vintera, J. "The Facts About an Orientation." *Prace*, February 26, 1967. In *Czechoslovak Press Survey* No. 1900, Radio Free Europe Research, pp. 7-9.
"Visegrad Talks Detailed." LD1602063591 Budapest MTI in English 1730 GMT 15 Feb 91. In FBIS-EEU-91-033, February 19, 1991, pp. 9-11.
"Visit with Hungarian Workers." *Pravda*, June 10, 1986. In *CDSP* 38 (July 9, 1986), p. 6.
Voinov, A. "Ekonomicheskie otnosheniia sotsialisticheskikh stran s razvitymi kapitalisticheskimi gosudarstvami" [Economic Relations of the Socialist Countries With the Developed Capitalist States], *Planovoye Khozyaistvo*, March 1973, pp. 110-20.
Voznesenskii, Nikolai. *Voennaia Ekonomika SSR v Period Otechestvennoi Voiny* [The War Economy of the USSR in the Period of the Patriotic War]. Moscow, 1948.
Wagrowska, Maria. "Membership Must Be Realistic." *Rzeczpospolita*, September 12-13, 1992. In FBIS-EEU-92-183, September 21, 1992, pp. 23-4.
Walencik, Ireneusz. "Hopes and Fears." *Nowy Swiat*, July 4-5, 1992. In FBIS-EEU-92-132, July 9, 1992, pp. 27-8.
Waltz, Kenneth. *Theory of International Relations*. Reading, Mass.: Wesley, 1979.
Wandycz, Piotr S. "Recent Traditions of the Quest for Unity: Attempted Polish-Czechoslovak and Yugoslav-Bulgarian Confederations 1940-1948. In Lukaszewski, Jerzy, ed. *The People's Democracies After Prague: Soviet Hegemony, Nationalism, Regional Integration?* Bruges: De Temple, 1970.
Wasilkowski, A. "Comecon Countries -- Differences and Prospects." *Gazeta Bialostocka*, November 27, 1968. In *Polish Press Survey* No. 2167, Radio Free Europe Research, pp. 1-4.
Weber, Steven. "The European Bank for Reconstruction and Development." *International Organization* 48 (Winter 1994), pp. 1-38.

Weitz, Richard. "The Expanding Role of the Council of Europe." *Report on Eastern Europe* 1 (August 24, 1990), pp. 49-57.

Weydenthal, Jan B. de. "Prospects for Soviet-Polish Trade." *Report on Eastern Europe* 1 (November 2, 1990), pp. 23-25.

"What is Slowing Us Down?" *Izvestia*, October 10, 1987. In *CDSP* 39 (November 11, 1987), p. 7-8.

Williamson, John. *The Economic Opening of Eastern Europe.* Washington, DC: Institute for International Economics, 1991.

Wirski, Wieslaw. "Poland's Commerce with the Countries of the Common Market." *Zycie Gospodarcze*, August 11, 1963. In *Polish Press Survey* No. 1575, Radio Free Europe, pp. 3-8.

"The Work of Comecon." *East Europe* 9 (April 1960), pp. 3-9.

Wroblewska, Agnieszka. "Is There A Need for CMEA." *Zycie Warszawy*, February 25, 1991. In FBIS-EEU-91-041, March 1, 1991, pp. 21-2.

Wysocinski, Jerzy. "The Urgent Need for New Forms of Cooperation Among Comecon Member Countries." *Zycie Gospodarcze*, February 2, 1969. In *Polish Press Survey* No. 2176, Radio Free Europe Research, pp. 1-6.

Yakov, Valery. "It Has Been Decided to Preserve a Single Customs Space." *Izvestia*, April 11, 1992. In *The Current Digest* 44 (May 13, 1992), p. 22.

Yartayev, Vladimir and Anatoly Shestakov. "Asian Gas Will Flow West." *Nezavisimaya gazeta*, May 13, 1993. In *The Current Digest* 45 (June 9, 1993), p. 17.

Yergin, Daniel. "The Next Oil Surprise." The Business World, *The New York Times*, December 2, 1990, pp. 8, 26.

Young, Oran. "Regime Dynamics: The Rise and Fall of International Regimes." In Krasner, Stephen, ed. *International Regimes.* Ithaca: Cornell University Press, 1983.

Zahradnidek, Tomas. "Poland Cannot Speak on Behalf of the Others." *Lidove Noviny*, October 9, 1995. In FBIS-EEU-95-200, October 17, 1995, pp. 10-11.

Zamora, Stephen. "Voting in International Economic Organizations." *American Journal of International Law* 74 (July 1980), pp. 566-608.

Zanga, Louis. "The Balkan Foreign Ministers' Conference in Tirana." *Report on Eastern Europe* 1 (December 7, 1990), pp. 1-4.

Zarev, Kiril. "Forms of Socialist Integration." *World Marxist Review* 14 (May 1971), pp. 71-6.

Zavolzhsky, S. and L. Lukin. "Bourgeois Criticism of Socialist Economic Cooperation." *International Affairs* [Moscow], January 1967, pp. 8-13.

Zdziechowski, Stanislas. "The Impact of the Common Market on the Soviet Union." *Studies on the Soviet Union* 11, no. 4, pp. 50-59.

Zeman, Karel. "Development in the Position of the Comecon Complex in the World Economy." *Zahranicini Obchod* 1974, no. 2. In *Soviet and East European Foreign Trade* 10 (Summer 1974), pp. 30-59.

Zhagel, Ivan. "We're Being Studied and We're Studying." *Izvestia*, August 5, 1990. In *CDSP* 42 (September 5, 1990), p. 22.

"Zhelev Greets Black Sea Ministers Meeting." AU0912134093 Sofia BTA in English, 1143 GMT 9 Dec 93. In FBIS-EEU-93-236, December 10, 1993, pp. 1-2.

Zhmyrev, L. "Good Foundation Laid. -- *Pravda* Interviews N. I. Ryzhkov." *Pravda*, January 11, 1990. In *CDSP* 42 (February 14, 1990), pp. 18, 36.

Zhukov, Igor. "Turkmenia is Cramped by the Limits of the Commonwealth, but Objective Circumstances do not Permit it to Leave the CIS." *Nezavisimaya gazeta*, October 7, 1992. In *The Current Digest* 44 (November 4, 1992), pp. 27-8.

Zhukov, Yur. "Aiding or Undermining the Reconstruction of Europe?" *Pravda*, August 18, 1947. In *Soviet Press Translations* 2 (October 15, 1947), pp. 160-63.

Zolotarev, V. "Integration of CMEA Countries and the Development of the World Socialist Market."

International Affairs [Moscow], January 1972, pp. 15-22.

Zotova, N. "Improving the Structure of Foreign Trade." *Planovoe khoziaistvo* 1967, no. 1. In *Problems of Economics* 10 (July 1967), pp. 34-9.

Zwass, Adam. "The Economy of the Comecon Countries in 1962." *Zycie Gospodarcze*, March 17, 1963. In *Polish Press Survey* No. 1505, Radio Free Europe Research, pp. 2-8.

______. *The Council for Mutual Economic Assistance: The Thorny Path from Political to Economic Integration.* Armonk, NY: M. E. Sharpe, Inc., 1989.